PRAISE

MW00810735

"This incredible book simply blew me away. It's filled with love, magic, and inspiration. Heavenly descriptions transported me into the scenes, and woven into the story are breathtaking epiphanies, nail-biting suspense, many lines that made me laugh out loud, and situations to which many of us can relate. It's exactly what the world needs. I can't wait to read it again!"
—Anisha Durve, DOM, AD, author of *The Power to Break Free* and founder of the Marma Institute of Ayurvedic Acupressure

"A feast for the senses. Vivid descriptions and rich imagery immerse readers in alluring, exotic settings, providing a truly immersive armchair traveling experience infused with the undeniable power of love and magic. The story takes you on a journey that is as much internal as external; you will travel inside yourself."
—Laura Sgroi, author of *In Our Thirties* and host of the En Los Ta podcast

"If you love traveling and spirituality, you'll want to live in these pages. A series of adventures around the world and an internal journey of self-discovery, sharing love along the way. This book reminded me to see life as a gift."
—Fatima Gholem, author of *Les Cendres et les Papillons*

"Genuine, courageous, and heartfelt—I loved this book. Sonya masterfully inspires readers to seek their own path, stay true to themselves, and never settle. A must-read!"
—Maria Gangat, author of *Tales of Horror & Happiness in Hospitality*

some kind of magic

A TRUE STORY OF LOVE, LIFE, AND WANDERLUST

SONYA MOORE

First published in the United States of America in Lavergne, TN.

Editing by Jocelyn Carbonara
Cover design by Sonya Moore
Cover art by Filo, Gliuki, and VoinSveta (IStock)

ISBN 979-8-9882817-1-9 (paperback)

Library of Congress Control Number: 2023917889

THE LIBRARY OF CONGRESS HAS CATALOGED THIS EDITION AS FOLLOWS:
Moore, Sonya.
Some kind of magic: a true story of love, life,
and wanderlust / Sonya Moore.
ISBN: 979-8-9882817-1-9 (paperback)
979-8-9882817-2-6 (ebook)
1. Moore, Sonya—Travel. 2. Southeast Asia—Description and travel.
3. Asia—Description and travel. 4. Spiritual biography. I. Title.
LCC DS522.3.M66 2023
DDC 959—dc23

www.sonyamoore.com

For the thirsty souls.

Dear Reader,

As you've probably noticed already (since it says so on the front cover), this is a true story. Before you read any farther, I want to let you know that it's not simply *based* on a true story. None of the events described in the following pages are fictional, exaggerated, or embellished, with the exception of some occasional heavy sarcasm. The spelling of a few names has been changed for phonetic reasons. A few other names and descriptive details have been changed to protect the privacy of some innocent and some not-so-innocent characters, organizations, and establishments involved. Apart from those exceptions, everything between these covers is true to life. As viewed from my perspective, of course.

I'm putting that on the record here, because above all, this story is about a specific kind of magic, and I want you to know that this magic is real. So, if you find yourself asking at any point, "Is this part really true?!" — the answer is yes.

I hope you enjoy the journey!

Sincerely,

Sonya

P.S. Some spectacular places—and occasionally, beings—are described in the following pages. If, while you're reading, you want to see pictures of some of them, visit sonyamoore.com.

And above all,
watch with glittering eyes the whole world around you
because the greatest secrets are always hidden
in the most unlikely places.
- *Roald Dahl*

Chapter 1

A toms of sunlight filter through the burgundy curtains, tinting the room with dim, atmospheric light. I'm lying naked on the wooden table. Three dark-haired women in colorful saris stand around me, holding golden pitchers shaped like Aladdin's lamp. The pitchers are filled with steaming medicated water, which the women are pouring repeatedly across my body, drizzling it back and forth in rhythmic, repetitive motion. The sensation of the hot liquid spilling onto my skin is hypnotic. Lulled into a semi-trance, I'm wondering hazily if this is what it would feel like to be transported a few centuries back in time, into the body of an Arabian princess being prepared for a lavish royal wedding…or would this be just a normal everyday ritual for a sixteenth century Arabian princess…?

But that's not where the story starts. It starts nine months earlier, in a far away and much less sultry, less decadent setting.

Nine months earlier (March 2017)
Johannesburg, South Africa

The calm silence of my hotel room is abruptly shattered by a furious yell.

"I don't want to do this anymore!!!"

1

The yell comes from me, and it's directed at my laptop screen. The defenseless laptop narrowly escapes being hurled across the room. But, luckily for both of us, I restrain myself from throwing anything and instead focus on the words that just came out of my mouth, which, until the moment I yelled them, I didn't realize were true. *I don't want to do this anymore.*

This startling epiphany is followed by a second one.

Nobody's making me do this. If I don't want to do this anymore, I can just stop.

As the full impact of this revelation dawns, I sit frozen in shock and awe. Invisible shackles around my wrists crack in half and shatter into a thousand pieces at my feet, as if made of glass. *"This"* referred to devoting approximately 90% of my waking hours, thoughts, and energy to my job, with its impressive but ridiculously over-inflated title of Senior Vice President of International Sales for a dermocosmetic company not large enough to respectably be handing out titles that long.

The company has exciting potential and manufactures exceptional products, but it's headed by an unstable genius and its management team consists mostly of incompetent men with oversized egos who specialize in making terrible business decisions. (Nothing against men in general, these particular incompetent egomaniacs just happen to be men.)

I've been with the company for a year and half. For the first fourteen months or so, things had gone extremely well in spite of those undesirable colleagues, and the job had been a rich, rewarding experience in many ways. But in recent months, doors had begun shutting in my face, one after another. Unrelated situations had begun plunging downhill for reasons out of my control, inside and outside the office.

It was odd. I had started to get the feeling that Life was nudging me in a different direction. But, until about ten seconds ago, I had remained committed to working towards a successful turnaround, feeling a sense of obligation to my goals, my employer, and my clients. The idea of leaving had never crossed my mind. My mind isn't wired that way. I'm not a quitter. I don't leave when things get tough.

The proverbial last straw that triggered my angry yell and apparently obliterated that internal wiring was the discovery of the three emails I found waiting at the top of my inbox when I got back to this hotel room after a long, exhausting, excruciatingly boring day with a potential business partner who had turned out to be a complete waste of time. All three emails were from upper management and cannot be accurately described by any polite adjective so I must call them what they were: asinine. Totally void of common sense, announcing ridiculous business decisions that would undo months of work on my part. And they were only the first three. Beneath them, five hundred more unread emails sat neatly lined up, waiting for my attention. They had accumulated during my two-week South Africa vacation, even though I had been skimming emails every day for anything urgent and keeping myself available by phone at all waking hours in case of any emergencies.

Now, as my head wraps itself around the astonishing concept that I want to part ways with my job and that no one will prevent me from doing so, the next question presents itself. *If I don't want to stay here, what do I want?*

I could look for another job in my field, with a more competent management team. My resume is strong; I could probably find one. But that idea makes me feel heavy and tired. I don't want to find another job like this one. I want to leave my whole career. I want to leave life as I know it.

This is another shock.

For the past thirteen years, ever since I graduated college, my life had revolved around my job. I wasn't career-driven by nature, but I was committed to success, and success took a lot of time, energy, and focus. For a long time, I didn't mind, because I loved the job. My career over the past twelve years was my adolescent dream come true: get paid to travel the world. When I was a young and inexperienced teenager, I didn't know anyone else who got paid to travel the world and that seemed like an impossible dream. But I got a degree in International Business, and my wish came true. My job took me everywhere from Paris to Bogota to Cairo to Singapore to Sydney, and to gorgeous Caribbean islands. I loved discovering the world, and

I loved the work too: it was exhilarating, interesting—and exhausting. I worked my ass off, through different time zones and airports and long airport lines, flights and taxi rides and sometimes a different country and hotel every night, meetings, store visits, keeping up with hundreds of emails a day, and occasionally three to four hours of sleep per night. "I'll sleep when I'm dead" became my motto.

Over the past few years, my workload has lightened. I get more sleep now, but the years of intensity have left me drained. This life used to be my dream, but it isn't anymore. It's started to feel empty. Actually, if I'm to be honest, it started feeling empty years ago, but recently it's become increasingly, undeniably soul-starving.

So now, sitting here alone in front of my laptop in the solitude of this quiet hotel room, I ask myself: *what's my new dream?*

True love, fairytale style, has secretly always been my other lifelong dream, but I haven't found that yet, and unfortunately, I can't snap my fingers and make my personal Prince Charming appear. So, what else do I want?

I don't know. Really, I have absolutely no idea. I know only two things: One, I don't want to look back at my life when I'm eighty and see that I did nothing more interesting than sell shampoo my whole life. And two, I don't want to deal with bullshit from upper management and/or colleagues anymore. Or from anyone.

"I want a year without bullshit," I announce to the room.

The room appears unaffected. But I'm not. From the starting point of that tiny seed of clarity, an idea begins to take shape.

There is one other thing I know: I still want to travel the world, but in a different way. No longer at the high-speed pace of a day or two per country, staying in the capital, meeting with business contacts, experiencing some great restaurants and if I'm lucky a little taste of local culture, then getting on a plane back home. I want to travel slowly now. I want to go beyond capital cities. I want to stay in one place long enough to discover the culture—to learn what's beneath the surface. I want to discover other sides of life.

I know it's possible to do this kind of thing, because for years I've been meeting people who do things like quit their jobs and travel for a year, or fly to Portugal on holiday and stay forever. But I always thought I personally could never do something like that. I need to be responsible, have a job, and pay my bills, right?

But, a year ago I met Crystal from Seattle. I met her in Playa del Carmen, just a few months before she got divorced, quit her job, and took off to Asia, where she's been wandering through Laos and Thailand for the past eight months, discovering outrageously beautiful waterfalls, rock climbing, learning to weave and speak the language and selling Thai tea and fabrics at the night markets. I'm enthralled by her Instagram photos and consumed with curiosity about her experience.

Since she could do it, I could do it. I have no children, pets, or spouse to hold me back. Savings will get me by for a little while, but I'll eventually need another job. What line of work will keep me clear of all bullshit for a full year?

A vivid memory floats back to me. When I was twenty-three, I spent a month working at a summer camp in Belgium, teaching English to cute kids. The kids were bullshit-free and impossible not to adore. I still carry my favorite ones in my heart: vibrant ten-year-old Sophie from Belgium, sweet little Charles from Germany, gentle brown-eyed Aurelie from the Netherlands who's now all grown up and in med school.

So, I could teach English for a year. Maybe in Asia somewhere. But wait. I won't start teaching right away. First, I'll take some time to be free as a bird and do whatever most pleases my heart.

And what would that be?

My mind pauses, searching. The first answer that arrives: *Go back to Bali.*

Oh yes, *Bali.* The closest thing to heaven on Planet Earth, as far as I know. I know this because I went to Bali for work a few years ago, and it was incredible. However, it was a very short trip, because I'd planned to take two weeks of vacation afterwards to stay and luxuriate in Balinese bliss, but an important buyer in Florida scheduled a meeting that thwarted those plans. Now, with no buyers to get in the way, I can go back for as long as I want. Or as long as the visa regulations will let me, however long that is. I'll figure those details out later. But definitely at least a month or two.

Now I'm starting to get excited. Next question: when will this happen?

Not immediately, that's for sure, because number one: I own a house that's an almost-completed Work In Progress. For the past three years, most of my free time and disposable income has been dedicated to transforming said house from a dated eyesore with some bizarre paint choices into a gorgeous zen sanctuary. (The movie *The Money Pit* pretty much describes my experience.) Thanks to my ex-boyfriend Ryan (and when I say "thanks," I mean it with sincere, palms-together-down-on-my-knees-bowing-forehead-to-the-floor immense gratitude), I did a lot of the renovation work myself. That is to say, we initially did a lot of the work together, then we broke up, and I carried on alone with my specialties (painting and tiling) and hired a Peruvian contractor/savior named Miguel to do the rest. This massive project is almost done—actually the house is finished, but I'm working on the backyard now, and its transformation from untamed wild jungle into urban tropical oasis is nearly complete. Obviously, I can't leave until it's done. And then I'll need to find a tenant.

Then there's factor number two: my job. A lot of people around the world have significant time, money, and potential invested in projects that I'm responsible for. I'll need to make sure they'll be left in a new pair of good hands.

Clearly, my leap into freedom won't happen tomorrow. According to my calculations, I'll need about four months to wrap up the house and job situation.

The details will take a while to come together, but from this moment, my mind is made up. There will be no wavering or second guessing. And just so you know, this bold, unwavering decisiveness is not exactly the typical me. I can be found more often hanging out noncommittally on the indecisive side of the spectrum. But there are times in life when what you want is so crystal clear that there is no room for doubt, hesitation, or second-guessing. This was one of those times.

In the months that follow, many people will tell me, "You're so brave for doing this!" That will surprise me every time, because a) I thought everyone would tell me I was crazy. And b) it wasn't brave. Bravery is a quality I respect enormously, because it's admirable, it's heroic, and it's hard. Bravery is when you are afraid to do something and you do it anyway.

In making this choice, I didn't feel any fear. I just suddenly realized what I wanted, and chose that. And you could say this was a selfish choice, because I made it entirely, 100 percent, for me. Because it's what I wanted to do, not because it was what anyone else wanted or expected me to do. I chose this because it was what my whole heart wanted. It wasn't the hard, scary road. It was the sparkling, enticing, irresistible road.

I didn't realize this at the time, but later it occurred to me that it's often at moments like these in life that things start to happen. Put into a formula, it would look like this: A (your whole heart intensely wants something with zero doubts, resistance or reservations—and often you have to get shaken forcefully to get to this stage) + B (your mind taps you on the shoulder and presents you a preview of What Other People Will Probably Think About This and you pause to look at it, shrug your shoulders, and with one dismissive swoop of your hand brush that scenario out of your mind and return to focus on What You Want) + C (you take some form of action in the direction of what you want, even if just one tiny step) = BOOM! As the magic starts showing up in your life in sometimes small and sometimes mindboggling ways, you, in starry-eyed wonder, ride the flow in the direction of the course your heart set for you.

But it's not all magic, rainbows, and butterflies. Oh no. This is real life. There will be curveballs.

CHAPTER 2

And you? When will you begin that long journey into yourself?
—RUMI

April 2017, Delray Beach, Florida

Preparations for my departure are unfolding. I'm wrapping up work and house projects and making my way through an online TEFL English teaching certification course. I have not, however, started looking for teaching jobs, because I've realized there are several other things I want to do with my free time first, even before going to Bali.

This realization was mainly thanks to a recent phone call from my friend Kim from Tampa. She called to ask if I was interested in doing a yoga teacher training in Key West. Kim, by the way, is the one who got me into yoga in the first place, a little more than a decade ago, when I was in my mid-twenties. I had recently tried yoga for the first time: by renting an advanced yoga DVD from the library and attempting to follow along with it in my living room. The only thing I remember about that experience is that I fell over a bunch of times.

Next, I tried a yoga class at the gym. When Kim heard about that, she scoffed. "Don't go there for yoga! I'll bring you to a real yoga class."

Shortly afterward, she brought me to my first real yoga class. It was at the home of the teacher, Tony, an Eastern European with a thick accent who could gracefully mold his body into postures requiring incredible strength, balance, and flexibility. The room fit a max of five students plus Tony, and the classes were physically challenging. We held each posture for a long time while breathing deeply. Once, I unexpectedly started crying in the middle of the class and had to leave the room. I didn't know where the grief came from, but suddenly it was there. And then the tears came, and when they stopped, the grief was gone too.

Over the years, I tried other studios and other teachers, and gradually I was hooked. I didn't do yoga every day, but I couldn't not do it for long. I had thought about taking a yoga teacher training course, not to become a teacher, just to deepen my personal understanding of this practice that had such a profound effect on my mental and emotional state. But I never had had enough free time.

Now, finally, I do. But, in Key West?

"Why don't we take one in India?" I asked Kim. "That's where yoga started, and everything's cheaper over there."

That's not a viable option for Kim, because she can't take that much time off work. But I have no such constraints.

That night at home, I google "yoga teacher training India." The first option the search engine presents me is a yoga school in Dharamsala. Their website is well done; the school looks good. Perfect, actually. The photos, the videos, the description, the testimonials, all of it. It seems like a perfect balance of traditional Indian and modern-day Western culture. And the price is a quarter of Key West's.

I know nothing about Dharamsala, so I google it next. To my pleasant surprise, Google reveals that Dharamsala is home to the Dalai Lama. I know essentially nothing about the Dalai Lama either, except that he is widely revered for reasons unknown to me, and his name (or is it a title?) has an exotic allure. A couple weeks earlier, I happened to see a YouTube video of him speaking and I liked his vibe. I had instantly decided he was someone I'd like to meet.

Google also reveals that Dharamsala is in the Himalayas of North India. Normally I'm drawn to beaches and the tropics, but for some reason lately I've been craving mountains. In the photos on my screen, the town of Dharamsala itself looks a little drab, but the panoramic mountain views around it are breathtaking. And, as it so happens, the Dalai Lama will be leading four days of teachings in Dharamsala at the end of August. They're free and open to all, and they'll end two days before the start of the teacher training.

I feel that rare and exceptional click of: *This is it. This is meant for me.* I never look at another school. I register for that September yoga teacher training.

What is strange about this is that normally I am the girl who looks at every single available option and spends hours—or sometimes days—evaluating and comparing before selecting the best one, whether we're talking about hotels, shampoo, jars of peanut butter, anything. But not this time.

There's one other thing I want to do before the teacher training: a ten-day Vipassana silent retreat. There are fourteen Vipassana centers in the US, but since I'm going to India, I might as well do it there. I already have a business visa that will give me four months in that country.

I find a Vipassana center near Delhi offering a ten-day retreat whose dates fit perfectly in the three-week window between my other plans: my friend Carolyn's wedding August 4th in San Francisco, and the Dalai Lama's teachings. I apply and they accept me.

Everything has all come together so conveniently … except for one problematic detail.

My beloved house.

I've decided to rent it furnished, because I have no idea when I'll be back. Everyone is telling me it will be snapped up immediately, but months pass, and every interested tenant falls through. I'm not sure what this means. Am I going to hate India and come home after a month? In any case, my realtor is fantastic, and if anyone can get it rented, she will.

People ask if I'll sell it. "Never!" I say. After all the years of work and love I poured into that house, I never want to part with it.

It's my last week of work. Carlos, who's the head of the Mexico division and one of my favorite people in the company, comes into my office to say goodbye. On his way out, he pauses and looks back at me to say, *"Este es el momento, el cielo te está hablando."*

"This is the time; heaven is speaking to you."

Carlos doesn't seem like a spiritual, metaphysical person, and I don't know why he said those words, but they make me feel that he knows something I don't and that some kind of magic is brewing under the surface. I smile and reflexively glance at my computer screen as he walks out the door. It's 4:44.

Goosebumps cover my arms, because for a little while now, repeating numbers on the clock have been showing up at significant moments in my life like winks from the universe.

Later that week, I'm in Bogota for a trade show. The last night of the show, we host a dinner for some of my favorite colleagues and clients, and it's a night that will forever stand out in my memory like a sparkling diamond. A night of cheer and well-being with the undercurrent of a celebration of life—the perfect ending to this corporate chapter of my life.

In the final weeks before I leave Florida, I get two readings. The first is a tarot card reading from a woman named Kim Kennedy. I met Kim through a mutual friend, and the first moment I saw her I felt that I was looking at my higher self in human form. She was in her early fifties I think, bright and beautiful, with sky blue eyes, a cascade of wavy blond hair, and a fairy-like energy of lightness, warmth, and wisdom. She glowed with a radiance that seemed more than human. From the instant we met, I felt that I already knew her.

When I learned she does tarot readings, I decided to get one from her, even though I didn't know much about tarot. I'd once had a reading from a woman sitting behind a folding table in a New Orleans plaza. The cards told the woman I was highly organized, which didn't give me a strong faith in tarot cards. But Kim inspires faith.

Kim does my reading over the phone. Everything she says resonates as spot on. While describing my near future, she tells me, "Trust your intuition, go with the flow…you won't be able to see the path ahead, but you will be guided, one step at a time. It will feel like you're blindfolded and being led by spirits."

It will feel like you're blindfolded and being led by spirits. Those words will come back to me many times during the journey to come.

The other reading is from my astrologist and psychic medium friend Rose. When Rose learned of my upcoming departure, she volunteered to read my chart. I've never had my chart read before, but I have great respect for Rose's physic powers, and by extension it seems fair to assume her astrological powers are formidable as well, so I accept her offer.

One thing my chart reveals, according to Rose, is that my near future includes neither death nor hospitals. That's a relief, since my mind likes to always have something to worry about, and what it has currently chosen as its biggest concern is the possibility that I'll become violently ill on my journey, end up in a sketchy, horrible, overcrowded Indian hospital, and possibly die unhappy and alone, far from everyone I know and love.

Then Rose says, "Now let me tell you about the man you're supposed to marry."

Oh, there's a man I'm supposed to marry? That's exciting.

"He's a Gemini," she says. "Or a Scorpio."

"Hmm, really? Alex is a Gemini…"

Alex is the man in my life at the time, and he's wonderful. But the situation is complicated, and when I leave the country, our relationship will end. Or so I think at the time.

If only it were that easy. Spoiler alert: it's not going to be that easy. You're going to be hearing more about Alex, and that being the case, I better explain how it all started.

How It All Started:
I met Alex in a bar on Halloween, eight months earlier. (An auspicious occasion to meet a man, I know.) It was an open-air bar in Delray Beach. I was there with two girlfriends, dressed in a last-minute turquoise Arabian costume that came in a package labelled "desert beauty." I was at the bar ordering drinks for my friends and me, and Alex came up next to me. The first thing I noticed about him was

his tallness, because he was taller than everyone else in the bar. Taller, and bigger. Everything about him was just bigger, in the most attractive way possible. His bones, his muscles, his features, his energy. He was dressed as some rockstar I couldn't identify, in jeans and a wig, with a guitar strapped to his back and an open vest without a shirt, partially revealing his tanned, chiseled torso. Not overly chiseled like he spends all his time working on it, just naturally chiseled like: oh, the outlines of these abs just happen to effortlessly be here. Like he was probably born like that and those effortless abs have been there all his life.

I looked at him and said, "Nice guitar." He looked me up and down and said, "Nice everything." We kept talking. He was down-to-earth, and funny. There was nothing pretentious or superficial about him. Something about him felt comfortable, familiar. At some point I realized he was the sexiest man in the world—and not because of the abs, because a man can have sexy abs and be a sorry excuse for a human (I know this from personal experience). It was a combination of everything: the abs, the tallness, the masculine energy, the sense of a click, and something magnetic and indefinable.

A few minutes into the conversation I felt some kind of flash, almost like a flash of…recognition? Recognition of what, I don't know—past, or future, or that we somehow matched each other. A flash that my soul seemed to recognize but my mind didn't understand. I don't know if he felt the same thing but apparently he felt something, because he suddenly kissed me. His kiss matched his energy: strong, masculine, and devouring.

We kept kissing for the next two or three hours. I don't make it a habit of making out with strangers in bars, but with him … what can I say? The rest of the world disappeared and it was just us in a dense cloud of attraction. He was so much bigger than me, so much stronger, and he smelled so good. He exuded masculine energy and vitality. Something inside me melted in his presence. Any walls and defenses I had learned to construct over the past thirty-six years of my life suddenly weren't there anymore.

An hour or two later, while we were taking a break from our makeout session to talk and he was cracking me up with his off-the-wall sense of humor, a voice yelled from somewhere off to our left, "Jasmine and Aladdin!!"

I looked over at the owner of the voice and then around to verify that he was referring to us, which indeed he was. In our costumes, we were in fact the spitting image of Disney Jasmine and Aladdin, if you ignored Alex's guitar and my blond hair. (We googled this to check.) My "desert beauty" costume was a copy of Jasmine's, and Alex's shaggy wig was the same cut as Aladdin's. Although Alex was wearing jeans instead of harem pants, the open vest was the same.

We laughed at our unintentional joint costume and I secretly loved the romantic coincidence.

We started seeing each other shortly afterwards, but sporadically, because at any given time, one of us was usually out of town. After a few weeks, my spidey sense of something-isn't-quite-right-here clicked on. During our third encounter, Alex told me, "You never asked me if I'm in a relationship."

Considering that the night we met he made out with me for three hours in plain sight of everyone in the bar *and* everyone walking down the street, it never occurred to me that I should ask if he was in a relationship.

He explained. They'd been together thirteen years; she was sixteen years older than him, she wasn't in good health, she'd kind of given up on living; she'd had open heart surgery last year, she almost died.

Maybe the appropriate response would have been anger, but I didn't feel any anger. Maybe it was easier because I had already sensed there was something going on and he strategically chose the moment that my emotions were buffered by post-coital bliss to reveal this information. Whatever the reason, the only emotion I could feel was what I imagined he must feel in this situation. He was forty-nine, which surprised me when he told me. He was thirteen years older than me, but he looked so much younger than that, and his spirit was so full of life.

What did it feel like for him to be with someone so much older, who'd already given up on living? I didn't have words for what I felt; I only understood that he was so full of life and he needed to live.

But fidelity was part of my moral code and I didn't want to be the other woman, complicit in the betrayal of his partner. So we said goodbye that night, and that was meant to be the end.

But it wasn't the end, because reasons kept surfacing that required him to come over to my house. Like, for example, he'd cut down a branch of fresh coconuts; did he want me to drop them off? (How could I say no to fresh coconut water?) Or, he was trying to help me find siding to match the existing siding on my house for a small section in need of replacement, and he needed to come over and measure. (Because there was no sense trusting the measurements I'd already taken.) And then to deliver the siding, which he did, almost miraculously, manage to find. And every time, the strong current of attraction was still there and we couldn't resist it.

And so it went on. My inner moral guide didn't approve, but something inside me was overruling her disapproval. Until a few months later, when I was suddenly fed up with being the other woman and I told him I didn't want to do this anymore.

He didn't argue, and for a month we had no contact. I went on a Tinder date and had a horrific experience. (You want to know the details? I'm giving you the chance to skip the rest of this paragraph and avoid being scarred for life … keep in mind you will never be able to unsee these words … never ever EVER …) but if you must know, the day after our date, this guy, who I went on ONE DATE with and didn't even kiss, sends me a Whatsapp message saying: *Thinking of you*. It's accompanied by an audio recording of himself jerking off.

Ewwwwwww!!!! Whyyy???

A week later, I heard "our song" on the radio. (Alex's and mine, to be clear, not insane Tinder guy's and mine.) I took it as a sign I should forget about Tinder and contact Alex. Plus, by now I'd decided to leave the country in a few months. What was the point of getting involved with someone new?

I believe in the sanctity of relationships. If two people are together, I don't believe in being the illegitimate third. But … I know what I felt with him. I know that the hours with him were like oxygen after my head had been under water until my lungs were empty. I know that to continue seeing him until I left felt unequivocally right.

I know he was real. I know that I loved every minute with him. I know that he was a reminder to appreciate the present moment, because with him there was no future but there was so much to relish in the present.

When I told him about my plan to leave the US, he said, "And what about me? What am I supposed to do then?"

"You'll meet someone else, or you'll be happy with your partner," I said matter-of-factly.

I never asked questions about his partner—almost never—because as long as we didn't talk about her, she didn't seem real. I could pretend she didn't exist.

Occasionally, I took a break from pretending and asked the universe: *Whyyyyy? Why does it have to be like this? Why couldn't we just be free to be together?*

One day I understood the answer, or what felt like the answer. I shared it with Alex. "I think it had to be this way. I think I could only meet someone I have no future with here, because otherwise I wouldn't leave, and I think I have to leave."

He listened, and he didn't say anything. I can't know for sure, but I think he knew I was right.

I say goodbye to Alex a few days before my flight, because he's going out of town. I say goodbye, he says see you later. It feels strange. I want closure, but he wants to stay light-hearted. He doesn't acknowledge that it's the end.

As he's about to leave, we notice my deck of oracle cards sitting near us. (I only found out about oracle cards a year or so earlier, from my friend Lauren. She gave me this beautiful Native Spirit deck for my birthday. They're amazing. You can pull one—or more, but usually one— and either just see what message comes up or you can ask a question before you pull the card. It's the craziest thing because if you ask a question, 99 percent of the time you'll get a perfect answer. I don't understand what magic makes this happen. But I love it.)

Alex pulls a card from the deck. Interestingly, he gets the Flowing River card, the same one I pulled the night before. *Everything is falling into place, because you aren't resisting the drift of the great river of life. It's time to let go,* the card says. *Let go of the shore and enjoy the ride.*

"I felt that card," he tells me, in a rare moment of seriousness. "I was thinking of you when I pulled it."

Well, the message to let go is crystal clear, but my heart doesn't know how to follow those instructions. After he leaves, something feels unfinished, not right. I don't understand it. It's disturbing and uncomfortable. But whatever. I'm going to the other side of the planet; my heart will have to unattach soon enough. Some things just take time.

July thirty-first arrives. My bags are packed, and all my personal items are neatly packed in storage. I look around my beloved, tenantless house for the last time, and my friend Tracy drives me to the airport. We have no idea when I'll be back.

CHAPTER 3

August 2017, Woodside, California

Carolyn and Jono's wedding is a fairy tale. The venue is a grassy hilltop overlooking miles of vineyards that stretch out to meet hazy mountains in the distance. The weather is perfect. A gentle breeze is blowing and the early evening sun tints everything and everyone with a soft golden hue. Musicians send hypnotic notes of cello and violin into the air, lulling the small group of guests into a mellow state of well-being. The bride is stunning. Tears appear in the groom's eyes as he watches her walk toward him, between the symmetrical rows of white chairs.

The ceremony is short and sincere. The bride and groom face each other under a vine-wrapped trellis, hands joined. The officiant reads these words by James Cavanaugh:

> *To love is not to possess, to own or imprison,*
> *Nor to lose one's self in another.*
> *Love is to join and separate, to walk alone and together,*
> *to find a laughing freedom that lonely isolation does not permit.*

A chord vibrates in my soul. *That's what I want.*

This moment, this hilltop, this wedding where the love is so real you can feel it ... it feels like magic. It feels like the Universe is smiling down on these two lovers, as if this perfect weather and all this beauty is a gift and a blessing just for them.

Wine and champagne and conversation and laughter flow freely during the reception and dinner that follow. At the dinner table, I chat with one of Carolyn's friends, a pretty brunette named Jess. Laughing, Jess tells me this perfect evening is the polar opposite of her own wedding, where everything that could possibly go wrong went wrong. She relays the story in hilarious detail.

It's a tale of chaos and disaster—but, in spite of everything, she and her groom had a good time through all of it. Today, they have two kids, are still happily married, and are still having as much fun as ever.

It's as if life is showing me two sides of the coin of Love: the fairy tale and the messy, the thick and the thin. And they're both beautiful. Somehow it feels like I am supposed to be here and see this on the eve of my departure into the great unknown.

Two days later, I'm in India.

The Vipassana center is a two-hour drive from Delhi and a world away from everything. It's simple and quiet, full of trees and green spaces. Our accommodations are private cabins with attached bathrooms. The cabins are tiny but charming and the privacy is an unexpected luxury, considering we're all here by donation, and we won't even have the chance to make any donations until the end of our stay. That was one of the things that drew me to Vipassana: it's not about money. It seems to exist from a sincere and genuine desire to help other human beings. In an overly jaded, profit-hungry world, this seemed rare and amazing.

At check-in, we're required to turn in our cell phones, laptops, and all reading and writing material. The idea is to remove all forms of distraction, leaving us with no choice but to be alone with our own minds.

The evening of arrival, we're still allowed to speak, allowing us a short reprieve from the looming appointment of solitude with our own minds. I chat with a couple women during dinner. Everyone is Indian except for me and one Brazilian girl. One woman, Anju, is friendly and speaks perfect English.

After dinner, the silence begins.

My soul craved coming here. The idea of stillness, quiet, and peace—a break from the exhausting speed and noise of the outside world—it called to me like a lush green oasis in the eye of a marathon desert sandstorm. My mind, on the other hand, was terrified of a few things this Vipassana experience would entail. Specifically:

1) waking up at 4 a.m. every day (sounds like hell on earth—bordering on impossible)
2) not having coffee for ten days (will I survive?)
3) not being able to speak for ten days (I can't even imagine what that will be like. My former boss, upon hearing of the program's non-speaking requirement, had immediately burst out laughing and told me, "They'll throw you out on the first day. You won't be able to do it.")

Ironically—and, as usual—the things I worried about are not the things that go wrong. Thanks to jetlag, I wake up every morning before the 4 a.m. gong. I don't miss coffee—and I won't miss it for a while afterwards. Not speaking, in this environment, is easy, natural, and a relief.

Also as usual, the things that are difficult are the things I never saw coming. Mainly one thing, really. The meditating-for-ten-hours-a-day part.

Halfway through Day One, five seated meditation hours in, my meditation cushion has become a torture device. Sitting, in any position (and believe me, I tried them all), is physically excruciating. My spine is screaming in agony, my legs are on fire, and my mind is a feral Chewbacca thrashing and howling to break free of this insufferable prison of agony and boredom. Until now I'd never tried to meditate for longer than twenty minutes at a time, so I had no idea it could be this painful. On the verge of tears, I ask the teacher for a backrest. He gives me one. After that, the pain recedes to a level of Tolerable.

These ten days are the hardest, longest days of my life—but woven in between the hours of silent struggle are small stretches when sitting quietly is peaceful and effortless, and occasionally even blissful. Most of the time, it's a roller coaster through an avalanche of emotions and mental torture: boredom, restlessness, fatigue, mental turbulence, anger, resentment, curiosity, more boredom, fatigue again, perplexity, impatience, anger again. There are innumerable moments when it seems impossible to keep sitting there, when I ask myself: *how can I do this for another hour and a half, let alone eight more days? ... six more days? .... four more days?* But I'm not going to quit, so I have no choice but to sit there and keep breathing. And that's the way to survive anything, isn't it, when there's nothing else you can do. Just keep breathing, and no matter how slowly time is passing, it does pass, and eventually the suffering is nothing but a memory.

Even in the worst moments, when I hate everything and every cell of my being is begging to run out the door, somewhere deep down in some unidentifiable part of me is a feeling that I'm supposed to be here, that this suffering has a purpose. That my psyche needs to go through this purifying fire in preparation for the rest of my life.

The brightest points of every day are mealtimes (the food is unfailingly delicious, colorful, and nourishing), bedtime, and any time the peacocks come to grace us with their presence. There are five of them, three males and two females. They saunter unhurriedly across the grass, and every once in a while one of the males caws and displays his magnificent feathered cape. There is something about this environment, silent, devoid of distraction and sensory stimulation, that heightens the senses and intensifies the effect of beauty. When those peacocks unfurl their dazzling feathers and the sun's rays land on them, highlighting the blue, green, purple, and gold, it's beyond breathtaking, beyond earthly beauty. The sight bathes my heart in bliss every time.

I will love peacocks forever.

There is no such love in my heart for spiders. I was born with an irrational fear of spiders that has lasted my entire life thus far. I know it makes no sense to be afraid of such tiny creatures, but logic has no

SONYA MOORE

persuasive power in the presence of hard-wired irrational fear. Growing up in the US, I was only familiar with American-sized spiders. When I was ten, someone told me that in Australia, there are huge spiders with bodies the size of golf balls. I promptly vowed never to go to Australia.

Later, I reneged on that and went to Australia a few times, but I never came across any golf ball-sized spiders. Here, however, almost every day, one or two very large arachnids take up residence in my cabin. Luckily for me, my new roommates are on the smaller side as far as Indian spiders go (a fact I'm unaware of at the time), but they're three times bigger than any other spider I've ever seen, and I'm not thrilled about having to share my tiny cabin with them.

One night, I'm walking back to my cabin when the Brazilian girl rushes down the sidewalk to meet me. "I need your help!" she whispers, breaking the solemn vow of silence. "I'm so sorry, but it's an emergency!"

She leads me to her cabin and explains the emergency. Geckos! Cute little geckos have been getting into her cabin every day. She's deathly afraid of geckos. She chases them out with a broom whenever she sees them and has barricaded the entrance against them, but somehow one has found a way in. He's hiding somewhere under her bed. She can't find him and she won't be able to sleep until he's removed. On the other hand, she has no fear of spiders, but her cabin is spider-free.

And I love geckos. I'm surprised anyone is afraid of these adorable little lizards, but given my irrational spider fear, who am I to judge? I help my Brazilian friend move the furniture around until we locate the sneaky reptile and sweep him out of the cabin. It's fun surreptitiously whispering.

I wonder why she's getting the geckos and I'm getting the spiders. Why couldn't it be the other way around? The geckos would be welcome to sleep over at my place, and she wouldn't mind the spiders.

It seemed Life was forcing us to face our fears, for some reason. Maybe it was offering us an inoculation: exposing us to small doses of our unreasonable fears so we could become immune.

CHAPTER 4

Tell me,
what is it you plan to do
with your one wild and precious life?
- MARY OLIVER

During the interminable hours of meditation, my mind has plenty of time to wander through the lanes of my memory. One day it revisits an event from nine years ago: a job interview.

I hadn't been looking for a job at the time—I already had one I was pretty happy at. But one afternoon, a headhunter called and told me about an opportunity: a fast-growing hair care company down the street from my current employer was looking for an International Sales Manager. I had never heard of this company, so I investigated by buying one of their products at the supermarket: a tea tree mint conditioner. After one wash, I was in love. The conditioner smelled heavenly, left my hair lusciously smooth with plenty of swing and volume, and the bottle it came in was adorable. When the company proposed an interview, I agreed.

The night before the interview, I sat on my couch trying to prepare, feeling underqualified and devoid of confidence. I was four years out of college. I didn't have enough experience. They surely had plenty of other more qualified candidates. They would never hire me.

But in the interview the next afternoon, I was calm and confident. The right words came out. Mostly.

The recruiter had told me the interview would be with the VP of

Sales, Stu Hamilton. I had googled him and the rest of the management team, but there was a second man at the table with Stu—an unknown mystery man. His name hadn't come up in my research. He didn't tell me his title or give me a card, but he was the one asking most of the questions. After twenty minutes of this, I finally asked him point blank, "I'm sorry, but who are you?"

In retrospect, I could have phrased the question more eloquently. Luckily, the mystery man just laughed. He was Ross Reback, the CEO.

While describing the responsibilities the position would involve, Ross told me, "We're looking for total domination of the hair care world."

That sounded like fun. I said, "Okay."

They hired me, and within a few years we achieved total domination of the hair care world. I'd love to take full credit for that, but it was very much a team effort. I had the invaluable support of some awesome colleagues and fortunately, everyone wanted our brand. It's pretty easy to sell a brand everyone wants, although the process of getting hundreds of thousands of bottles of hair care products produced, shipped, and delivered to their final global destinations, complying with all relevant international regulations, and putting out the endless fires that inevitably arose along the way was a lot of work, but I loved it. It also must be noted that none of the sales domination would have happened at all without the singlehanded path-clearing work of the VP of Sales, Stu Hamilton. Stu was a big, gruff, broad-shouldered man in his early fifties with an imposing moustache. He barked rather than spoke, his words coming out in fast staccato. He didn't smile much during the interview, if at all. I thought he would be a tough boss.

I couldn't have been more wrong. Stu turned out to be the best boss I ever had—and not only because he almost never told me what to do. He trusted me to get the job done, but if I ever had a question, he had an immediate answer. He barked loudly, but behind the bark was a huge heart and a ready laugh. As the company owner observed one day, "Everyone loves Stu." Stu had little time or patience for detail and his political views were the polar opposite of mine, but he consistently rewarded each and every employee with genuine appreciation. He had a natural gift for making everyone in the company feel genuinely seen and valued and a solid aura that made you believe, as soon as he walked into the room, that everything would be okay.

A year after I joined the company, annual sales broke $50 million. That day Ross opened a bottle of champagne in the boardroom for our small team of nine office staff plus two warehouse managers. Four years later, annual sales surpassed $250 million. Our corporate team had grown to a staff of sixteen; we were selling in forty-one countries and both in the US and globally, our brand had become the hottest drugstore hair care brand in the market.

The corporate world gets a bad rap sometimes, but in the early years this was the best of the professional realm—a fun, irreverent, passionate place to work, and our team was like an imperfect but fun-loving family.

Things started to change a year later, when a leading private investment group bought a 49 percent share of the company. By then, Ross and the company had parted ways. In spite of their minority share, the investment group held a majority of seats on the board, so they controlled the decision-making. And under their control, the company's heart began to disappear. Everything became about the bottom line, and the bottom line only. Company decisions were made with no regard for their human cost. Compassion had no place in the boardroom and often, common sense didn't either. We were experiencing yet another year of record sales growth. Our corporate team was lean and efficient; costs were low, profits were high. But the investors' job was to make costs even lower and profits even higher, so they did. From a numbers perspective, they did their job well. But some of the decisions they made had crippling effects on many of the loyal business partners who had gotten us to where we were. They didn't care.

I know this is a common experience in the corporate world. "It's just business," is the phrase we frequently hear to absolve all corporate crimes against humanity. But business can include basic human decency and compassion, and still be profitable. When a fraction of a percent of profit becomes more important than the fair and decent treatment of partners and employees, something is wrong.

It wasn't all terrible. I still had some wonderful colleagues and clients, and my direct bosses were great people. We still had good times. *I'm lucky to be here,* I told myself; *it could be so much worse.* But my motivation and sense of purpose were draining away. I was starting to feel less and less a fit with this organization.

But they dangled a carrot in front of us, those they designated as "key employees." If we stayed until they sold the company or went public, we would be rewarded with a generous incentive payout. The greater the company's profit, the greater our personal profit would be. However, if we left before the sale or IPO happened, we would forfeit 90 percent of that incentive.

For me, the minimum payout would be a seven-figure sum. It was a tantalizing carrot. Okay, it wasn't a carrot. It was a giant slice of cocoa-dusted tiramisu with an extra shot of rum on the side. And although the details were mostly hush-hush, all signs indicated that the payout-triggering event would be happening very soon. So, I told myself, *I just need to hang in there for a little while longer.*

But one day I got a phone call from a headhunter. He told me about an opportunity with a dermocosmetic company—a publicly traded company with offices in Miami, Europe, and Mexico, with disruptive products and an exciting future. They were looking for a VP of International Sales. The position would report directly to the Chief Commercial Officer, who had been the VP of Global Sales for Procter & Gamble for many years. He was on the University of Miami's Board of Leadership. I could learn so much from him, I imagined. I researched the company. What I found was impressive: their ads and PR looked great; celebrities recommended their products. I was intrigued enough to agree to an interview.

The interview was with Manny, the CCO, an intelligent, fast-talking guy who answered all my questions satisfactorily and gave me more exciting details. The company was poised for tremendous growth. Within the past few months, they had brought on a brand new management team: a new CEO and CFO along with himself.

I left their office feeling more excited about the opportunity than

I had expected. When I got into my car and turned on the ignition, the time on the dashboard clock was 1:11.

A lucky repeating number. *Maybe it's a good sign,* I thought.

Manny had given me a bag of product samples to try. I washed my hair with their shampoo that night. That shampoo, Revita, was their number one product. It was the best shampoo on the planet, according to Manny. It was a hair growth shampoo that actually worked—it made hair grow, made it grow faster, and left both hair and scalp healthy and perfect.

I had been in the fast-moving consumer goods side of the hair care industry for over a decade at that point. Over the years, I had tried hundreds of shampoos. This one amazed me. It was exceptional. It *was* the best shampoo I had ever tried. It left my scalp feeling delightfully refreshed and invigorated, and after a quick blow dry, my hair looked like I had just stepped out of a salon. Every strand was in perfect condition: smooth and light, with volume and swing and a glow of healthy shine. I was genuinely impressed.

I told my friend Michelle about the situation and showed her the products. She picked up the anti-dandruff shampoo. "My husband has this shampoo in our shower!" she exclaimed. "He loves it!"

One more point for Company #2. In spite of myself, my excitement about this potential opportunity was growing. It was a career move that made sense. I was stagnating at my current job, and that's a horrible feeling. This new company was close to what I had come from, but with the dermatological aspect, different enough that I could learn and grow. They were offering a very attractive salary and bonus package, and stock as well. If the company reached a certain threshold, that stock would be worth just as much as the incentive my current employer had offered. But it was the riskier choice, of course. And meanwhile, office whispers indicated that the sale or IPO of my current company (aka, "the payout-triggering event") would be happening very, very soon.

Luckily, I didn't have to decide yet. There would certainly be a second, and probably a third interview before they would potentially offer me the job.

Wrong! Two days later, my phone rang, precisely at 3:33pm, according to the time on my phone screen. It was the headhunter calling to tell me they would be sending an offer letter soon.

Sure enough, the offer letter arrived in my inbox the following Monday. Now I had to make a decision.

That night I sat at home in my living room, weighing my choices. There was a very high probability that accepting the job would mean walking away from a seven-figure payout that would be coming in the next few months. Would that make me certifiably insane, or just really stupid? There were a lot of things I could do with that much money. But … would it make me happier? Maybe. It could mean financial freedom and financial security. Two very attractive things. There was a secret irrational fear that had always lived somewhere deep inside me, that someday I might end up unemployed, homeless, and starving. With this payout, I wouldn't have to worry about that ever again.

Or would I? Are we ever really guaranteed security in this world? What if I invested the money and lost it all as quickly as I earned it? (See, my mind can find something to worry about in any scenario.) But with that much in the bank, I would be feeling reasonably secure. And I would be able to do pretty much whatever I wanted. I could take nicer trips, fly first class, stay in more expensive hotels, and buy more shoes and clothes. I did love beautiful things. I could also stop working if I wanted to. But then, wouldn't I get bored? I wanted to keep learning and evolving as a person. If I quit this job, I would want to find another one.

On the other hand, what would I be giving up to stick around for this sugar-coated carrot/tiramisu of a payout? The other job opportunity seemed perfect, and if I passed this one up, there was no guarantee something this good would come along again.

Sitting in stillness and thinking about it, I recognized that the big lump sum of money wasn't the thing I wanted most. I liked money. I liked there to be lots of it in my bank account so I didn't have to think about it. But at that moment, more than lots of money, I wanted to keep learning and experiencing life and growing as a person. And I had a feeling I would have other chances to make money.

I also knew, deep down, that if I chose to stay with Company #1, it would be out of fear. It would feel like selling out. Actually, it would feel like selling my soul, and I wouldn't respect myself for it. Even if it was completely illogical from a financial point of view, I just couldn't do it. My gut told me the second path was where I was meant to go. Besides all that, quite honestly, I just wanted to take the job. The idea of quitting felt like the chance to walk out of a prison door. So I decided to kiss the future payout goodbye, and take the job.

Once the decision was made, I felt that click that happens when you know you've made the right choice. It felt good.

Before I formally accepted, Manny called one more time. I was on a layover in Washington Dulles airport when we spoke. When we hung up, my attention was caught by a digital clock to my right displaying the time in huge white numbers on a black screen. 2:22.

Three in a row of those repeating numbers at these key stages of the interview process? What were the chances of that? Maybe they were just three timely coincidences … but they felt like something more. They felt like winks from the universe, a friendly cosmic reassurance that I had made the right choice.

Less than three months later when the sale of the company was about to go through, my former employers exercised their option to buy back the remaining ten percent of my incentive shares for a fraction of what they would have been worth after the sale. It didn't matter. They kept their money; I kept my happiness.

The first few days at my new job were exceptionally great. I felt exhilarated and engaged—sensations I hadn't felt at the office in so long I'd almost forgotten it was possible to feel this way. It felt like coming back to life after a long hibernation.

And then, exactly two weeks after my first day, all hell broke loose. That day, the management team filed a report with the SEC disclosing that the company's prior year financial statements had inaccurately recorded equity transactions and inflated revenue by close to a million dollars. Simultaneously, they announced the termination of the company president for his alleged involvement in the fraudulent financial reporting.

The CEO addressed this bombshell publicly with soothing words, describing a company that had gone off course but was now being steered back onto the respectable, law-abiding path towards a bright future. And that may well have been how things would have gone, except that the president, who was also the founder of the company and the chairman of the board, didn't take kindly to this attempted coup. He fought back like an incensed lion, resulting in a very messy, very public power struggle. He filed suit claiming the termination was invalid, launched his own internal investigation, had the IT director cut off the CEO's access to her company email, and began issuing regular press releases which read like episodes of a lurid soap opera. Among other details, he revealed that the CEO, the head of the audit committee, and the lead attorney had defrauded investors by conspiring to issue each other two million shares of stock within days of the "attempted" termination of the president. Meanwhile, stock plummeted and multiple class action lawsuits were filed against the company on behalf of injured shareholders. After a week and a half of this drama, Nasdaq halted trading of the company's stock.

There are several morals to be found in this story, and clearly one of them is that if you plan a corporate takeover, you should make sure the head of IT is on your side. Another is that if you choose to follow your heart, you aren't guaranteed protection from life's curveballs. I would be lying if I said the thought that maybe I made the wrong call never entered my mind during that turbulent time. But even during those weeks of chaos when the solid ground under my feet seemed to have disintegrated, something inside me insisted I had made the right choice. Even if this career choice ended in catastrophe and I ended up jobless in a few days.

But it didn't come to that. After about a month, the storm calmed. When the dust settled, the company founder was the one left standing. He fired the management team and appointed his long-term business partner, Fernando Tamez, as the new COO. However crazy and possibly illegal any other actions of our newly reinstated corporate leader may have been, that last one was a smart choice. Fernando was a young, highly intelligent entrepreneur and medical doctor who was personally responsible for the company's legitimate and thriving business in Mexico and Europe.

Fernando and the president, who reprised his role as CEO and chairman of the board, liked my vision for the future of the company's international business and my roadmap to get us there. The rest of the year went well—amazingly well. My global contacts were panning out, things were falling into place, business prospects were looking very promising all over the globe. I met fantastic people, went exotic places, learned, grew, evolved.

In the midst of all of that, something surprising stood out brightly. Many of the business contacts I met during these months shared life stories that in broad strokes were identical to mine. Repeatedly, I heard different versions of the same story, from diverse places: Spain, Chile, Mexico, Italy. He or she had a stable job with a successful company—and then the time came they didn't want to be there anymore. They made the decision to leave, to leap, to try something different and riskier. The choice was a scary one; not the most prudent from a financial point of view, but the one they had to make to feel truly alive. None of them regretted their choice. They all had the same light in their eyes when they told their stories.

My experience wasn't unique, I realized. Something about this was, if not universal, at least widespread.

Then the new year came. January 2017. Abruptly, my good fortune seemed to invert itself. Doors began to close around me. Everywhere I turned, another one slammed shut. The future started to look darker. The most ominous shadow was thrown by the company's cash flow position. Thanks to past mismanagement, they had reached a point where they couldn't afford to buy the raw ingredients needed to manufacture the goods to meet customer demand. Out of stocks were becoming more frequent, and longer lasting. Customers were angry—constantly. Meanwhile, I was expected to continue developing new business. But my confidence in the company's ability to deliver on any new business I brought in was rapidly eroding. If we couldn't deliver on time, the delays would create serious negative ramifications for our new overseas partners who would be investing significantly to launch our brand in their respective territories.

That was the chain of choices and circumstances that led to that fateful moment in my Johannesburg hotel five months ago when I decided to leave my job and life as I knew it.

Sitting here in India on my meditation cushion, I have no regrets.

On Day Seven, I wake up thinking: *Lucky number seven. Something magic could happen today.*

And it does.

It happens during the afternoon Power Hour, which is what I've silently nicknamed the afternoon one hour meditation sessions during which our assigned goal is to not move a muscle for the entire hour. These daily hourlong stretches are painful, but not impossible, and the part of me that thrives on challenges loves them. They are a test of sheer willpower and endurance. If you move, there are no negative repercussions—no one will punish or reprimand you. Most likely no one will even notice. Your only opponent, coach, and cheerleader is yourself. After a half hour or so, it becomes astonishingly painful to hold the same position—and yet it is possible to grit your teeth, keep breathing, and stay frozen in place.

This particular hour, something unexpected happens. I've been sitting immobile for around thirty minutes. Pain is burning in my legs. My hands rest motionless on my knees and my arms are itching intensely to move. Suddenly, intriguing thoughts surface in my mind.

What if there's something beautiful under this pain and discomfort? What if other times in my life when I was confronted with pain or discomfort, there was always something beautiful waiting on the other side, if I would have just gone far enough through it instead of turning around too soon and running back to comfort? What if pain and discomfort is a layer that we just have to dive through, just have to go far enough or deep enough to get to the other side and that's where something amazing has always been waiting for us?

The thoughts are an enchanting Pied Piper. As my mind follows them, curious to discover where they lead, my awareness of physical pain gently fades away and a sense of wellbeing rises in its place. A vivid scene rises up in my mind. I see a river, a wide, flowing, silvery-blue river, with a current that's strong but gentle. The current represents the current of life, and I understand how it's meant to pull me forward through life. Large boulders are scattered throughout the river, and sometimes the current deposits me up against them and leaves me there for a while, but sooner or later it tugs me forward again. And I see how in my past I sometimes got comfortable on those boulders and tried to cling to them for too long. I fought against life's current when it started to pull me forward, but the river was stronger than me and it always pried me loose in the end. I understand how sometimes I suffered unnecessarily for trying to fight the current of Life, for trying to hang on to things and situations and people too long when they weren't meant for me anymore. I see how much easier and more pleasant life can be if I just go with the flow. I also see that I'm not powerless in this river; I can swim with the current to move ahead faster or steer myself to one side or the other. But when a strong current comes along, it's beyond my control.

I'm blissfully absorbed in the unfolding epiphanies and time floats by without me realizing it, and before I know it the hour is up, and I am light and joyful and triumphant.

That was the first part of the magic. The rest comes right afterward, when the teacher calls our small group over to him and asks us how we're doing. (We get these tiny windows of authorized vocal cord usage a few times during the ten days.) When it's my turn to answer, I tell him that right now I'm great but it's been a roller coaster, up and down.

The teacher replies, "Yes, up and down, and this is how it will continue through the course. Later, you'll be like her" (he gestures toward a woman who just told us she was feeling heavy), "and she'll be like you. This is like life also—sometimes it's easy, sometimes it's hard; it's like a flowing river. Sometimes we make ourselves suffer unnecessarily because we crave the good things too much, and we try to cling to them too hard, instead of letting go and going with the flow of the river."

As if he could see into my mind; as if he was describing, practically word for word, what I just saw. I stare at him, speechless, wondering if he has psychic powers.

I decided later that he probably didn't. He was probably very intuitive and very tuned in, but I think some higher force nudged him to speak those words, to spark yet another divine coincidence. If déjà vu is a glitch in the matrix, I think divine coincidences are a bell for our attention—the Universe's way of underlining and highlighting a message, a person or an opportunity that will take us farther down the path that's meant for us. To make sure we notice.

Somehow that day, the message about letting go reached deep enough into my psyche to change me. And I needed that particular transformation, because it would make the rest of my journey possible.

CHAPTER 5

A good traveler has no fixed plans and is not intent on arriving.
- LAO TZU

August 2017

After Vipassana, I'm supposed to fly to Nepal. Distracted by the excitement of being allowed to talk, I mix up my departure time and miss the flight by forty-five minutes. I try to rebook at the airline counter, but strangely, there are no available seats on any flight to Nepal for the next four days. The Wi-Fi in the airport is barely functional and I have no idea what to do instead. I decide to book a hotel in Delhi for the night and figure out Plan B once I have internet.

"You should go to Ladakh," a Jet Airways employee tells me as she's escorting me across the airport to the exit. "It's more beautiful than Nepal and the people are nicer."

The people of Nepal might beg to differ, but this woman's words remind me that a few months ago, an Indian friend of mine back in Florida told me Ladakh was a beautiful place. So that settles it. That's where I'll go instead.

A few hours later, I'm seated on a comfortable couch in the lobby of my Delhi hotel; showered, relaxed, and researching Ladakh on my laptop. Ladakh looks mountainous, remote, and stunning. I glance up from my screen when a crimson-robed monk with a pleasant face sits down across from me. We start chatting. It turns out he's just arrived from Nepal. *(Hello Nepal, I couldn't make it to you but thanks for sending a representative.)*

I mention I just finished a Vipassana course. The monk replies: "Oh, that's why you seem so calm."

Me: "I seem calm, really? You can tell?"

Him: "Yes, I noticed that about you. Because most Americans are not calm."

If being told by a Nepalese monk that you seem calm is not the ultimate compliment, then I don't know what is. All those brutal hours of meditation were not in vain.

This monk turns out to be a cool, interesting guy. He shows me pictures of his family's beautiful homestay in Kathmandu, where his niece teaches Tibetan guitar and yoga and they have an altar for meditation. They're five minutes from two World Heritage sites and he knows the father of Kumari, the living goddess, so he could easily arrange for me to see her. This sounds fantastic. I'm starting to be glad I missed my flight. I'll go to Nepal later and stay at the monk's homestay and it will be incredible. For now, Ladakh.

The next morning, I wake up to incomprehensible news.

It arrives via text message from Stu, my former boss. It's the link to an obituary for our former CEO, Ross Reback. It gives no information other than that he passed away August 17th, with contact information for the funeral home. Stu has no other information either.

My mind can't process this. It has to be a mistake. Maybe it's a different Ross Reback. I just saw Ross two weeks before I left Florida. We had stayed in touch after he left the company and we usually met for lunch a couple times a year when I was back in Tampa. Last time, as usual, he was fully, vibrantly alive, engaged in multiple fascinating projects, full of hilarious stories and plans for the future. As always, he was also genuinely interested in what was going on in my life. He always got me. My own father didn't get me and wasn't particularly interested in my life, so Ross kind of filled the father-figure void. He once volunteered to walk me down the aisle at my wedding. (A hypothetical future wedding, in the event I ever had one.) We didn't always agree on work issues and business strategy, but he had a lot of wisdom in his own street-smart way and was people smart in ways I wasn't.

During one of our lunches, in the middle of a story, I paused to acknowledge, "Well, I am a little crazy."

"Anyone who's not a little crazy is boring as hell," he replied.

It struck me instantly as profound truth. "Right? They totally are! Boring as hell!"

We used the word crazy, but neither of us meant bonafide insanity, just a fun-loving, unorthodox, irrepressible refusal to sacrifice living fully for the sake of conformity, tucked in there under a thin surface layer of level-headed responsibility.

That last lunch was our goodbye lunch because I was going to Asia for God knew how long. Ross said the nicest thing. "Be careful out there. If you ever need anything, call me. I mean it. I'll get on a plane…"

He said it twice, so I knew he meant it. And he hated flying, so that meant a lot. I wasn't scared, but it was still nice to know someone was willing to come to my rescue in case I ever needed to be rescued.

His presence was too vivid to disappear just like that. Refusing to believe the outrageous news on my phone's screen, I text him. *Ross, are you okay?*

No reply. Maybe he's busy, or something. In the merciful numbness of denial, I go on with my day, which will be spent in Delhi. My flight to Ladakh is booked for the next day.

At breakfast, the Nepalese monk is eating with his white-bearded American friend from Louisiana. They invite me to join them. The monk's name is Tsering (the T is silent) and his American friend is Neil. They met twenty years ago when Neil spent six months in a monastery in India where Tsering was the only monk who spoke English. Now Neil spends six months every year in India, with Dharamsala as his home base. Tsering lives between Nepal and Dharamsala. For the past twelve years they've been bringing groups of pre-med students and social workers to India for mindfulness training retreats. They'll both be in Dharamsala while I'm there.

I know essentially nothing about Buddhism and I'm curious to learn more. I ply them with questions and a fascinating conversation ensues. Tsering explains that there are many different forms of Buddhism because there are many different personality types. (Later, I will discover the same concept in the Bhagavad Gita—many paths for many personalities.) People are wired for different things, people learn in different ways, some people need rules, some people don't—etc. There are many paths to enlightenment. This is in stark, refreshing contrast to the strict Christian philosophy I was taught during the first eighteen years of my life: one right road to salvation, one right interpretation, all other paths lead to hell and damnation.

Neil and Tsering describe a few different methods of Tibetan Buddhist meditation. In one, you are taught different plays that your mind has to run through, while using beads as assistance. In others, you're given mantras or mandalas to focus on, or you imagine yourself as a certain deity or character and see how you feel in that role.

Those all sound like way more fun than the austere Vipassana method.

I ask them if Buddhism has anything to say about why some people are just awful and why people sometimes do horrible things, which is something I've wondered about my whole life.

Neil replies in his relaxed Louisiana drawl. "Buddhism would tell you that they are all enlightened beings just acting out their roles in a big play that was written for you, to teach you whatever lessons you need to learn to bring you to enlightenment."

His answer leaves me spellbound. The next day, on the plane to Leh, I'm still thinking about it. It's a novel, liberating way of looking at things, a perspective that could release all animosity, anger, resentment, and bitterness from one's reaction to people who do bad things—all those heavy emotions that weigh us down. It removes the need to spend any time or energy trying to figure out the answers to questions like "What's wrong with him/her? Why would they do that? What are they thinking?" Seen from this vantage point the situation could remain light and playful, sort of like a challenging game. The challenge being to look inside and figure out, *okay, what am I supposed to learn here*, or *what is this showing me about me*. Also, if I'm in this big play that was written just for me, it's like I'm on stage or on camera, with all eyes waiting to see how I'll respond. As multiple studies have shown, human performance improves dramatically when we know we're being watched.

The first time I did ayahuasca a couple years earlier, a cryptic message kept repeating in my head: *Be the star of your own movie.* At the time, I had no idea what that meant. Maybe it meant something along the lines of this Buddhist theory. I have no proof that this theory is valid, but it sure is a fun, comforting way of looking at this majestic, bewildering mystery that is Life. So I choose to embrace it. I decide that from this moment on I will assume that I am being filmed at all times by a crew of celestial enlightened beings—sympathetic enlightened beings who are all rooting for me to do well and who are here not only to film but also to support and protect me and to nudge me in the right direction when needed, keeping me on the path I'm intended to be on, heading towards some mysterious, unimaginably beautiful destination.

CHAPTER 6

What is the purpose of life?
To live. But live fully.
- MATTHIEU RICARD

August 2017

Leh is quietly magnificent.
  It's Ladakh's capital, a small town set in the lap of India's northernmost Himalayas, surrounded on all sides by sand-colored mountains resting peacefully under a cornflower blue sky. The streets of the town center are vibrant with backpackers, and colorful wares beckon in shop windows: fabrics and scarves, jewelry, singing bowls, statuesque teapots and gold Buddhas and dancing Hindu deities. They aren't cheap souvenirs—they're all beautiful, exotic, and good quality. I want to buy everything. But everything I buy has to be carried in my suitcase, so I stick to jewelry and scarves.

  Typical Ladakhi architecture is attractive at first glance and exquisite up close. Buildings are made of white stucco garnished with ornately carved wooden window frames, porches, and overhangs. Ladakhi wood is the color of caramel-tinted gold. Bright flowers are everywhere. My favorites are the tall red and pink hollyhocks.

  Life is simple here. The local people seem unworried and happy. I notice a large number of shockingly handsome Ladakhi men around, mostly working in small shops. They're tall, well-built, and olive-skinned, with strong jaws, chiseled features, and great hair. They seem totally unaware of their uncommon good looks. I come across the first of these beautiful beings in a quiet corner of the market, selling handbags and coin purses. His attractiveness startles me. *What are you doing in this little shop?* I think. *Shouldn't you be out on a movie set somewhere?*

When I realize how many of these gorgeous men are here, I wonder if I should go find modeling contracts for one or two or five of them. This kind of beauty shouldn't be hidden from the world. Then again, they might be happier here, sheltered from the spotlight of the world's attention.

I spend my first couple days wandering, exploring everything. Bliss finds me in small, simple moments. At a table in a small outdoor plaza, sipping a hot honey lemon ginger tea and savoring veggie momos with an orange sauce whose flavor is perfection while slow music and cool breezes float through the air, blending with the muted laughter and voices of locals and backpackers who meander through the square, nonchalantly whiling away the day's last hours of sunlight. Watching them, I'm lulled into contentment by this place where stress doesn't seem to exist.

Bliss sneaks in again as I'm lying in a hammock in the grassy courtyard of my peaceful hotel, gazing up at a circle of tall sycamore trees under a blue sky. It feels like the garden of a classy Southern estate. I'm thinking, *this is India?*

India is many things, I will come to discover.

I receive two energy healings these first two days in Ladakh. The first is from an Indian journalist I meet in my hotel lobby. Our casual conversation reveals that he's also a teacher and practitioner of Vipassana, kundalini, and tantra. As we're talking, he spontaneously starts reading my energy. Everything he says is eerily spot on. (Among them: "You just went through a breakup, right?" Although that could be a lucky guess and I'm not sure if I technically went through a breakup or not.) He offers me an energy healing, at no charge.

Energy healings are mysterious, non-scientific, and enticing. I am both skeptical of and drawn to them. Depending on who's doing the healing, they can be nothing or they can be life changing. Here in this setting, I'm open and curious, and the journalist/teacher's spontaneous energy reading was convincing enough to hook me.

That afternoon, he comes to my hotel room to conduct the healing. Before we begin, he spends a long time explaining the three different healing options he can offer. He wants to be sure I feel comfortable with whichever one I choose. The options are:

Level One: no touching.
Level Two: some touching.
Level Three: he will use his lingam in my yoni to remove all of my energetic blockages.

(In case you're not familiar with this sacred Hindu terminology, lingam = penis and yoni = vagina.) The journalist/healer also explains that Level Three is not sex. He shows me pictures of his wife and young daughter to help make this clear.

This scene couldn't get any more sketchy and cliché if it tried, but my intuition tells me he's sincere and means well. I don't sense any threat. However, I stick with Level One.

Level One begins with us standing very close to each other while the journalist/healer slowly blows air out of his mouth onto my body. Then he instructs me to lie down on the bed while he hovers over me and continues blowing breath on my face and body. It would have been nice if he had brushed his teeth or used mouthwash or chewed gum or all three before this treatment. I try to inhale as little as possible.

He asks me to take my clothes off for the lying on the bed part. I keep them on. It's all very strange and I can't say that I notice any energy shift, except that I feel relaxed because I'm lying down. At the end of the treatment, he starts spontaneously reading my energy again and throws out some predictions for my future. "You're going to lose something of material value in two to three months, like a phone or a TV will break and have to be replaced, something like that. You'll start working again in the future, although not necessarily the same job, but you'll go back to work and you'll feel good working. Actually it's important because you feel better when you're working."

Me: "Well, I'm feeling pretty good not working right now."

Him: "Yeah, but it's just a break. And you needed it because if you didn't come here definitely you were going to collapse."

Hmm, interesting. It's true that I was exhausted quite often. Actually, I had been chronically exhausted for years. If not for coffee I probably wouldn't have made it this far.

He continues with his last prediction: "You'll be in courtship again soon. That courtship will begin no later than six months from now, and this guy loves your soul. It's going to last, because when you love someone's soul you'll never detach. He can love your body too but it's really about your soul. It's someone from your past that will come in your life again with new energy, and it will be very good."

That surprisingly beautiful third prediction lights a warm glow in my heart. I tell him I'll write these down and see if they come true. To his credit and my surprise, over the next couple years, he'll text me a few times to ask if his prophecies have been fulfilled. I lose things on such a regular basis that it will be difficult to know which item prophecy number one might have been referring to. Number two will come to pass as he described: I will start working again, and it won't be the same job, and I will feel good working.

As for number three … that remains to be seen.

Energy Healing Number Two takes place the following day at a small yoga shala in town. I go there in the morning for a drop-in yoga class. I'm the only student and the teacher is a balding Eastern European swami with a heavy accent and warm brown eyes. He's shorter than me, has one missing tooth, and can put his legs behind his back. I enjoy the class. It's challenging but relaxing.

After class, the swami proposes that I come back that afternoon for a reiki healing session and Level One training. Since I'm interested in reiki and on a roll now with healing sessions, I take him up on it.

When we begin, he has me sit in a chair in the center of the room and asks me to take my shirt off—not normally a requisite for reiki, in my experience. What is it with all the energy healers in India wanting me to take my clothes off?

"Why?" I ask.

"Sometimes there can be other people's energy on the clothing," he replies. "They can be contaminated."

"This shirt just came from the laundry," I tell him cheerfully. "I'll keep it on."

He doesn't have an argument for that. My shirt stays on, and he proceeds with the reiki. Thankfully, he doesn't blow on me, but he tells me repeatedly that he has enlightenment (he pronounces it "light-ment") and that I need light-ment. Halfway through the session, he becomes very happy and informs me that I remind him of his ex-girlfriend—I have the same energy and I look like her. At the end of the session, he asks me with glowing eyes, "Aren't you feeling more love than you ever have in your life?"

No, I can't say that I am. Just mildly uncomfortable and eager to leave. I stand up. He hugs me and kisses me on the forehead and the cheek and then tries to kiss me on the mouth. I extract myself from the embrace, hand him the required rupees, and make for the door while he tells me I should come study yoga with him at his ashram—my hips need to be opened.

Um, no thanks.

Free of the shala and the overly affectionate swami, I return to my state of relaxed contentment. A day later, as I'm wandering through the streets of Leh feeling light and wonderful and loving life, I realize I haven't felt this blissful and carefree since I was about seven years old. This isn't a feeling I want to give up anytime soon, and there is so much more to see and do in this part of the world. It occurs to me that I probably won't be going back home anytime in the near future—this adventure is just getting started.

That afternoon, halfway through a yoga class in a high-ceilinged shala (a different shala this time, with no hip-opening swamis present), my mind drifts to the one thing holding me back from total happy carefreeness. My still unrented house in Florida, sitting there empty, slowly draining my bank account with its monthly mortgage payments.

My house, my sanctuary, my beloved private oasis I had thought I would never part with—all of a sudden, it feels like a ball and chain. In that split second I realize the house is one of those boulders from my Vipassana flowing river vision, and the current is tugging me away from it, toward something else ahead and unseen. It's time to let go.

Suddenly I know I'm not going back. And I want to sell my house.

The sudden desire to set myself free of my former sanctuary is so intense it takes every ounce of my willpower not to jump up immediately and run outside to call my realtor. Invoking all my inner strength, I wait for the class to end first.

My realtor must be thrilled to hear the news, but she accepts my decision calmly and professionally. We agree on a price and she lists the house. Three days later, I have an offer. The buyer's credit is stellar; the bank approves the offer. We'll close in six weeks or so.

The years of home renovation paid off. The house sells for $110,000 more than I bought it for—enough to fund many years of travel at Asian prices. I traded my house for freedom.

For as long as I could remember, letting go of things and people I loved—and even some I didn't love anymore—was one of my biggest struggles in life. But I never felt a moment of sadness or remorse about letting go of my cherished house, neither then nor afterwards. It gave me so much happiness while I was there, and now, letting go of it gave me more joy. It was time for the house to become someone else's sanctuary. Meanwhile, other happiness and other sanctuaries waited ahead for me, somewhere new and unknown.

I don't think it would have happened without my flowing river miracle lesson. That was Vipassana's biggest gift to me.

In Leh, I also finally let go of my denial that Ross is really gone.

It was a heart attack that took him. Some of my former colleagues went to the funeral service; they said it was beautiful. One of them wrote a moving tribute to him and emailed it to everyone in the company.

I didn't get to say goodbye! I thought for a second—and then I realized that we did say good-bye. It wasn't goodbye forever, but it was *goodbye, I have no idea when I'll see you again.* One of the last things he said to me was, "I love you—you know that, right?" The words *I love you* were easy for him to say. He said them often to many people, because he was connected to his heart and he recognized that love is part of life and it was comfortable for him, and I knew he meant it.

"I know—I love you too," I said back. They're easy words for me to say if someone else says them first, and I meant them too.

I am infinitely grateful for that goodbye. He was a unique, legendary, and unforgettable human. He will always remain vividly alive in my memory.

CHAPTER 7

Don't look back, you're not going that way.
- CARD SEEN IN A DHARAMSALA CAFÉ

August 2017

In Dharamsala, it was the clouds that got me first.

The ocean of clouds that stretches out below the city as far as the eye can see, always moving, shapeshifting, forming an ethereal buffer between this mountaintop sanctuary city and the rest of the world. The clouds that occasionally ascend to envelop the town's colorful buildings in a thick fog, and sometimes pause overhead to unleash buckets of rain onto everything and everyone below. During monsoon season, the rain can continue for days, even weeks at a time. But always, eventually, the sun reappears, sending its sparkling rays over the lush, rain-cleansed mountain landscape.

The city rises above the clouds like something out of a fairy tale—if you look from far away. Close up, you can't see all the beauty.

Dharamsala (or *Dharamshala,* as pronounced in India) is made up of Upper Dharamsala and Lower Dharamsala. Upper Dharamsala includes three villages: McLeod Ganj, Dharamkot, and Bhagsu. The Dalai Lama lives in McLeod Ganj, and that's where I stay my first week here, in a simple homestay with stunning views of the lush misty mountains and two enormous spiders in the bedroom.

These aren't the harmless spiders from my Vipassana cabin I've made my peace with … these are the legendary golf ball-sized spiders of Asia with thick, hairy legs. They're way too big to kill, and there's no way I'm going to sleep with them in the room. The cook removes them for me, scooping them up in his bare hands, laughing at my terror.

The first two days, McLeod Ganj depresses me with its drabness, its concrete, and the trash (mostly plastic) that litters its streets and forms an entire waterfall of garbage down the side of one mountain. The manmade waste is a stark contrast to the natural beauty of the scenery around us. I complain about this to Neil when I meet him for lunch. (He and Tsering are back in Dharamsala now.) He tells me, "If you blur your eyes, it looks like flowers."

That strategy doesn't work for me. I miss the cleanliness of my homeland.

My second day in Dharamsala, I meet Sam in a coffee shop. Sam sounds and seems American but he's Mongolian—a New York-educated, West Point-trained Mongolian army officer. He's twenty-five, which is a little more than a decade younger than me, but he has a natural presence that's been enhanced by his military training. He's fun, attractive, and multifaceted. He tells stories that are fascinating or hilarious and often both. He's missing the USA too.

That night we take ourselves to LaBooze, the closest thing in McLeod Ganj to a western nightclub. We drink cocktails at the bar while familiar dance music vibrates around us and we're temporarily transported back to the US. On our walk back to our respective hotels we find our path blocked by a giant black cow sitting in the middle of the street and we realize we're still in India.

By the third day, Dharamsala's charm is starting to bring me under its spell, pulling me beyond my first impressions. I start to notice its peaceful energy. I discover enchanting little restaurants and meet more nice people. I keep hanging out with Sam, who loves restaurants and hiking like I do. (When you're traveling alone, there's something incredibly delightful about having a friend to meet up with on a regular basis.) Sam introduces me to some fantastic off-the-beaten-track places. One is a waterfall that pours into a river with giant boulders that reminds me of my Vipassana vision. We climb on the boulders. Sam peels off his shirt to dive into the river, which is how I discover he has the rock-hard six pack you would expect of a West Point-trained military officer. I don't jump in the river because the water's freezing.

I visit Tushita, the Buddhist center Tsering told me about. During a guided hourlong meditation, my mind drifts back to a personal goal I set before I left Florida. *I want to become comfortable with discomfort.*

Two seconds after the thought passes through my head, the teacher intones, "Become comfortable with discomfort."

The silent bell of synchronicity. Okay, Universe, noted.

It's the first morning of the Dalai Lama's teachings. The temple is beautiful, full of pillars, bright colors, and golden Buddhas. Every morning of the teachings, it's packed full with a thousand or so people seated closely together on cushions on the floor, both monks and lay people. As we wait for His Holiness' arrival, the vibe is peaceful and patient. The monks are chanting and the melody is soothing.

Ni me tse waydeh chen chen ray zee
Ti may kyen bay won boh jon bel yung
Ken chen kyeh bay tsu kyen zoba bah
Lo san tra bay, shaba so wah day.

Later Tsering tells me it was the "Ode to Tsongkapa."

When the Dalai Lama appears, walking slowly, supported by other monks, smiling and raising his hand to the faces around him, the effect of his presence is ... unexpected. There is something about him, something about the energy he emanates that immediately touches the heart. It brings tears to my eyes. Never in my life have I been affected this way by anyone's sheer presence.

Sam tells me afterwards that he too teared up a little at the Dalai Lama's arrival—and he's a tough-ass Mongolian military officer. So it wasn't just me; there is something real and powerful about the energy of this self-described "simple monk." It's as if he's filled with so much genuine peace, love, compassion, and lovingkindness that it can't be contained within his body, and the vibrations of those qualities spread out to fill the room he's in and touch a chord inside the hearts of those around him. The quiet admiration and devotion that the Tibetan people feel for him intensify the effect.

Part of it is that the Dalai Lama isn't pretending to be anything he isn't. He's real. Besides all this wonderful compassionate lovingkindness, he's wise, curious—and hilarious. Every time he straightfacedly says something funny and then starts snickering at his own joke, it kills me. I love him. In a world filled with hypocritical, power-hungry spiritual and religious teachers, he is a rare diamond. He makes me want to be a better person.

The night before my yoga teacher training begins, Sam and I have dinner in a cozy restaurant. We order a bottle of Indian red wine— Sula 2016 Cabernet Shiraz—and it's good! We're shocked. No one told us there was such a thing as good Indian wine. We go through a bottle and a half and take the remaining half bottle back to my room. I moved to a new hotel in Dharamkot for three nights and it's a little piece of heaven. A treehouse-like heaven, with tall glass windows on two sides, bright red curtains, a big balcony, and spectacular views of the green mountains and the clouds. I splurged on this one; it was $40 a night.

A soothing rain has started. My room has one double bed and a twin bed. We pull the twin mattress out onto the balcony, where the hypnotic night rain falls around our dry, comfortable open air shelter. We trade kisses and laughter in between swigs of wine from the bottle. It's sensual, playful, fun, and that's all. Something in me won't let me sleep with him. I'm not sure how much that has to do with his age, or how much it has to do with Alex, who's still texting almost every day, and how much it has to do just with me, but I'm happy and safe in my current balanced emotional state and this sense of balance feels fragile. I don't want to mix my energy with someone else's in that intimate way right now. But our makeout session is fun and he's a good cuddler.

We fall asleep on the outdoor mattress. In the morning we lay relaxing in our open-air nest for a long time as the cool sun slowly rises. Birds chirp around us and clouds drift by in slow motion. Time seems to slow down in India, and it passes by deliciously.

Later that morning, I discover three massive hickeys on my neck. They can be hidden by my hair, except when my hair needs to be tied back—such as during a yoga class, for example. Oops.

Oh well. Life happens.

CHAPTER 8

Gam zu l'tovah.
Even this is for good.
— THE TALMUD

September 2017

Today, the yoga teacher training (YTT) begins: four weeks of uninterrupted spiritual bliss guided by fully enlightened beings— but no, I'm kidding. That's not *quite* how it goes.

The YTT takes place in a hotel that may once have been beautiful, but its dingy interior exudes a palpable aura of neglect. Not one single time do I ever see a smile cross the faces of the front desk staff. Maybe smiling is forbidden here because the two young Indian yoga teachers don't smile either when they come to greet me. The hot water in my shower (and everyone else's, as it turns out) lasts for precisely two minutes per shower. And it's cold here in the Himalayas. I take the fastest showers of my life, but they always end with freezing water pouring over me.

But the yoga shala is lovely, with floor-to-ceiling glass walls at the front and back that offer a view of the forest on one side and the mountains on the other, and I like the other students right away. We're a small, international group, mostly women; from the Czech Republic, Mexico, Australia, Holland, Germany, Hungary, Russia, India, and there's one other American. There are four teachers: the Indian director, the Japanese head teacher, and the two young initially unsmiling Indian girls (who, fortunately, reveal their smiles later on). The energy and the music during the orientation are uplifting and transportive, and the director says some beautiful, inspiring things. Like at Vipassana, I have the vivid feeling that I'm supposed to be here.

Our days begin early, with three hours of pranayama, meditation, and ashtanga yoga prior to breakfast. In case you're wondering if that's an enjoyable schedule: no, it's not. We're all starving well before those three hours are up. There's no coffee or tea to start the day, but Sam—God bless his soul—gave me Vietnamese coffee and a little metal drip coffee maker before he left for New York, so I can make coffee in my room. Later, in an effort to become more zen, I buy a kettle and switch to tea.

The daily pranayama (breathing techniques), kriyas, chanting, and the occasional dynamic meditations are all new to me and mildly life-changing. Pranayama is a magic pill for my mind. Kriya is pranayama with some form of repetitive physical movement added—like next-level pranayama, you could say. After a kriya session, my body feels weightless, as if I'm hovering above the ground. My mind is still and meditation is deep. Chanting is blissful, calming, and fills me with a sense of connecting to something sacred. The dynamic meditations are a mix of silence, music, sitting, standing, and dancing, and some of them transport me to a state of pure joy.

The ashtanga practice is physically challenging—both stretching and strengthening. By three weeks in, my flexibility has increased dramatically. The daily philosophy classes are a window into yoga's history, lineage, and depth, revealing many ancient concepts woven into classical yoga texts and theory. These classes are taught by the oldest of the young Indian girls, and it's clear that she genuinely loves the subject. Her eyes shine while she teaches.

Occasionally the director, Rakesh, teaches the philosophy classes instead. During one such occasion he discusses *Ishvarapranidhana*, one of the key concepts described in Patanjali's *Yoga Sutras. Pranidhana* is most commonly translated from Sanskrit as "complete surrender." *Ishvara* is the Source—or any other word you may choose to use for this indefinable Higher Power: the Divine, Infinite Intelligence, God, the Universe, etc. Ishvarapranidhana is the idea of surrender to a Higher Power—to a force greater than yourself. It means to accept that a Higher Force is in control, and to trust that it's looking out for you. Essentially, it can be translated as: Relax. Trust the Cosmos. You're in good hands.

Explaining why we might believe that an unseen Higher Power exists and is looking out for us, Rakesh points out that none of us, with our conscious minds alone, can keep ourselves alive. We can't even consciously control the basic physiological functions of our own bodies: the beating of our own hearts, the blood pulsing through our veins, the levels of oxygen circulating in our blood. All of that is totally out of our conscious control. And yet we are alive. Some Force we can't see is keeping us alive.

This discussion resonates on a visceral level of my being like a vibrating bell, grabbing my full attention. Rakesh makes a valid point. I am alive, and most of the factors responsible for my aliveness are out of my control, and mostly beyond my understanding. Some invisible intelligence has orchestrated—is orchestrating—the incredibly complex dance within and between the trillions of individual cells that make up my body, and the essential oxygen/carbon dioxide exchange between me and the plants around me, and the slow twirling of the moon around Planet Earth, and of all the planets around the sun. It's so vast, complex, and intricate I can't even fully comprehend all the details involved, much less control any part of the process on my own; but it's all somehow working together perfectly, without any of my conscious doing.

Long after the class ends, I continue turning this concept over in my mind.

I was raised in a devout Christian family, so the idea of trusting a Higher Power isn't new to me. For the first twenty years of my life, I went to church three times a week, and from approximately age seven, I read the Bible every day. I was very familiar with the Biblical version of Ishvarapranidhana. But the Biblical version came with strings attached. God—our Heavenly Father, who created all of us humans and considered us His children—cared about us and would look after us … as long as we believed in Him, loved Him, and obeyed Him. If we failed to do any of those things, after death we would be consigned to a punishment of eternal pain and agony, as vividly described in an alarming number of statements in the Bible from Christ and his apostles about eternal punishment, the lake of fire, and the especially vivid "fiery lake of burning sulfur" into which those who didn't follow the gospel of Christ would be tossed on the day of judgment. Because apparently our Heavenly Father would not have been satisfied with, say, instant annihilation of his wayward children.

A loving, caring, omniscient, all-powerful God willing to consign a few trillions of His children to eternal agony and damnation if they happened not to believe in His existence or serve Him exactly as He wanted? This doesn't make any sense to my brain. That group of the damned would include many of my friends and acquaintances, whom I personally knew to be wonderful people.

When I was young the idea terrified me, but eventually I concluded it was too outrageous to be true; and even if it were true, I couldn't in good conscience love or worship a God capable of such horrifying cruelty, much less trust that God to look after my well-being. I know other people can—I have many Christian friends who are phenomenal people—but I cannot. So I parted ways with the Christian faith a long time ago. That was a choice that rendered me a pariah in the eyes of my immediate family, with the exception of my little sister.

But I was never able to part ways with the sense that there was Something out there: some Higher Power, some God-like entity behind the dazzling beauty and complexity of this life. I couldn't believe in the Christian God, but I also couldn't believe existence was nothing more than a meaningless accident. I didn't know what I believed in, but I didn't believe in nothing.

Now, suddenly, Ishvarapranidhana is offering me a viewpoint of existence that makes sense. Ishvarapranidhana isn't attached to any threats of hell or damnation. It's just an open invitation to let go of anxiety, to trust an unseen, invisible force greater than myself, delivered along with a persuasive reason why. I also recognize this message, or pieces of it, from other sources: Buddhist teachings, Paulo Coelho's writing, Joe Dispenza's talks on YouTube, and

Eckhardt Tolle's *The Power of Now*. It was the starting point of the *why* that brought the message home to me this time: that, on our own, we can't even keep ourselves alive. That like it or not, we're already relying on this force that I usually refer to as the Universe, Life, or the Divine. Call it what you will—call it God if you like—it's all different words for the same thing, a vast magnificent Force beyond our comprehension.

And whatever this mysterious Force is that the *Yoga Sutras* have named Ishvara, it's intelligent and powerful enough to keep my incredibly complex human body functioning in this dizzyingly intricate, magnificent world. So, I might as well trust that, a) there is some reason for it doing so, b) there may be a deeper purpose behind the events that unfold in my life, deeper than what I can see on the surface, and c) this Force is more than capable of sorting out whatever other complicated situations I face in life, without me needing to stress about everything or figure out every detail on my own. I'm not alone. I can relax.

It's a message I need, because it's in my nature to worry about everything. When there's nothing to worry about, I worry that something I should be worrying about might have slipped my mind. Ishvarapranidhana is the soothing antidote to all of my worries.

That doesn't mean that from this moment on I shift to living life with zero anxiety and perfect trust. But the seed is planted in my mind.

I'm starting to love the little village of Dharamkot, with its casual vibe, unmarked hill paths that substitute for roads, charming cafés, and laid-back shop owners. There is something common in the shops here that amazes me—the concept of "pay me tomorrow." If you try to pay for something with a large bill (and by large bill I mean something like 500 rupees; US$8) and the shop clerk doesn't have or doesn't want to give small change, they tell you, with a casual wave of the hand, "Pay me tomorrow." While you're obviously a foreigner and they don't know you from Adam, and they're completely unconcerned about the possibility that you might never come back and pay. This trusting, serene attitude bolsters my hope for the future of humanity. Imagine if the entire world operated this way…

But India, like the world, is a place of contrasts. I find the darker side of humanity here too, primarily embodied by Rakesh, the yoga school director.

His shadow side reveals itself gradually. He can be funny and jovial when he wants to be, but from the beginning, there is something off-putting about him. Something heavy and dark lurking just underneath his smile and jokes and beautiful philosophical words. At first I think maybe our energies just don't click. He's arrogant with an ego that fills the room; that's clear from the beginning. He loves talking about himself and he doesn't welcome open discussion in class. Any opinions that differ from his are abruptly quashed. We catch him in lies, some small and some big.

Then he begins harassing the youngest student in our class, a sweet, beautiful Indian girl. When she rejects his advances, he threatens to withhold her yoga teacher certificate and occasionally screams at her in class for terrible crimes such as, for example, having her hands angled the wrong way in a yoga posture. We learn later this wasn't the first time something unsavory had gone on in his trainings. Oddly, the school is in the middle of a name change for the third time in less than ten years, and Rakesh is planning to change his first name as well.

He's a shady character, but fortunately he isn't around much. After the first few days, he leaves the teaching to the three women. They're good teachers, especially the older two: sincere and experienced.

It's confusing to be in this place where it feels I'm meant to be; living an experience of beauty and connection and the peeling away of external layers, while knowing that the person in charge is a reprehensible character. If I apply Neil's Buddhist theory to this situation, maybe Rakesh is just playing a role to further my—or our—spiritual growth. After all, I wished to become comfortable with discomfort, and Rakesh's strange negativity and creepy behavior make me very uncomfortable. Negative vibes are like the spiders in my Vipassana cabin; they both disrupt my comfort and peace of mind.

Maybe this is another inoculation, bringing me closer to immunity to people with bad vibes.

After deciding that this was probably the divine reason for Rakesh's appearance in this part of my personal journey, I curl up for some reading time with a book a local café graciously allowed me to borrow because something about it called to me: *Intuition: Soul Guidance for Life's Decisions*, by Sri Sri Daya Mata. My eyes land on these words:

> *Every one of us can learn to move through life enjoying a radiant peace and serenity. Instead of permitting the inevitable complexities and demanding situations to make us nervous or upset, we should use each of them as motivation to open in ourselves a new window onto the Divine Consciousness.*

I take this as confirmation of my theory. And after the end of the YTT, a few classmates and I report the facts of Rakesh's behavior to Yoga Alliance, and the rest is out of our hands.

And not even Rakesh is all bad. One day he gives us a beautiful gift. He walks into our 8 a.m. class and announces, "There's a clear sky today. Classes are canceled. We're hiking to Triund."

The hike to Triund is about two hours, a moderately challenging trek over dirt trails and rocks and increasingly steeper terrain. When we reach the top of the mountain, we find ourselves in another world. A world I've never seen before, one I didn't imagine existed. It's made mostly of sky—a sky of hazy white clouds suspended against an azure canvas. The clouds are the whitest white and the sky is the bluest blue. Below them is a lake of green and silver mountaintops, stretching on and on until they are swallowed by clouds in the distance. The mountains are at once so close and so far away, blanketed with green grass and pine trees woven among patches of gray and silver granite. The world looks enormous. The clouds are constantly moving, sometimes descending to wrap around the peaks like an ephemeral crown, sometimes enveloping us in a hazy fog. Mountain goats and gentle horses graze peacefully nearby.

It's a Monday afternoon. Sitting cross-legged on top of a boulder in the middle of this wonderland, I imagine what I would be doing if I hadn't quit my job and was back home on a typical Monday afternoon. Probably I would be trapped in front of my computer screen or maybe going to the coffee machine for another acidic coffee to keep my eyes open through the afternoon post-lunch slump. Or maybe in a meeting, or on a plane to a meeting. But instead I am here, in this magnificent new world I never knew existed, and it's incredible beyond belief. The world is so huge and so beautiful and this place has always been here and I had no idea.

If I wasn't perched on a precarious boulder high above the ground, I would be dancing in circles. But my heart is dancing.

One day my friend and fellow student Vero and I visit Men-Tsee-Khang—the school of Tibetan herbal medicine and astrology where my monk friend Tsering told me they can try to find our previous incarnation—for a Tibetan astrological reading from the astro science department. What Vero and I really want to learn about is our past lives, but it turns out that's a very small part of the reading. The only thing the kind Tibetan astrologer can tell me about that subject is that I was a carnivorous animal.

I pause to take this in, then ask, "Are you sure?"

Tenzin: "Yes."

Me: "Because ... that doesn't feel right. I feel like I was human."

Tenzin: "Well, it's not bad. Some people have been plants, insects..."

Me: "You don't know what kind of carnivorous animal?"

Tenzin: "No."

Me: "Well ... maybe I was a jaguar then. Yes, probably a jaguar."

Later I ask Tenzin what she was in her past life. She was an elephant. Vero, it turns out, was a deer.

The funny thing is that Vero has an unusually strong love for deer. And Tenzin, after revealing my carnivorous animal past, asks me if I eat meat.

Her question is interesting, because in spite of the frequent thinly veiled or blunt pressure in the yoga world to be vegan or vegetarian, I've never been either because I don't feel good on a diet without meat.

"Yes," I say.

"It's because of your past life," Tenzin tells me.

Overall, the readings are 95 percent accurate for both of us, in surprisingly specific ways. However, Tenzin's forecast on my love life is pretty vague. "Your fortune is looking average. It depends on the fortune of the other person as well. If you meet a fortunate person, it could go smoothly. Don't get distracted quickly, confused quickly, bored very quickly. Be more stable-minded. When you fall in love truly, you'll make everything perfectly—you'll make your home very full of love and warm. You're lighthearted and open; that's good. Be stable and you won't face major problems."

Well, let's hope I meet a fortunate person.

Meanwhile, on the other side of the world…

In the capable hands of my realtor, the requisite steps to finalize the sale of my house are underway. Everything is proceeding smoothly, more or less, punctuated by occasional challenges like spotty Himalayan Wi-Fi and the hunt for a notary in Dharamsala willing to notarize my signature on a power of attorney.

One night, I'm on the phone with my best friend Sarah in Orlando. I tell her the house sale news. She asks immediately, "Who's going to pack up all your stuff?"

A very good question; one I had been ignoring because it is my nature to put off dealing with undesirable tasks until the last possible moment.

"I have no idea," I reply. "I should probably fly back to take care of this, but I can't leave in the middle of the yoga course."

"I'll do it," she volunteers cheerfully.

Sarah lives three hours from my house, has two daughters aged two and three, and is going through a complicated divorce. None of those factors make her pause for a second thought or so much as blink an eye. To my effusive gratitude, she responds, "This will be a

60

fun mini-vacation!" True to her word, the following week she packs up the girls, talks her mom into coming along, and in five days, somehow miraculously has every piece of my furniture and assorted miscellaneous items sold, and everything else neatly boxed up—*and* she cleans out the garage, and that alone, I assure you, was a medal-worthy feat. She did it all with such tireless joy-infused efficiency that I am left speechless in awe and my realtor wants to hire her.

There are times in life when you see pure selfless love in action and this was one of them. I'll never forget it.

Alex helps a lot with the house too. He's still texting almost every day, regularly offering to check on the house, and once Sarah has everything packed up, he drives two truckloads of stuff to my storage unit. It takes Tetris-honed skills to get it all to fit. Between him, Sarah, and my realtor, who's been watering my plants since I left, I feel incredibly well looked after.

And then Hurricane Irma materializes, grows into the largest Atlantic hurricane on record, and heads straight for Florida and Puerto Rico, threatening to pulverize everything in its path. Floridians are used to hurricane warnings, and the typical reaction involves a sharp spike in sales of bottled water, long lines at gas stations, and windows boarded with hurricane shutters or plywood, but I've never seen a panicked response like the one Irma has triggered. My Facebook feed is a reel of photos of empty Florida store shelves. Everyone in South Florida is evacuating. Alex puts up my hurricane shutters before he leaves town.

My house has one major flaw: the roof isn't attached with the right kind of hurricane-proof nails. Because of this tiny detail, my home insurance is sub-par, and theoretically the roof will blow off more easily if exposed to hurricane force winds. I envision Irma brutally demolishing my home, the house sale falling through, and me left high and dry with no choice but to abandon my plans of travel and freedom to go back home, deal with this catastrophe, and get another job. For days, I forget my anxiety-erasing Ishvarapranidhana tool while my mind tortures me with horror films featuring My Miserable Future.

As usual, the fear and anxiety turn out to be a waste of energy. Irma veers away from the south coast of Florida and my house is safe. But two weeks later Hurricane Maria demolishes Puerto Rico, wiping out the island's power grid, destroying homes and businesses, and leaving much of the island without water or power for months. A year later, Hurricane Michael will destroy many homes in the Florida panhandle, including my friend Holly's. Two days after the destruction of Holly's home, a friend of mine in Texas will lose hers in a house fire. I will learn this scrolling through my Facebook feed, where I see their posts back to back. In spite of the devastating losses, both react with joy. My Texan friend, a devout Christian, writes that God is good and getting back to the basics makes you realize how He provides and how much she appreciates all the love everyone has showered them with. Holly posts a selfie with her boyfriend. Her smile is radiant. Her caption reads, *We may have lost our home, but we're alive and kicking and loving the water.*

As I read their posts, tears slide down my cheeks. I sit motionless, feeling their losses acutely because they could so easily have been mine, and in awe of their joy and resilience. Sometimes the human spirit is so beautiful.

CHAPTER 9

Creation is light and shadow both, else no picture is possible.
— PARAMAHANSA YOGANANDA

September 2017

The YTT has ended, my long-awaited house closing has finally gone through, and the world is once again my oyster. At the moment India specifically is my oyster, since my visa allows me two more months here. My next stop is Rishikesh — destination chosen because Krishna Das will be performing there October 4th.

I arrive in Rishikesh by bus and hate it immediately. After five weeks in peaceful Dharamsala, it's a shock to my senses. It's hot, crowded, dirty, and loud, with horns blaring incessantly. As if that wasn't bad enough, the hotel I booked for my first two nights notifies me just before I arrive that they're overbooked and can't accommodate me. The Osho ashram, where I'll be staying next, is also fully booked tonight. I have barely existent Wi-Fi and nowhere to go.

But I remember that a couple weeks ago, a friend from Miami mentioned that I should check out Sattva Yoga in Rishikesh. I had googled the name and noticed that they seemed to operate as a hotel as well as a yoga school. I grasp at that wisp of a memory like a lifeline. Google Maps shows a Sattva Yoga across the river, so I tell the rickshaw driver to take me there.

This Sattva Yoga turns out to be no oasis. Its unimpressive lobby is almost as loud as the street outside, filled with the sounds of voices, humming engines, and impatient horns. But the man at the front desk tells me there's another Sattva Yoga twenty minutes away. Away from this horrible noisy city is all I want. He calls and makes a reservation for me, and in a couple hours I'm there.

At this second location, it's a different world. It's a heavenly sanctuary on the banks of an offshoot of the Ganges River: quiet, peaceful, and more luxurious than I expected. Its white-walled two-story buildings are spread out across a wide grassy lawn shaded by tall oak trees and clusters of slender bamboo, areca palms, and rose-purple allamanda. One quiet corner features a pristine, sparkling pool. My room is big and beautiful, the shower is wonderful, and I'm not exaggerating when I tell you they have the world's best smelling shower gel.

I've magically been transported back to dreamland. I'm a little dazed at how I ended up here in this secluded paradise, but I gratefully accept this turn of events as part of Life's new standard operating procedure of miraculously bringing me to wherever I'm supposed to be. It feels like being blindfolded and led by spirits, like Kim Kennedy's reading said.

At dinner, I meet a nice Italian guy who works here. We chat for a bit. He tells me there's a yoga teacher training going on at the moment. It seems I'm the only guest who's not part of the YTT. For a brief moment, the nice Italian looks at me thoughtfully and I see in his eyes that he senses there is something he should do. With the disclaimer that he has to check whether this is okay, he invites me to come to the 8 a.m. yoga class tomorrow. Except he doesn't say class, he says "journey."

The powers that be give their permission, so I join the class the next morning.

Afterward, I stagger outside, overwhelmed and speechless, and I understand why they call it a journey. It was intense, indescribable. Repetitive, strong, rhythmic pranayama was woven in between the poses, and the rush of energy that poured into me during the practice was unlike anything I'd ever experienced in any other yoga class. Maybe unlike anything I'd ever experienced anywhere. It transported me to another realm and then brought me back to earth to take it in.

Even the Krishna Das concert two days later can't compare.

KD's baritone voice is resonant and marvelous, but I don't feel mind-blowing transcendent energy here. Even at the end, when we're on our feet swaying to the music, I am not transported back to that ethereal post-journey realm.

But it's nice to be there hearing Krishna, and Nesha is with me. Nesha is my beautiful Indian friend from the YTT, and she's joined me here because she loves Krishna Das too. Nesha is a decade younger than me and we grew up on opposite sides of the planet, but we have concluded that our souls are twins. We think and say the same things at the same time on a regular basis and we are both an eclectic mix of beauty-loving sensitivity, inquisitive spiritual curiosity, and fun-loving goofiness. We crack ourselves up on a regular basis.

We're staying at the Osho ashram. We both loved the Osho dynamic meditations during the YTT, but we don't love this ashram. The staff here exude a strange, mildly zombie-like energy. Their eyes are a little too intense and too far away at the same time. As if they've spent too much time in that other realm and their consciousness hasn't fully made it back to planet Earth. And consciousness, apparently, is all that matters. When I chat with the young Indian guy who leads the meditations, the topic turns to sex (not sex between us, but in general terms.) He says dismissively, "It's just your body."

Later, when I watch the insightful and appropriately named documentary *Wild Wild Country*, it will all make sense. But for now, we're just weirded out.

The setting of the ashram is beautiful though, along the banks of the sage-green Ganges River, with large boulders in varying hues of taupe and light gray scattered along the sandy riverside. By daylight, it's zen and soothing, and at night, hypnotic and otherworldly.

Tonight, there's a full moon. Obviously, what would pair perfectly with this magical moonlit riverside setting is a bottle of wine.

But Rishikesh is a dry city, so no alcohol is sold here. We learned this disappointing fact only after our arrival.

Nothing will make you crave a glass of wine like being told you can't have one—especially if you just spent a month-long yoga teacher training not drinking wine. We're determined to find some. A man in a restaurant tells us about a hotel outside of town that will sell us a bottle. A twenty-minute bone-rattling rickshaw ride brings us to the location shown on Google Maps, but there's no sign of any hotel. We've ended up on a long empty road in the middle of nowhere, with nothing to be seen in the vicinity except one large, white, unmarked building that very much resembles a prison. After driving back and forth a few times, we ask the driver to stop at the scary prison building. We wonder if this could be part of a set-up ... we walk inside, ask for wine, and they promptly incarcerate us right then and there.

We decide to take the risk.

It turns out not to be a prison, and there's a restaurant inside. It doesn't have a normal, familiar hotel restaurant vibe. We conclude it's probably run by the Indian mafia. Fortunately, they sell us a bottle of Jacob's Creek Cabernet Shiraz for 4000 rupees (US$64). Because it's dark by the time we start our return journey, the driver refuses to take us all the way back to the ashram. The road passes through the jungle, and he says there are wild animals that come out at night here. Mountain lions, tigers, etc. He leaves us on the side of the road to walk the remaining thirty minutes through this predator-infested jungle.

Chivalry ... apparently a concept he's not familiar with.

Everything seems so ridiculous and over the top here, we take this situation as part of the adventure. Plus, our ashram is in the jungle and it's not enclosed by any fences. It doesn't seem reasonable to worry.

Our thirty-minute walk brings us back to the ashram with no jungle cat encounters. We have no glasses, so we seat ourselves on boulders beside the moonlit River Ganges and sip the wine straight from the bottle. The immense pleasure this gives us is well worth the $64 and our high-risk journey.

Rishikesh has some redeeming qualities, we discover. We fall in love with the Beatles Café, a fabulous hideaway with a spectacular view of the Ganges and an unforgettably delicious salad called Morrison's Salad. (If you're ever in the area, you should definitely try that salad.)

We ended up at the Beatles Café thanks to Alex, who has been my unofficial travel advisor ever since I arrived in India, via Whatsapp texts relaying fictitious tales of his past experiences in all of my destinations. For example:

> Me: *Taking a bus to Rishikesh tonight.*
> Alex: *Check out Café Delmar/Beatles Café. I helped George Harrison write a couple of tunes there.*
> Alex again: *By the way the Beatles were a band in the 60's. Also Little Buddha is a good spot, I could never fit in. I had to settle for XL Buddha.*
> Me: *Oh I thought Beatles were a kind of insect. For sure you would need XL Buddha.*
> Alex: *Did you go to the marahashi mahesh yogi hashram yet? Cool graffiti from Beatles. Pretend you're Indian you get deep discount for the entrance fee.*

Most of his messages were like this, goofy ones that made me laugh mixed in with travel tips in disguise. The travel tips, always delivered in the form of his mythical past travels to wherever I was at the time, were really helpful, because throughout my entire first year in Asia I was plagued by insanely slow Wi-Fi which made travel research a serious challenge.

So we end up at the Beatles Café thanks to Alex (and also later, at Maharishi Mahesh Yogi's abandoned ashram, which does have spectacular graffiti from the Beatles era, and if I could have passed for Indian I would have gotten a steep discount on the entrance fee.)

Next door to the Beatles Café we find a travel agency where a nice guy named Akash is working. We buy tickets from Akash: a train ticket to Jaipur for Nesha, a bus ticket to Delhi for me. There are no tickets to Jaipur the day Nesha planned to leave, so we decide to stay in Rishikesh an extra day. Then we notice that the travel agency offers a sunrise waterfall hike. We book that too, for 4:30 a.m. the next day.

Akash is our guide for the hike. The whole day is spectacular, starting with a pastel sunrise on top of the mountain and an expansive view of the Himalayan foothills all around us, then the hike down to the waterfall, which just keeps going and going and going … an endless cascade of meandering crystal water. The falls occasionally form turquoise pools, some deep and some shallow. I swim in the deep ones, luxuriating in refreshing coolness. In the shallow pools, some ingenious locals have set up plastic tables and chairs to create an incredible outdoor café experience. We sip masala chai with our feet ankle deep in clear water and marvel at how we only got to experience this magical place because there were no tickets to Jaipur on Nesha's planned day of departure. Once again, things worked out better than planned.

The next day, I'm comfortably ensconced on a Volvo bus to Delhi. The six-hour journey gives me lots of time for reading. (One of the best things about quitting your job is that you finally have lots of time to read books.) The book that keeps me company on this leg of the journey is *The Book of Joy*, by Douglas Abrams. It's about a weeklong discussion between the Dalai Lama and Archbishop Desmond Tutu on the subject of joy and suffering.

The book is a treasure. There are so many gems of profound wisdom woven lightly into every page that I want to read it over and over until all of it is absorbed into every cell of my being.

Reading a book is its own kind of journey. The right words can weave their way into your heart, tug blinders from your eyes, alter the direction of your path, and leave you forever changed. There will be a handful of books that do that for me during my time in Asia and this is one of them.

In its pages, these words catch my attention:

Joy, it seemed, was a strange alchemy of mind over matter. The path to joy, like with sadness, did not lead away from suffering and adversity but through it. As the Archbishop had said, nothing beautiful comes without some suffering.

CHAPTER 10

The breeze at dawn has secrets to tell you.
Don't go back to sleep.

- RUMI

October 2017

I've come to Kerala in search of beautiful beaches and ancient Ayurvedic wisdom. My first stop is Kochi, a coastal city perched about halfway down the southernmost state on India's west coast.

In Kochi, there are no more mountains and no woolen scarves needed. Instead there is an abundance of vibrant color, spice, and European colonial architecture. It's a comfortable, creative, artsy town. I linger here for a few days, reading, writing, and falling in love with colorful cafés full of delicious food. In one of them I chat with a friendly young Indian waiter. He tells me his story. He loves cooking and his dream had been to open a little guesthouse with a small restaurant. One opportunity led to another and his dream manifested into reality. He shows me pictures of his cute little café with two backpacker-style guest rooms.

But one day, it all burned down in a fire—set intentionally, he thinks, by someone who was jealous of his success. He lost everything. He had no insurance. He doesn't have money to start over from scratch, and that's why now he's here working as a waiter at this restaurant.

I'm horrified for him, but he tells the story matter-of-factly, without bitterness. It just is what it is. I wish for life to be kind to him, for his future to hold success and happiness.

From Kochi I make my way south to explore the coast. I find sleepy, pretty beaches dotted with quiet villages where the pace of life is barely above stillness. Hidden in those villages I find well-equipped Airbnbs with kind, caring hosts, delicious homemade meals, and dreamy hotels erected in sandy gardens. But the beaches are unremarkable, until I arrive in Varkala.

Night is falling as the taxi reaches my hotel, but even in the dim light I realize that Varkala Beach is more than beautiful—it's magic. It's partly the magnificent views of the long beach and the rhythmic rolling waves seen from the cliff above, partly something in the air, and partly my hotel, Mad About Coco, with its marvelous Balinese décor and down-to-earth German-Indian owner Anita.

Anita makes me feel immediately at home with her relaxed friendliness. When we finish the check-in, it's dinnertime and I'm hungry. She invites me to come along to Darjeeling Café, which is also part of Varkala's magic, with mandalas painted on wooden tables, ocean views, and a bohemian Cheers-like atmosphere where everyone seems to know each other.

Serendipity strikes again my second day here. I listen to a *Yoga Girl* podcast in which Rachel tells the hilarious story of her long-ago first experience teaching yoga to a big group of strangers. She's an amazing teacher with a huge following, so it's comforting to hear that even she, at one moment, was nervous about teaching. Because I've been thinking that I should probably put my newly acquired yoga knowledge into practice and offer classes here, but the idea scares me. For years I've attended yoga classes and listened to teachers' calm, confident voices and thought: *I could never do that.* I stumble over my words even when I'm standing still on two feet. Eloquent, inspiring words could never roll easily off my tongue like they do from the mouths of these gifted teachers, while I simultaneously balance my body in various contorted shapes, keeping an eye on a roomful of students with my mind full of a seventy-five minute yoga sequence and a bunch of long Sanskrit names. No. Other people can do that, but there's a strong possibility my brain is not wired for yoga teacher success. The positive feedback I got after the one class I taught at the end of the YTT gave me a little confidence boost, but still, it's highly possible that if teaching to strangers, I will make a complete fool of myself and they will have a miserable experience and never try yoga again.

That afternoon I take a hatha yoga class in town. It's taught by an Indian guy and it's okay but, just okay. I think to myself, *I could teach a better class than this. I should just get over my fear and go for it. There are mats and a gorgeous rooftop space at Mad About Coco and I'm pretty sure Anita wouldn't mind. Yes, I want to do a 300-hour training before I start seriously teaching, but teaching some free, casual beach classes would be good practice.*

Next thought: *But what if I suck? What if it's horrible?*

Me: *Ohhh, good point. Yeah, maybe this is a bad idea. Maybe I should just do the 300-hour first….*

Me again: *Seriously, this is NOT that serious. You're just scared. You've been practicing yoga for twelve years. You should do this. You need the practice. You could teach at the hotel rooftop; it's beautiful. Ask Anita if you can put up a sign or something.*

Me: *Okay, yeah, you're right. I'm just scared. Well, we'll see. I'll think about it.*

After class I walk outside with my yoga mat tucked under my arm like an oversized baguette, and just as I step onto the sidewalk, a young French couple is passing by. "Are you going to a yoga class?" the guy asks me eagerly.

"I just came from one," I reply.

"Oh, we're looking for one. We've never done yoga but we want to try it," he tells me.

I hesitate for a split second, but when Synchronicity holds up a blinking neon sign, it's best not to ignore it.

"Well, I just finished my yoga teacher training a few weeks ago and I was thinking about offering a class at my hotel rooftop," I tell them.

They're thrilled. "We're definitely in!" they tell me. We tentatively agree on 5 p.m. the next day.

That evening I find Anita at Darjeeling Café and ask her permission. She loves the idea. She immediately invites everyone at the table to join and says she'll tell all the guests. Before you know it, half of Varkala might be there.

Four students show up—the French couple plus two hotel guests, and that's plenty enough for me. When I'm nervous I talk fast, so I talk too fast—especially for first-time yoga practitioners whose first language isn't English. But no one dies and they're sweating but still smiling at the end. And when I look at the clock at the end of class, it's 5:55.

The French couple tells me the class was great, but they're nice people so they might be politely lying. A couple days later the hotel guests request me to teach another class and that's my favorite compliment.

Because of Anita's social nature and Mad About Coco's communal ambience at the breakfast tables, I meet a lot of nice people in Varkala. Among my favorites are Helen and Helen, two British yoga teachers who are here for a few days, and Joanne, an American who lives in Varkala with her Spanish boyfriend. Joanne and her boyfriend have The World's Best Job: they are employed to search out the best locations in the world for new hotel development.

OMG, sign me up for that, I'll go back to work immediately.

The Helens leave before I do. One of them—the blond, vivacious one with the irrepressible laugh—is planning to go to Bali soon, like I am, but neither of us have nailed down exact dates. We exchange Facebook contacts and agree to try and meet up when we're there.

In Varkala, everything is picture-perfect: gorgeous beach town, great coffee, cheap, delicious food and drinks, fun people, Ayurvedic massages, great things to do like sunset stand up paddleboarding, good books to read, plenty of yoga around. But for some reason, after a few days here, a strange thing happens. I transform into an irritable, short-tempered grouch.

I don't know what's wrong with me. I'm free as a bird, luxuriating in this beautiful paradise with zero reasons to be stressed and a thousand reasons to feel immensely grateful, and instead I am not feeling good and there's no excuse for this and I know that, which makes me feel guilty, and the heaviness of the guilt makes me even more cranky.

It's hot here, so the Ayurvedic explanation would probably be that there is an excess of *pitta*—the "fire" component of the human constitution—in my system, and that may be true, but it's not just the weather. Something is off, and I think it's something internal and physical. I've addressed my mental and spiritual self here in India, but it feels like it's time to give attention to my physical self. It's time for a little detox—or something.

I've been hearing good things about Ayurvedic treatment centers. A Dutch guy in Ladakh told me he went to a center in Kerala, not far from Varkala, and to his surprise his chronic knee pain totally disappeared. And a Russian girl in Varkala told me how an Ayurvedic doctor here got rid of her chronic acne. But for some reason neither of those centers are drawing me. I do a little research online, but still nothing grabs me. Then Serendipity shows me where I need to go next.

I've booked a ten-day side trip to the Maldives, because that spectacular island nation is only an hour flight away, and therefore I am basically morally obligated to pay it a visit. The day before I leave Varkala, I think to myself that I would have liked to talk with Joanne before I left, American Joanne with the Best Job in the World. A couple hours later I take myself to Tibetan Kitchen for lunch and voilà, there is Joanne, sitting at one of the tables. She invites me to join her and we fall into a long conversation over delicious momos and Tibetan soup. She mentions that she did a forty-day panchakarma at an Ayurvedic center in Kerala and it transformed her health and her life.

She tells me her amazing story:

"I was living in California at the time, and I had gotten these mysterious hives all over my body. They were so bad I had to go on medical leave, and no doctors or allergy tests in the US could figure out what was causing them. I went to see so many doctors, and none of them could help. Eventually I went to a functional medicine doctor who recommended this place. At that point I was willing to try anything. So I went.

"The center was amazing—I wish I could go back every year. It's in a beautiful place by a river. The doctor meets with you every day to check on your progress, and they're so loving and caring there—I felt like a baby." She laughs. "They wouldn't even let me dress myself. They serve you wonderful, nourishing food and you get massages every day. During the panchakarma, the hives went away, never to return. I felt like I was given a new body."

While I'm listening to her, some little light is ignited within me. *That's where I need to go.* A butterfly disguised as a thought dances through my mind: *if I looked at the clock right now, it would probably be 1:11 or one of my repeating numbers.*

The next time I see the time is when I look at my phone back in my room. It's 2:22.

I immediately google this heavenly treatment center, preparing to cringe at its price tag. It must be expensive with all of those daily doctor visits, massages, yoga, treatments, etc. I'm shocked to find that the single occupancy price is ninety-two euros per day, all inclusive. And the daily rate goes down for longer stays.

They have three locations, and availability at the smallest one, somewhere in the mountains of central Kerala, so I book that one. My stay will begin two days after I get back from the Maldives.

The Maldives are as stunning in real life as they are on postcards and screen savers. Crystal clear water, white sand, curvy palm trees, and baby blue skies. The public islands are full of charm and delight: fresh fish dinners roasted over coconut shell fires, open air dining rooms with sand floors, a prevalent interior design style that gracefully blends indoor and outdoor living. Macrame hammocks are strung between palm trees and schools of dolphins swim playfully in the crystal clear ocean. So many dolphins. I see them every day.

But the private islands are outrageously expensive, and on the public islands, residents and visitors alike are subject to strict Islamic law, which includes a prohibition of skimpy attire such as bathing suits on some of the beaches and a strict ban on alcohol.

I can survive nine days without drinking, of course. That's what I'll voluntarily be doing soon enough at the Ayurvedic center. But here on this exquisite island, in the sand courtyard of my guesthouse, with fresh sea breezes around us and a black sky full of diamonds overhead, savoring a magnificent dinner of pasta and salad with fish grilled over a coconut shell fire, I miss wine.

The beauty of the Maldives makes my soul dance, but its restrictions remind me how much I cherish freedom.

CHAPTER 11

Breathe in experience.
Breathe out poetry.
- MURIEL RUKEYSER

November 2017

It's the morning of my transit to the Ayurvedic retreat center. I'm back in Kerala, at crowded Ernakalum train station, pulling a small mountain of luggage behind me. I'm looking for three pieces of vital information: at which track will my train arrive, what time will it arrive (almost guaranteed to be different than the scheduled arrival time) and where, in the chain of 25+ cars, will my coach be—because if I'm waiting at the wrong end of the track, that would mean a very long sprint, and I'm not in the mood for a mad dash with my 800 pounds of luggage.

An electronic screen overhead shows train arrival times and track numbers, but mysteriously, my train isn't listed. It's currently just past its scheduled arrival time of 9:30 a.m., so if it arrives anytime soon on the opposite track, I won't make it. And that wouldn't be good, because there are no other trains to Calicut today.

There are no uniformed station personnel to be seen, and long lines of people at every ticket window. I'm roaming the long station looking for answers when a smiling Indian man in business casual attire walks up to me.

"Where are you going?" he asks.

"Calicut," I reply.

"Train number?" he asks.

"12076."

"That's track one," he informs me, still smiling. (Great news! That's the platform I'm on.)

"Car number?" he asks.

"C3."

He holds up four fingers. "That's four cars from the engine— waaaay down" and points toward the north end of the track.

"Thank you so much!" We part with smiles and I continue toward the end of the track with a lighter step as the analytical side of my brain tries to calculate the statistical probabilities of a total stranger walking up to me right at that moment and giving me exactly every piece of information that I needed without me asking for it. Granted, my face probably announced that I was lost and he didn't need psychic powers to guess what information I would need. But that information wasn't listed; how did he know it all? He unhurriedly walked away from the track, so it seemed unlikely that he was waiting for the same train. And especially, how did he know where my car was? The coach numbers are in a different order on every train, so you can't just figure it out from the letter and number, although it seems like that would be a smart idea that some train station administrator should think about implementing. So who was this guy? Does he memorize train and track numbers and full coach charts for fun and then walk around train stations looking for people who need that information? Was he an undercover rail station employee with a photographic memory? Or some sort of male Mother Theresa of the transportation industry who devotes his days to saving travelers from missing their trains?

All of those scenarios seem unlikely. As far as I can see, the only reasonable explanation is that divine forces were involved. Especially because this kind of thing has been happening in my life on such a regular basis lately that I've finally accepted that this must just be how the Universe works. It's possible that this kind of divine intervention happens to me more often than to most other people because celestial forces have realized that leaving me to my own devices would lead to more chaos and disaster than anybody wants to deal with. For the greater good of all, they might have deemed it necessary to dispatch a special team to look after me full time; which if so, was really very thoughtful of them and I'm sincerely grateful. At some point, I decided the team consists of four angels, all very masculine and well built. Four angelic bodyguards, and they are awesome. Always on the ball. Exactly how they operate, I don't know. Did one of them just nudge this nice stranger and whisper in his ear that he should go talk to me? Or did one temporarily manifest in human form as the nice helpful Indian man? I lean toward the whispering-in-the-ear theory, but who knows? Also, I'm curious whether everyone has a personal team of angels, and if so, how many angels do most people have? I'm guessing that many people are more responsible than me and less likely to put themselves in situations where divine assistance would be required, so one or two might be sufficient. But again, who knows? And who needs to know? Mystery is part of the magic.

A minute after the conversation transpired between me and the divinely-sent messenger, a voice over the loudspeaker announces in Malayalam and then in English that train 12076 will be arriving shortly at Track One.

I station myself at my best guess of what would be four cars from the engine, with the expectation that since angelic forces are watching over me, car C3 will roll to a stop directly in front of me. And that is exactly what happens.

It's like the Universe has rolled out a plush red carpet just for me. I step onto that train full of delight, sending a river of gratitude to the mysterious unseen forces of the Universe and their messenger.

A driver picks me up from the crowded Calicut station and takes me on a four-hour ride to the Ayurvedic center, through mountains and flowers and clouds and betel nut trees whose trunks are so tall and skinny they remind me of matchsticks. Very tall matchsticks. Monkeys are playing on the roadside. The journey is so beautiful I don't want it to end.

But when we reach our destination, I'm glad we have.

An elaborate gold-plated gate marks the entrance. I step through it into another world. It's a dreamlike haven of peace and stillness, infused with the harmony of the forest that surrounds it. Native Keralans dressed in the traditional local garb of *saris* and *dhotis* greet me with smiles and sparkling eyes. Taking my luggage, they embrace me not with arms but with genuine warmth of spirit as they lead me to my assigned cabin.

The cabin that will be my home for the next three weeks is all wood inside and out, the doors emblazoned with intricate gold etchings, but I hardly notice the doors because the view from the spacious wood porch takes my breath away. It's on the second floor. Hibiscus and banana trees rise around it, so close I can reach out and touch their leaves from the edge of the balcony. Through the leafy trees I see the valley spread out below, dotted with the tiny rooftops of a small village, and beyond the valley, hazy ridges of mountaintops rise in tiers like distant waves in the ocean. Above all of this is a dusky blue sky. The air is filled with a gentle humming chorus of birds chirping.

My mind settles into serenity. An inner knowing of: *yes, this is what I was looking for,* rises from somewhere deep in my soul. A place where I can just relax—where I can just be. This is the inner peace I was craving in Varkala—the peace I couldn't even find in the Maldives. Finally, nothing to do, nothing to explore—I can just be still and let nature and Ayurveda rejuvenate me.

During my first consultation, the kind female doctor with bright eyes tells me what will happen here. "The treatments will get your body back into a rhythm with nature, then it can take the good from everything and not the poison. You should be relaxed and happy at every moment. You should enjoy everything."

The words are a lullaby. I start to cry, as if my subconscious realizes we have finally reached a place where it's okay to let go; to stop pretending to be strong and acknowledge the sheer exhaustion I've been hiding for years—exhaustion and the fear that I don't have enough energy to face life, and knowing I have to find the energy somehow because if I collapse, no one's going to catch me.

Or that's what I used to feel. Now I'm starting to believe that Life was actually always there for me, with a giant, invisible safety net waiting if needed.

There is a small group of other people here for treatment. A nice cozy group that fluctuates as some depart and others arrive. We bond over shared treatment experiences and shared love of the food, nature, and massages. One of the patients is a pretty Swiss girl who just spent two months in Bali. She gives me two Bali recommendations: ecstatic dance at Yoga Barn, and a restaurant called Kismet.

I write them down in my phone, and they stay in my mind too since there are only two and they're easy to remember. At that moment, neither of us have any idea how memorable those two simple recommendations will become in my future.

My three-week panchakarma begins blissfully. Massage every day—a synchronized four-hand abhyanga massage by two therapists. The massage table is wooden, but strangely it's not uncomfortable. Here in this ambience where everything feels sacred and steeped in ancient tradition, they have to be made of wood.

For five days, the daily massage is followed by a luxurious twenty-minute medicated hot water pouring, which involves me lying naked on the massage table (we're always naked for massages here), while three women in colorful saris pour steaming medicated water from golden pitchers that look like Aladdin's lamp over my body in rhythmic, repetitive motion while I lay there feeling like an Arabian princess. The experience is sublime.

Then the treatments become less enjoyable, culminating in the most unpleasant one of all: Vamana. This cleansing treatment involves drinking enormous quantities of milk and licorice tea to induce controlled, therapeutic vomiting. If you think this sounds like a bizarre, twisted, horrific idea for a therapeutic treatment, I completely agree with you. Vomiting and drinking milk are two of the things I hate most in the world, and also I've never in my life been able to force myself to vomit with my finger, even when sometimes I really wanted to.

During my initial consultation, I informed the doctor that I would be skipping this one, thank you very much.

She looked at me with her warm brown eyes and said kindly, "You can skip it if you want to, but then your treatment won't be perfect."

Did I come all this way to cheat myself out of the perfect treatment? I sighed and agreed to Vamana.

For some people, Vamana is a cakewalk. Drink and purge, done, easy. For me, it turns out to be a walk through the valley of shadows, an epic battle of willpower and discomfort, possibly the hardest thing I've ever voluntarily done in my life.

Vamana takes place in a room with a doctor and two assistants, who are there supposedly to assist me and hold my hair back while I therapeutically vomit but, I suspect, also to restrain me in case I decide to run out of the room or throw something at someone.

I lose track of how many glasses of milk and licorice tea I chug down. Twenty? Twenty-five? A hundred? By the halfway point, I'm uncomfortable. A few more glasses later, my mind starts revolting and my head is filled with smoldering hatred. I suddenly want to announce to everyone in the room, "Just to let you know, I hate you all right now."

But I keep that information to myself and keep drinking. They keep pouring me more glasses, and I'm impossibly full but I keep drinking, and the hatred turns to rage. Simmering rage mixed with intense, searing discomfort. Interestingly, the feeling of fullness is awful, but the feeling inside my brain is even worse. A state of indescribable, agonizing suffering.

This sucks this is awful I don't want to be here I hate this I can't stand it ... I can't do this. I can't take one more sip. I need to get out of here. Then my thoughts fixate on how what I'm experiencing right now is nothing compared to what uncountable billions or maybe trillions of people throughout history have suffered. War, torture, hunger, pain, disease

… the collective suffering of humanity is incomprehensible, unendurable. Despair floods my mind. This is no longer just about me, this is about all of us, all of humanity; anyone who's ever suffered.

"Why does there have to be suffering in the world?!" I yell at the doctor, glaring at him as if he's personally responsible. "Isn't there an easier way?"

His face remains expressionless and he answers without hesitation. "There are no shortcuts."

At this moment, something that's either a premonition of the future or my vivid imagination rising to the occasion to get me to the end of this dark tunnel flashes into my mind's eye—a flash that is part words, part hazy vision. It tells me, *there's a beautiful future waiting for you—but this is part of your path and you have to go through it to get there.*

I want the beautiful future. Somehow I finish the tea, and then mercifully comes the purging, and then it's over.

Little by little I discover more waiting for me. I didn't have to search to find it or fight to have it. Letting go of the racing, spinning, trying to keep up, gave me a deep sense that everything is ok as it is.

Those words were written by my friend Lauren Ziegler, and goosebumps cover my arms when I read them on Instagram because she found the perfect words for what I've been feeling.

After Vamana, my time at the center is easy and peaceful. The days flow by filled with pleasure and relaxation. I haven't felt so thoroughly pampered and taken care of since I was four years old. I've never felt so content to simply sit still for extended periods of time, admiring the nature around me. There seems to be something magic in the air here that dissolves restlessness. Everyone here feels it—most of the time.

The food is so good here I want the recipe for almost everything. Meals are always delicious and filling—dosas and curries and rice and samosas, sometimes banana-leaf wrapped packages, sometimes a chili-like dish with kidney beans, sometimes savory sautéed veggies like long beans, and sometimes a little dessert. The only sweetener used here is jaggery, an unrefined sugar made from sugarcane.

There is yoga every day: a meditative but physically challenging morning class, blissful yoga nidra at noon (during which I fall asleep every time), and an optional gentle 4 p.m. class. The classes are led by Ranjeev, a quiet, sincere, extremely flexible South Indian man. On days he's out of town, he's replaced by the jovial, good-natured Aru.

The yoga shala is a striking artistic masterpiece. Its four walls are painted floor to ceiling with vibrant, intricate depictions of Hindu deities and scenes from epic moments in Hindu mythology. I admire them daily, ignorant of their identities, until one day the artist (the founder's nephew) stops by and gives me a personal tour, explaining the story behind each image.

It's like a mini Hindu Mythology 101. There is Annapoorna (or Annapurna), the goddess of food and nourishment; Shiva, the destroyer/renewer; Surya, the sun god, wearing a garland of lotuses (because he loves lotuses); saints performing *tharpanam* (making a water offering) to Surya asking for blessings for the day; Vishnu and Lakshmi sensually entwined together representing the creative sexual energy of the sacral chakra, balancing a jug from which water flows, because all life comes from water. Then Lakshmi alone, as the goddess of beauty, holding a mirror, because she takes the form that represents each person's idea of beauty; an ascetic yogi meditating, oblivious to beautiful Lakshmi just a few feet away; the earth goddess, who takes the face of a pig when she's angry, otherwise she's a beautiful woman; Ganesha, the remover of obstacles; the moon god, seated on a lily; Shakti, painted in different stages of her life, like the seasons of the earth, and Prince Rama, his wife Sita, and loyal Hanuman.

Although the Hindu religion includes a dizzying number of deities, most Hindus are monotheistic. They believe the individual deities are simply different aspects of the one true God, expressed individually as poetic, allegorical symbols to bring us to a deeper understanding of the complex nature of God—and also of these same aspects present in ourselves. They're not meant to be taken literally.

The poetry of this concept captivates me. One of the beautiful things that Rakesh told us in Dharamsala is that the Vedic teachings are poetry. It's their poetry that makes them beautiful, but some people take them literally and then they mess it all up. Because I come from a family who takes the Bible as literally as a legal document, this is an eye-opening thought for me.

What if all religion was meant to be poetry? What if all of life was meant to be poetry?

At night, all is quiet except for the sounds of the jungle—and the jungle makes a lot of noise. Monkeys occasionally scamper across the bungalow roof. In spite of the racket, I'm usually asleep by 9 p.m., and I have vivid, eventful dreams every night. Most of us do. Something about this place, or the treatments, makes us dream.

Alex is never in my dreams at night. I only dream about him during the day. I'm annoyed that he's taking up space in my head—still. He was supposed to be one of those boulders that the current pulled me away from but somehow his consistent, hilarious, ridiculous text messages are a water-resistant super glue keeping me attached.

I tell only one other guest about him: Beryl, an elegant and proper retired British nurse in her seventies.

"Well, he should leave that horrible woman!" is her immediate reaction. "He probably wants to but doesn't know how."

I laugh and defend Alex's partner, assuming he wouldn't be with her if she was horrible. But maybe Beryl's right that he should leave her.

A week later I realize that the steady stream of text messages responsible for my lingering attachment are just nonsense texts that communicate nothing serious or meaningful. The last straw is Alex's Thanksgiving text to me—in reply to my coherent message in which all words were spelled correctly. *Enjoy your boba ganash turkey along side with taniki stuffing!*

Half of those words don't even exist and people aren't over here eating baba ganoush or tahini in India, Alex. And "along side with"?

How about you do me and the English language a favor and lay off the words for a while if all you can do is massacre them.

I realize my emotional response may be completely irrational but I don't care. What's even more irrational is that I have this ridiculous lingering emotional attachment to him and this crazy idea that one day he'll announce he can't live without me, leave his unsatisfying non-marriage, and come join me in Asia for an incredible adventure of exploration, joy, and fantastic sex. I don't really want him in my future anyway. He can't even spell.

Filled with sudden clarity, I open my journal and my pen dashes quickly across the page, filling an entire page with a list of exactly what I want, starting with "Someone capable of texting intelligent things." And then I forget about the list until I come across it three years later, and for a few weeks I stop responding to Alex's texts.

At the end of my twenty-one days in this Ayurvedic sanctuary, I have not transformed into the perfect version of me with all issues resolved that I was secretly hoping for. But I am lighter, fresher, and detoxified.

My final stop in India is Delhi, where I leave two suitcases full of cold weather stuff with my friend Anju from Vipassana, and she drives me to the airport. I leave India with less baggage than when I arrived four months ago, in more ways than one. But I'm still carrying some.

CHAPTER 12

The way back to love begins with understanding
how we disconnected in the first place.
— GABRIELLE BERNSTEIN

December 2017

My friend Kelli from Miami and I have arranged to meet in Bali December 2nd. She'll stay ten days; I'll stay for sixty because that's the maximum a tourist visa will allow me.

Four days before our scheduled flights, a volcano erupts on the island. Mount Agung. The news is filled with images of ominous ash clouds billowing from the mountain's cone. The airport shuts down, but the Indonesian government advises travelers it's still safe to come to Bali. Kelli and I take them at their word. We decide Plan B will be Thailand if our flights are cancelled, but we both have the same gut feeling that we'll make it to Bali.

Our gut feelings are right. Denpasar airport reopens just in time for our flights to depart as scheduled. My flight from Kuala Lumpur carries me and about six other passengers, because apparently most people aren't eager to fly to an island featuring a volcano on the verge of eruption. I luxuriate in a row of seats to myself.

At the airport, I'm greeted by an empty immigration section. There's not another soul here except the agent behind the counter. No lines, no waiting—no complaints from me.

The tourist visa costs $35. The credit card machine on the counter refuses to accept any of my credit cards. "There's an ATM machine over there," the agent says, pointing behind me.

"Okay, thanks." I turn around to head in that direction and immediately freeze in surprise, because there is now one other passenger walking towards me in the otherwise empty terminal and it's none other than one of the Helens from Varkala—radiant blond Helen who had been planning to come to Bali at some undecided future date when I last saw her.

"No freaking way!!" I yell. *"Helen!!"*

She sees me and screams. We have an exuberant, incredulous reunion in the empty immigration hall. "This is so crazy! What are the chances?"

We take a selfie, exchange abbreviated travel stories, and agree to meet up later.

I wait at the airport for Kelli, whose flight arrives two hours after mine. On the taxi ride to Ubud, our driver gestures at a tall green mountain in the distance, sitting peacefully under the clear blue sky. "That's Mount Agung."

That's Mount Agung? It looks nothing like the scary photos in the news. Not so much as a hint of smoke or billowing ash anywhere to be seen.

I have yet another unplanned reunion with Helen the next day when we both show up at the 4 p.m. vinyasa flow class in Yoga Barn's upstairs shala. We laugh and accept that we're meant to be in each other's lives for this stage of our respective journeys.

Our respective journeys are already surprisingly similar. We're both thirty-seven and both decided a few months ago to leave financially rewarding careers and sell our houses in order to wander through Asia for a while. She's a yoga teacher too, although unlike me she was already a yoga teacher before she left home, and she also had a relationship end this year.

In Bali, we're surrounded by beauty. Beauty is the fabric that Bali is made of. The lush green of nature and its exuberant flowers, our gorgeous Airbnb villa with its casually luxurious detail and private pool, the Balinese architecture and curvaceous stone statues, the colorful food. We find amazing lattes made with fresh coconut milk and mouthwatering Balinese dishes flavored with kaffir lime, galangal, and lemongrass.

Part of Bali's beauty is felt rather than seen. It's the energy here: a soothing, nourishing softness. It's subtle but ubiquitous in Ubud—in the gentle sweetness of the Balinese people, in the supple texture of the tropical plants, in the graceful curves of the stone goddesses standing by turquoise pools, in the quiet air that fills our lungs.

I was craving this softness without realizing it. The world is so loud, so tough, so demanding. I needed the opposite of that: this soothing, compassionate softness. The world needs more of this.

Bali whispers to me to look for those qualities in myself—to bring them out of hiding. To reconnect with that side of my own nature.

India was beautiful, but a lot of work, and very dusty. Bali is just bliss, beauty, and pleasure. And here, it only costs $12 an hour for real, serious bliss—if you indulge in the Royal Balinese Massage at the spa on the second floor of Clear Café. My massage standards are sky high and their therapists consistently surpass them. They have magic fingers. I'm never disappointed here.

There's a full moon a few days after we arrive and the astrologer Michael Lennox has this to say about it: "This full moon is a celebration of all the choices we have made along the way that have led us, inexorably, toward this moment."

That's exactly what it feels like. Kelli, Helen, and I celebrate the full moon and all the choices that brought us inexorably to this moment by drinking wine next to our pool in the glow of the moonlight, with our combined crystals all around us. We discover that Bali has some terrible wine and I managed to select the worst bottle of all: Aga Red. It's so spectacularly awful it should be globally banned. Luckily Helen brought a decent non-Balinese bottle.

When Kelli leaves, I move to a cheaper guesthouse, buy the month-unlimited yoga pass at Yoga Barn and dive back into yoga immersion.

Yoga Barn is yoga heaven. There are ten to eleven classes a day, including yoga and meditation and Shamanic breathing and more — an abundance of different styles and different teachers to try. I want to try everything. Sometimes I attend four classes a day, soaking up as much knowledge and inspiration as possible.

One mid-December morning, thirty or so students and I are in the middle of a vinyasa class led by the Indonesian teacher Murni in the spacious wooden second-floor shala. She has us all in a variation of *upavishta konasana,* the seated wide-legged forward fold, reaching for our left foot. Glancing forward as I lean into the pleasant stretch, my eyes land on an attractive man on the left side of the room. He looks intent but exasperated as he stretches his hands in the direction of his left toes. Limited flexibility keeps his foot well out of reach of his fingers. His profile is charmingly handsome and the pose accentuates the muscles of his back under his cotton T-shirt. I like his style immediately: baby blue T-shirt and beige cotton pants. He looks effortlessly good, casual, and comfortable. Something about him strikes my attention like a bell being struck, triggering a sudden jolt of attraction and interest. Something I haven't felt at the sight of anyone else in Bali…or anyone anywhere in a long time, for that matter. The sight of him makes me suddenly wish to have a man in my life again. His attitude of focus mixed with frustration is endearing from all the way across the room.

After the class, I walk downstairs and notice the handsome guy standing by the water cooler. I suddenly decide I'm thirsty and walk over to serve myself a glass.

"Did you like the class?" I ask him.

I hope he can't tell that I'm a little nervous to speak to him. I have a bright red scar next to the inner corner of my left eye from the recent removal of a small keratosis (by an excellent dermatologist in Delhi, just before I left India) and the scar makes me self-conscious.

I relax when he responds nicely to me, and we start chatting. It feels natural, no awkwardness. His name is Julien, he's French, and he's in Bali for a few weeks. He's been studying Balinese massage, just for the fun of it. (An excellent pastime, in my opinion.) He mentions the Yoga Barn ecstatic dance Friday—he went last time and says it was incredible. I was already planning to go since it was one of the two recommendations of the Swiss girl from the Ayurvedic center, and I'm happy to hear he'll be there too.

After a few minutes of chatting, we part ways.

This encounter pushes me to stop putting off the one hard thing I need to do in Bali, which has to do with Alex. I haven't replied to him in three weeks. After a week of silence from me, he texted Sarah asking if I was okay.

Yep! She's going to Bali! she texted back.

I have a feeling that nothing's going to happen with anyone else until I sever the energetic cord connecting my heart to Alex, and ignoring him won't do that. I know what I have to do, and it's going to be very uncomfortable. (Sigh. In spite of my ongoing aspiration to become comfortable with discomfort, my natural preference is still to bury my head in the sand or run the other way.)

But the avoidance strategy won't get me where I want to go, so I will have to walk the plank of discomfort, which involves: telling Alex how I feel and finding out how he feels. That's going to be uncomfortable because, a) it's probably going to lead to awkwardness and rejection, and b) Alex and I never talk about our feelings for each other. Except once, way back in the beginning, when I was trying to stop seeing him but not trying hard enough, and I asked him, "Do you feel guilty?"

He answered me the next time he came over. "You asked me if I feel guilty. I do. I think about you when I'm with her. I feel … emotions for you."

Then we agreed again that we should stop seeing each other, and again we didn't stop. But we never talked about feelings again. We lived in a comfortable bubble of avoidance, as if his partner and complicated human emotions didn't exist.

At this point, I have no idea what his feelings have evolved or faded into. I would rather relive getting my wisdom teeth pulled than bring up this dicey subject. But this is the only way. *There are no shortcuts.*

After a couple more days of emotional preparation, which

involves steeling myself for rejection and reminding myself that whatever his response is, it's meant to be, and what doesn't kill me will make me stronger, I leave him a Whatsapp voice message.

I tell him that I've been thinking about him too much. I tell him I thought it was over between us when I left, I didn't think I would keep hearing from him, and it makes me happy to hear from him but actually it makes me too happy. And he's taking up too much space in my mind and I don't want to have these feelings anymore if it's just one-sided. I just need to know if he's only texting me out of friendship or if it's something more. And if it's something more, is he going to do something about it, like get on a plane and come over here? It's not like he has to stay forever but he could just come check it out. I know that idea might sound batshit crazy and maybe such a thought never occurred to him, but, I just want to throw it out there. Whatever his answer is, it's fine either way. He doesn't need to worry about hurting my feelings. I know that whatever is meant to come of this, will be. No rush, but if he could just let me know.

It takes me a while to fall asleep that night. I drift off eventually, but wake up a little while later. I look at my phone and it's 1:11. I fall back asleep and when I wake up again it's 5:55.

I don't know exactly what that means, except that apparently I'm on the right path.

A few minutes after 5:55, Alex texts me. *Hey, can you speak?*

Uh-oh. He didn't need time to think. I'm pretty sure I know what that means.

He calls, and in his blunt, no sugar-coating New York style, gets right to the point. "When you stopped texting, I knew what was going through your mind. Yeah, all those texts and all the help with your house, that was just out of friendship. I know it's my fault for texting, but yeah, I wanted to know where you were going and stuff."

I wanted to be telling the truth when I said he couldn't hurt my feelings, but it turns out I wasn't. His response seems so casual and easy, and that hurts. But I don't let him see that.

"Okay, I figured as much. Thank you for letting me know," I reply brightly.

And that's all we say about that. We chat for an hour or so about life on our respective sides of the world. It's fine. We're fine as friends too.

After I hang up, I feel low—and a little confused. I didn't really think he was going to jump on a plane and fly to Bali, but I expected his response to be … different. To include some emotion or compassion or at least a tinge of regret. He seemed so unfeeling, so casual. So, it had been ridiculous of me to think it could have been anything more, to think there was anything special about our connection, to let him matter so much more to me than I mattered to him. But after all this time, after everything, how could his heart feel nothing more than friendship? Emotions change, feelings disappear all the time, I know that. I just didn't think his had.

So I'm free now—or supposed to be free—but I don't feel free. I feel unsettled, and sad. It wasn't knowing once and for all that it was over that hurt me. It was discovering that I was never anything special to him.

Night arrives: the night of the ecstatic dance. Helen, her friend Andrea, and I go together. The music is pumping; the shala is packed. Everyone but me is having the time of their lives, dancing their hearts out. But I can't get into it. I can't find any energy and my mind is elsewhere.

Nonetheless, even in this weird disconnected state, I don't want to miss my chance to see the handsome French guy. I make a tour of the shala but I don't see him anywhere. He must not have come. I rejoin Helen and Andrea near the balcony and resume going through the motions of moving to the music, while the words from the morning's conversation replay in my head. *It was just friendship.*

As the words cycle through my mind, something clicks. Why did he say "all the texting, all the help with the house, that was all just friendship"? I never said anything about the house. It's like he gave me a clue; a time stamp. I vaguely remember the tone of his messages around that time, and as I recall they weren't anything like the messages of just a friend.

Giving up on the dance, I tell Helen and Andrea I'll be downstairs. I find myself a seat on the cushioned swing in the courtyard and scroll back through Alex's messages until I find the ones from my second month in India, when Hurricane Irma was fomenting mass terror and evacuation in South Florida.

I reread the messages, and as I had thought, they could by no stretch of the imagination be construed as "just friendship."

I put the phone away and smile to the dark night around me, filled with a sense of peace and acceptance. My power and energy flow back to me. It's over with Alex, because we chose different paths, but our connection had been real. I think I know—more or less—the reasons he wouldn't follow me to the other side of the world, but for a short while, our paths had intertwined and it had been something beautiful. Now, it's time to let go. Now that I understand, the cord between us is severed. Now I'm free. Now I'm ready to move on. And now I feel like dancing.

But the ecstatic dance is ending, and the girls and I are hungry, so we go back to our favorite café, The Ubudian, for wine and food. We eat and drink and talk about men. We all went through breakups recently … but not too recently. We're all ready for a man in our lives. It doesn't have to be The One. It's okay if it's just a fling—but it has to be a fling with connection.

We're happy and laughing and fully alive, joyfully discussing our heart's desires. In the open-air restaurant, surrounded by the magic-infused breezes of the Balinese night, we join our hands and reach up toward the sky and send our wish out into the universe, out loud. "We wish for a fling, but a fling with connection!"

It rains that night, as it so often does these months, as if the rain is washing away the past, leaving us clean, fresh, and renewed.

The next day, Saturday, I am light and full of joy. I realize that as much as I was craving Alex's presence, I'm not finished yet with what I need to do alone. It's a luxury to be able to focus all my energy on me right now and to have the freedom to keep moving toward the future of my dreams.

The next morning I wake up early for the 7:30 a.m. kundalini class at Yoga Barn. At the end of the class, I stand up to put my mat away and I spot Julien near the middle of the room. We start chatting; he tells me he was at the dance Friday and he looked for me too. We're both surprised we didn't see each other. He asks if I want to get a coffee. Of course I do.

I'm secretly craving an Ubudian coconut milk cappuccino, so I'm a little disappointed when he leads me to the Yoga Barn restaurant. But luckily all their tables are full, so I tell him I know an amazing coffee spot if he wants to go somewhere else. He agrees and we take the five-minute walk to the Ubudian.

We sit across from each other at one of the low tables where you can sit cross-legged. Conversation flows naturally. The energy between us mingles and rises as it bounces back and forth between us. It feels good. He's open, easy to talk with, and interesting. Our conversation is a comfortable mix of English and French. (I've been in love with the French language since I first began learning it at age eleven, and some part of my brain lights up with joy on the rare occasions I get the chance to speak it.) Julien's interests are broad. He's well-traveled, passionate on some topics, and occasionally shares tidbits of wise advice. Meditation is part of his life. He's done meditation retreats with Thich Nhat Hahn. (How cool is that?)

At some point he comes over to sit next to me to show me photos on his phone, and he stays there. This is fine by me. Our legs are lightly touching.

Our coffees finished, I start looking at the food menu, but he says, "If you trust me, I can take you to another nice place. It's in the middle of a rice field: amazing view, a little far away. We have to go there by scooter."

This day is getting better and better. I'm thrilled for our spontaneous date to stretch on, and I love scooters. I don't have one, so he takes me on the back of his.

The ride to the restaurant is an adventure. Outside the city center, the off-the-beaten-track roads of Bali are skinnier than your average sidewalk, and they snake haphazardly between buildings and through rice fields. Julien is clearly an experienced driver; he navigates the tightrope of a path confidently. I hold on to his torso for dear life.

The restaurant is surrounded by rice fields and a grove of papaya trees. We take the stairs to the second floor and find ourselves on a big wooden deck with a thatched roof, open on three sides, surrounded by splendid views of the pristine countryside. There are no other customers.

We seat ourselves on floor cushions at a low wooden table. Our conversation continues over a delicious breakfast of tofu curries, with a fresh coconut for me and a passionfruit smoothie for him. I like his combination of qualities: natural, open, classy but adventurous, and at ease in this tropical setting.

He describes his journey to Bali, which was an adventure in itself. Mount Agung erupted while he was already in the air on the way here. His flight was redirected to an emergency landing in Chengdu, China. Determined to get to Bali, he booked a last-minute seat on a flight to Surabaya, on the island of Java. From Surabaya he paid a taxi driver a small fortune to drive him to Gilimanuk—a two-day journey. On the way, the driver suggested they stop overnight in Bromo so he could hike one of the active volcanos and see the incredible views. So they did. (It was phenomenal.) From Surabaya, he took a boat to Kuta, and thus, he was finally in Bali.

He spent a few days in Kuta and then visited Ubud, planning to stay for three days. Someone told him to check out Yoga Barn, so he did. He had never done yoga before. He tried a beginner-level class, and he was hooked. He decided then and there that this is where he would spend his remaining two weeks in Bali. He bought the Yoga Barn unlimited pass and, like me, started trying as many different styles and classes as possible.

He tells me that morning he woke up and thought, *Yoga Barn, baff.* He felt like staying in bed, but something made him get up and go to the kundalini class. (Secretly I thank whichever divine operators are responsible for that, who must have also put blinders on us at the ecstatic dance so he wouldn't find me when I was in my state of disconnected lowness, so we could have this beautiful day instead. It had to be today, because he's leaving Bali tomorrow.)

After breakfast, I lean back on my cushioned seat and feel a twinge of asana-induced pain in my glutes. "Ow."

"You have pain?" he asks with concern.

"My ass hurts," I reply, laughing. "From yoga."

"Do you want a massage?" he asks, very seriously.

He couldn't have known that I'm the world's number one fan of massages. Of course I want a massage—especially from him. It's starting to feel like I've entered a dream of the best day ever. As if the Universe Genie assigned a special team to create one absolutely perfect day for me and they scrolled through my unconscious mind to painstakingly select every single detail that would bring me the most delight.

Julien creates a little massage bed on the floor out of our seat cushions and I lie down on my belly. He proceeds to give me an excellent full body massage, starting with my ass. He clearly paid attention in his Balinese massage classes; his technique is excellent. The tension in my sore muscles melts away and I dissolve into bliss.

When he's finished, I slowly bring myself up to sitting. "It was so wonderful," I tell him. "How can I thank you?"

He laughs and says, a little shyly maybe, "You can let me kiss you."

Which of course I do.

The Perfect Day continues. We spend a long time kissing in the solitary privacy of our second-floor deck. Along the wall there are cushioned wooden benches with mattresses the size of twin-sized beds. At some point we move to one of them for greater comfort and continue our make-out session. It's sensual but relaxed. He stays polite and respectful.

At some point, a young backpacker comes up to our private rooftop. He sits down near us and the three of us chat for a while, me curled up next to Julien and Julien's arm still around me. The guy stays longer than we want him to, but finally he leaves so we can go back to kissing.

Eventually we leave our pleasant deck. Julien drops me off at my guest house so I can shower and change, but we make plans to meet up again a couple hours later for dinner. I suggest Kismet—recommendation #2 of my Swiss friend from India. Julien is happy to try it. There's a jacuzzi at his Airbnb, so we make a tentative plan for jacuzzi after dinner.

Dinner is as perfect as the rest of the day has been. We have a cozy corner table with a cushioned bench seat so we can sit as close together as we want to. Dinner is delicious and the wine is marvelous. (They don't serve Aga Red here.) My French date knows his wine; he gives me little tips on identifying the tasting notes. Blackberries and cherries and a little oakiness, this one has. We sneak more kisses in between sips of wine and conversation and laughter. An aura of happiness envelopes us and our table. He tells me that he noticed me too, that day in class, before I talked to him at the water cooler.

The rest of the night is as perfect as the day was. The man is a deep well of tireless passion and sexual energy. Lying on his bed, after a while in the jacuzzi, and a longer while of sensual, firework-inducing lovemaking, he lightly caresses the curves of my back.

"Tu as un corps pour faire l'amour," he says.

You have a body for making love. Words are richer and more seductive when you hear them in a language that's not your own and your mind translates them one by one, dwelling longer on their meaning than if they were the words of your mother tongue. In this moment and setting, after four and a half months of celibacy, I love the literal idea of these words: that my body exists for the purpose of making love. That is the main reason for the existence of my body: to make love. To this man. Right now.

Later, he takes me to a late-night second dinner because I'm ravenous. The chicken burger is the best thing I've ever tasted. As we're walking back afterwards, a taxi driver on the side of the road asks me, "Does he always make you this happy?"

"Oh yes, always!" I reply, beaming a smile of unfiltered joy back to the astute driver.

The next day, we're still wrapped in the glow of happiness. We want to spend as much time together as possible before he has to leave for the airport, but I have an appointment to visit a villa with Helen, because we've decided it would be ideal to rent one together for our last month in Ubud. Julien drives me to the villa. I introduce him to Helen and she gives Julien one of her radiant, conspiratorial smiles. "Thank you for taking good care of my friend."

He laughs, a charming, easy laugh, and smiles at me. "It's my pleasure," he replies, in his cultured French accent.

Helen and I don't love the villa, so we cross it off our list, but that doesn't diminish my happiness. On the scooter drive back, my lover lightly massages my ankle, the side of my leg. The amazing power of an affectionate touch, triggering that cascade of oxytocin in the brain, rekindling the warm glow of pleasure. I've already forgotten that ideal-man wish list I scribbled down a few weeks earlier when I was mad at Alex-who-can't-spell, so I don't realize at that moment that Julien is very nearly almost everything on that list, from Speaks French to Affectionate and Loves to Cuddle and Capable of Texting Intelligent Things and everything in between. At that moment I'm not thinking about any lists, or anything past or future. I'm just happy.

We stop at a wine store for a chilled bottle of rosé and go back to my hotel. We find two glasses and settle in at the long table in the alcove next to the pool. The Cape Discovery rosé is light, summery, and perfect. Overhead, capiz shell wind chimes dance in the breeze, sending a soothing melody into the air.

I learn a little more about this charming, hazel-eyed Frenchman. He was married for a long time, divorced a couple years ago, and has two grown sons. I don't ask his age; I guess he must be around forty-five. We discover that we both have a file of inspiring quotes saved in our phones. We compare notes. There is one that we both have: Steve Jobs' famous statement from his 2005 Stanford commencement address. "Have the courage to follow your heart and your intuition." Julien has only that first part of it and I have the end of the sentence: "…they somehow already know what you truly want to become."

And then the time comes to say goodbye. I walk with him to his motorbike, parked at the front entrance.

"It's hard to say goodbye," he says.

At this moment nothing can ruin my happiness, not even this goodbye. It all feels magical. Even though part of me wishes he would hint that I should come to France sometime, he doesn't, and it doesn't matter. We leave it as: maybe we'll see each other again one day, somewhere on planet Earth.

Whatever will be will be. For now, our thirty-six hours were perfect. The best early Christmas gift I could have wished for.

He leaves, and we keep texting for a while, and the texts gradually become less frequent, and all the while Bali remains beautiful and magical.

CHAPTER 13

The older I get, the more I think every problem is just fear.

- PEMA CHODRON

January 2018

Planet Earth has whirled into 2018. Helen and I spend a quietly festive New Year's Eve weekend on the tiny island of Gili Air, dancing by bonfires on the sand with fireworks overhead. DJs fill the air with music and we are filled with joy. We start New Year's Day with a vinyasa class on the beach, then rent paddleboards and paddle to the neighboring island of Lombok and back. This year is off to a bright start.

Back in Ubud, we decide we need faster transportation than our own two legs, so we rent scooters. Thus begins my love affair with motorbikes in Asia. (At some point I transition from the American term scooter to the Asian "motorbike.") I had a scooter in Miami, but I discover that whereas in Miami scooters are optional, for long-term stays in Asia, they're essential. Motorbikes give you wings. With a motorbike, you are free to go wherever you want, whenever you want—and thanks to Mount Agung, there isn't much traffic to contend with here. To be perched comfortably on a motorbike, riding along the gently curving roads of Ubud past lush green foliage and ornate temples and exotic statues, feeling the breeze on your skin— it's pure, unadulterated bliss.

Bali is known for its healers, and our two-month stay wouldn't be complete without at least one healing experience. Distracted by all the other amazing things going on, we haven't put any effort into finding one, but one day Andrea reports an incredible experience with a spiritual healer named Tunjung. Tunjung is a Balinese woman who owns a spa in the center of Ubud.

"She knows things," Andrea tells us. "I walked in there and the first thing she told me was, 'well, you need to fix that issue with your mother.' How would she know that?"

Helen schedules a session for herself and comes away equally awed. "She does know things. You can ask her anything," she tells me afterward. "While I was laying on the treatment table, I could feel her moving energy in my body. It was unbelievable."

So I in turn schedule a session with Tunjung.

It turns out the timing is perfect. Although I've been floating on a cloud of joy for most of my time in Bali, today is an off day. I've fallen off the bliss wagon back into the swamp of self-doubt and anxiety. I've started thinking about the future and worrying. Maybe this journey won't have a beautiful ending after all. Maybe I'll be a terrible yoga teacher. Maybe I'll never accomplish anything I want to; maybe I don't have the focus and energy and drive it would take, blah blah blah, and so on. Even though most of me doesn't believe any of that, the voice is loud and persistent today. I recognize this voice. I know she's the price I'm paying for too little sleep and too many cocktails during our festive holidays.

So I'm not feeling my best when I walk into Tunjung's spa for my appointment. The spa is lovely and inviting, with warm wooden interiors accented with fresh flowers. Tunjung sees me in a treatment room on the second floor. She's around my age, I guess: mid-thirties, dressed in Western clothes. She's genuine, direct, and no-nonsense. To give her psychic powers a fair test, I don't tell her much; I just ask what she can read from my energy. She tells me a few things, all of which are true. Then I tell her that most of the time I feel pretty great, but sometimes I feel a kind of heavy energy inside. "Like right now. I don't know what causes it and I don't know how to get rid of it."

I lie down on the treatment table while she does an energy healing for about half an hour. When it's finished, we go back to her desk and she delivers her assessment.

"Actually, you are still detoxifying from years of not really being yourself. Your confidence/third chakra, it's the one that really dropped right now. It's affected your body, it's affected everything. And your mind is really busy. It's like, always preparing things. If you try to just really go with the flow you're gonna be really fine though. Because what I see is that this is the one that's heavy. It's like subconsciously you know—you actually quite know—that everything is just going to happen in your life, everything you wanted actually. But there's another part of you that's always trying to prepare for the rainy day. That actually makes it heavy. You always try to prepare for how about if things not gonna work. Why you prepare to be hurt rather than prepare to just enjoy? For now, you don't need to prepare anything, you don't need to prepare how if things not gonna work. F-U-C-K-I-T. Okay? That's it, you don't need to prepare how if you're hurt, or how things not gonna work. You just need to, 'okay I'm just gonna do it.' And what if it's not work? So what. Let's see.

"That's what you need to be. Then you'll be fine. Because your energy is quite open but actually it's like it's wrapped up in this weight which is the fear of how things not gonna work. Maybe you're used to it because of your previous job or everything but no, it's not like that. Life, even in the job at a big company, it should not be like that. It should be like, let's do it and see. You don't need to prepare for it, for how things not gonna work. You just need to do it. Then you'll be fine."

It's as if she has peered into my psyche, seen everything, and delivered a perfect summary of my lifelong inner tug-of-war between joy and worry along with a permission slip to let go of the worry. As for her future predictions, only time will tell if they are true—but they feel spot-on.

Curious, I ask her if she's always had this gift, this ability to read people's energy. Yes, she says, she always had it, but she used to hate it and for a long time she tried to ignore it. "You know, in Bali people believe in this stuff, in spirits and energy, but I didn't like it. I didn't want it." It was only six years ago that she finally accepted her ability and started to work with it. And now she loves it, she tells me with a smile.

I like her empowered, comfortable authenticity.

An hour after the healing, I head to Yoga Barn for a shamanic breathing class. Before it begins, the teacher offers us the option to pull a card from a deck at the front of the room.

I pull the Power card. That feels perfect.

As we're lying on our mats, breathing deeply as the vibrations of tribal music and shamanic drums fill the room, I relax back into confident, playful, feminine power. By the end of the class, my energy has shifted completely. I feel light as a feather and on top of the world.

I can't say for sure how much of the shift is due to Tunjung and how much is due to the breathwork and how much to a serendipitous combination of both, but the impact lasts for weeks. It feels as if some old toxic energy has been swept out of my cells.

The experience reminds me of something I once heard Dr. Gabor Maté say. "The greater calamity was that you lost the connection to your true essence." It feels like that. It feels like the work of a true healer is to enable us to repair the connection to our true essence; to clear out the residue of old toxic energy that's been separating us from our true nature.

A few weeks later, Helen and I meet an Australian woman who's lived in Ubud for several years. She raves about another local healer, Tjokorda Rai (pronounced "Chuh-korda Rye"), whose grandfather was the last King of Ubud. He's now close to ninety years old and has devoted his life to healing for over forty years. He's quite well known in Bali and is considered a master spiritual healer.

"He's amazing!" she tells us. "People line up every day at his home to be healed. You should get there early, like before 9 a.m. The healing is out in the open. You just lay down on a table in front of everyone. You can talk with him and then he does something with energy. He always knows specifically what's wrong. A friend of mine went to see him and he started pointing at her belly and saying, "Get it out! Get it out!" She had an IUD. She went to get it checked out after seeing him and they found cancer around it."

A couple days later, a Spanish woman at my hotel happens to mention that she visited Tjokorda Rai a week ago. She had gone to see him because of her chronic tinnitus.

"He's amazing," she tells me. "He knew what my problem was without me telling him, and he gave me the best advice. It was so common sense, but I'd never thought of it."

That settles it—Helen and I have to go see Tjokorda Rai too. No matter that we don't have any actual pressing need for healing. After our festive holiday celebrations, my liver could surely use some healing, if nothing else, and Helen primarily wants to find out if the healer can help her father. Luckily, our destination appears on Google Maps under Tjokorda Rai, so it's not difficult to find him. Early one weekday morning we jump on our scooters and make the ten-minute drive to Tjokorda Rai's home, prepared to wait all day if necessary.

His residence is a spacious compound, laid out in typical Balinese style, with groups of independent buildings set in a grassy area bordered by a brick fence. We wander through the yard until we find a woman who appears to live there.

"Tjokorda Rai?" we ask.

She points toward the distant left. "You'll see many people!"

We head in the direction her fingertip indicates and find a small group of Westerners seated under a covered dais. One man is lying on his back on a raised platform and a thin, elderly Balinese man is tracing a short wooden stick over his body as the others watch in intent silence. We sit down quietly and join the group in fascinated observation.

Tjokorda Rai spends about ten minutes with each person. He begins by talking with them for a minute or two. Then he massages their face, head, and ears with strong pressure. Next he has them lie down. He presses a spot on the inner edge of their big toe with the edge of the wooden stick, causing some people to yelp in pain. He moves his hands through the air just above their body for a few minutes, his hands following different patterns, focusing on different areas for each person, sometimes massaging somewhere or applying pressure with the stick. Finally he presses the stick against the same area of the big toe, but the pain is gone. No one yelps or flinches now. The patient sits up and they talk for a couple minutes. The healer has a lively sense of humor and usually starts cackling with laughter at some point.

Helen and I chat with a British guy after the end of his treatment. "I have to say, that was incredible," he says. "I was having this intense pain, and then it was just gone."

When it's Helen's turn, she walks up to the platform and sits down in front of Tjokorda Rai. He looks at her and informs her there's nothing he can do for her.

"You should come back later," he adds.

We're both taken aback. We didn't realize that there was a possibility healers could turn you away. But after the initial moment of surprise, Helen acknowledges that, actually, she's feeling all-around really great already. I can attest to the fact that she's currently glowing with vibrance, health, and vitality. Tunjung's recent work had apparently been very effective. (Helen visited Tunjung twice, for the record.) Maybe two visits are the secret because I, as it turns out, have not yet reached such a perfect no-need-for-healing state. Tjokorda Rai doesn't send me away.

When I walk up hesitantly to sit in front of him, he looks at me for a second and says with a smile, "You are very happy!"

I laugh. "So are you!"

He gestures for me to turn around and performs the scalp, face, and ear massage. As he's pressing on the sides of my scalp, he exclaims, "Ooooh! You worry a lot!"

I laugh again. Spot on. "Yes, always!"

"Don't worry; worry brings doubts. Just be happy," he tells me.

He essentially paraphrased Tunjung's summary, I notice later.

He massages my scalp a little longer and then tells me to lie down. When he presses the wooden stick into the side of my toe, it's excruciating. "Aaiieee!" I yell, writhing in pain.

Luckily he doesn't maintain the brutal pressure for long. I close my eyes while he does something mysterious above my body—

moving energy around with his hands, I assume. After a few minutes, he presses my toe again. This time, there's no pain.

When I sit up, he announces, "Your hormones are low. You need omega-3."

I look at him in surprise. Omega-3 is the only supplement I take. In fact, it's the only supplement I've ever managed to stick to taking consistently in my life, but my supply ran out a couple months ago. Kelli brought me a bottle of my favorite brand from the US, but lazily I've not gotten back into the habit of taking the capsules daily. "Omega-3?" I repeat.

"Yes, omega-3. Just one capsule a day."

That's also interesting, since the recommended dosage of my capsules is two per day, but I only take one. Kudos to my intuition— and to Tjokorda Rai's mysterious powers.

"You will feel very good; you will be very happy!" he announces. "Then you come see me again!"

I thank him with a smile, leave a small donation, and Helen and I make our departure. And I go back to taking my omega-3 capsules religiously.

Two weeks later, one last Balinese healer comes into our lives. We find out about her from Karine, a bright, vivacious Belgian who manages a gorgeous hotel on the outskirts of Ubud. The healer is a shaman named Jero Made. (Made is pronounced "Maa-day" and it's one of the five most common names in Bali—as in, approximately one out of every eight Balinese you meet will probably be named Made. Jero is a term of respect.)

Karine discovered Jero Made through a Balinese friend. "She's the real thing," she tells us with wide eyes.

So of course we have to visit her too. Jero Made doesn't speak English, so Karine arranges for her friend/tour guide to take us to see her. He'll serve as our translator, too. He's named Agung, like the volcano, but Agung the person is much less threatening and far more charming than the lava-filled mountain. He has a great sense of humor and a wide, easy smile.

We could never have found our way to Made's home without Agung. Made lives in a village outside Ubud, past a maze of unmarked streets that lead eventually to her unmarked gate. There is no signage announcing her services. Her clients are locals who know of her by reputation.

I love her at first sight. She has a smile that radiates light and an energy that exudes warmth, love, and sweetness. She greets us as if we're dear friends, smiling into my eyes and pressing my hand warmly between both of hers.

She serves us tea, coffee, and Balinese pastries. We chat for a little while over the refreshments, with Agung translating. Then Agung explains how our visit will unfold. We can ask Jero Made any questions we want to. She'll relay our questions to the spirits and ancestors, and she'll transmit their replies. Afterwards, she'll do an energy healing on us.

She leads us into a small room where a Buddha statue stands silently at the front. We each sit on a square meditation cushion. Helen asks the first question and Agung translates for Made. She listens attentively, then stands up, walks to the Buddha, and murmurs words in a low voice. After a few minutes, she returns to sit with us and delivers the answers.

Apparently the ancestors had a lot to say on the subject. Made's first report is a six-minute torrent of Balinese. Finally Agung politely interrupts her, saying something that probably translates as, "Woah, Madam Shaman! You expect me to remember all this?"

She laughs and pauses for him to translate. He does, condensing her six minutes of Balinese into forty-five seconds of English.

This pattern continues for every question we ask. Made returns with a prolific Balinese answer, and Agung provides a short, concise translation. Typical male/female communication pattern, I think.

The ancestors give very specific answers. When we ask about health issues, they prescribe detailed recommendations for what to do, what to eat, etc. After our questions are answered, Made has us lie down on a mat outside, one by one, and she gives us a relaxing energy healing that takes about twenty minutes.

We leave feeling good: calm and light. Because we didn't arrive feeling unwell, it's hard to say definitively whether we experienced any supernatural effects, but in Made's presence I felt love; and love, I think, is the most powerful healer of all.

In any case, life is, I've come to believe, an ongoing journey of healing. There is no perfect fix, no final moment. There's always more to discover. All three of these healers were bright lights along my personal journey, and yet I continued with much more waiting to be discovered and healed.

I receive another gift from the connection with Karine: a house.

A few weeks earlier, in the midst of all these beautiful Ubud hotels and Airbnbs, I started craving a house. More than a house, what I was really craving was the grounded, comforting feeling of a home. With space to be alone and focus and write, and a closet with plenty of hangers for all my clothes, and a kitchen. Specifically, an indoor kitchen, because most houses in Ubud are villas with outdoor kitchens, which is fabulous if the weather is beautiful but less than ideal in the humid rainy season.

Helen liked the sound of a house too, so we decided to rent one together. We've looked at a few villas, but none of them have felt right.

It's Sunday, January 7th. We're in Karine's car and Karine is enthusiastically giving us a long list of local recommendations: best restaurants to try, best places to have a drink and watch the sunset, best things to do, etc. Everything she describes sounds irresistible. At the end of her list, she says laughingly, "Anything else you're looking for around here, just let me know!"

"Well," I say, "We're looking for a two-bedroom, two-bathroom villa to rent for a couple weeks. Do you know of anything?"

"What dates are you looking for exactly?" she asks.

"January 10th to around the 25th."

She starts laughing. "Well, I'm renting my house from January 10th to the 29th, because I'm going to Belgium those dates. It's a two-bedroom, two-bath, two-story villa. I was planning to put it on Airbnb but I haven't gotten around to it yet. If you want to come see it…"

She had described her house to us fifteen minutes ago while telling the serendipitous story of how she found it, and it sounded like a dreamy homey sanctuary. Just then I glance at the clock on the car dashboard. It's 5:55. Right then I know it's going to work out perfectly.

It does. Karine's house is beautiful. Spacious, open, full of light and color and the peaceful sound of birds and nature humming. The kitchen is indoors. The master bedroom includes a magnificent wardrobe with shelves and more than enough hangers for all my clothes. And the rental includes a maid who comes three times a week. It's literally my dream come true.

The house is on the outskirts of Ubud, a ten-minute scooter ride to Yoga Barn. Helen decides she prefers her location in the city center, so I rent the house myself—which is also perfect for Karine, as she tells me laughingly the morning she leaves. "Thank God you only took one bedroom, I wouldn't have had time to clean everything out of the other one!"

It's perfect for me too. With my own space, I transform back into a productive, focused human being. The project I'm determined to bring to fulfillment before leaving Bali is the launch of my website. Comfortably ensconced on the turquoise-cushioned seats of Karine's dining room table, nourished by beautiful meals cooked by Me in the indoor kitchen, it all comes together.

Our last night in Ubud, Helen texts me. *Fancy a glass of wine tonight to celebrate Ubud?*

It's 5:55 p.m. when I open my phone and see the message. Of course I fancy a glass of wine to celebrate our last night in this magical place. The location of our celebration lives up to the occasion; an atmospheric open-air table overlooking a majestic jungle-bordered river.

When I look at my phone back in my Balinese home after our celebratory evening, the time on my screen is 11:11.

CHAPTER 14

There are things all around us, and right at our very feet,
that we have never seen; because we have never really looked.
- ALEXANDER GRAHAM BELL

February 2018

I'm in the Philippines. I'm here for three weeks, and I arrived with
an ambitious plan to explore a large swath of its island territory,
including all of its best beaches and the chocolate hills of Bohol (they
had me at "chocolate hills.") But, as it turns out, I don't make it
beyond the province of Palawan. There's too much to do and explore
here in this giant tropical playground. I'm captivated by the
bewitching views of Kayangan Lake, the giant natural hot springs, the
majestic underwater coral gardens, yoga with ocean views, the white
sand beaches of uninhabited islands, and the paddleboarding among
jagged rock formations that rise from clear turquoise water.

I start my Palawan exploration in the town of Coron. Coron, by
the way, is the name of both a town and an island, and the town of
Coron is not located on the island of Coron: it's on Busuanga Island,
right next to Coron Island. Because there wasn't enough confusion
in this world already.

One night in Coron-the-town, I climb the thousands of stairs to
the top of Mount Tapyas to see the sunset. (Okay, technically there
are 724 stairs, but it feels like thousands.) I finally reach the top, out
of breath, and look out at the stunning sight of a shimmering silver

ocean dotted with hilly green islands under a sky streaked with shades of pink, coral, and blue. For a second, the view takes away my remaining breath. I know a picture won't do justice to the reality, but I feel obligated to take one anyway.

View seen, photo taken, I'm about to walk back down the 724 stairs when a thought comes into my head. *I climbed a lot of stairs to get here. Maybe I should stay for longer than two minutes.*

Out of a sense of obligation to this reasonable thought, I pause and look again at the view. As I hold my gaze fixed, the sight before me becomes more vivid, more clearly in focus, as if the first time I didn't really see it. All of a sudden, I'm mesmerized. It's so quietly spectacular: the still, glimmering sea, the tiny white boats resting quietly in the water, the lights of Coron sparkling far below, a horizon of island mountains resting peacefully under the pastel canvas of sky. It's so beautiful, tears come to my eyes. And then I realize I don't want to leave. The last thing in the world I want is to leave. I just want to sit here and absorb all the beauty in front of me.

I find a seat on the grass and keep staring. This place is so incredibly beautiful, and I am so lucky to get to see it. And at the same time, there are so many countless other incredibly beautiful places on this enormous planet of ours. I wonder, *why is this world so beautiful?*

The answer that comes to me is, *it's a gift.* For us. For humanity. An enormous, extraordinary, incomprehensible miracle of a gift.

A feeling of awe, deep gratitude, and contentment slowly spreads through me.

Then I notice something. I've seen so many other beautiful places before. Macchu Pichu ... Cape Town ... the coastal mountaintops of Rio de Janeiro ... two days ago, the spectacular lagoons of Palawan ... and so many others. All breathtaking, but even while I admired their beauty, my ever-present restlessness remained. Once I had seen the view, I was immediately ready to move on to something else, somewhere else. But here, now, I don't want to be anywhere else. I don't want anything else. I just want to be right here, exactly where I am, letting the dazzling beauty of this present moment dissolve my heart into bliss.

Then I remember something else I had forgotten: this state of contentment is something I had wanted more than anything—maybe even more than I wanted true love. I wanted that constant restlessness to be gone. I wanted to be able to just be still, and be content. To have this feeling of inner peace.

I sit motionless, luxuriating in this sensation. I imagine it won't last forever, this sublime peace and contentment. But now I know what it feels like, and now I know it's possible to have.

Two days later, Helen joins me in Coron for our next joint adventure: a five-day island hopping boat tour that takes us through the vivid turquoise water and majestic lagoons of northern Palawan. We feast on exquisite buffets of fresh grilled seafood, nourishing veggie side dishes, and fluffy, abundant rice—always rice. ("Filipino power!" the crew jokes.) We snorkel through stunning underwater reef gardens and camp on deserted beaches bordered by jungles of foliage straight out of Jurassic Park.

On the fourth day of our trip, a typhoon alert is issued for the Philippines and all boat day tours are canceled for the next few days. Thanks to that, we're almost alone on the water. As we draw closer to El Nido, pristine white sand beaches that would otherwise have been occupied by hundreds of other boats and tourists are left deserted for us to enjoy all to ourselves.

Volcanos, typhoons … so far, these close calls with natural disasters are working out well for us. The closest conditions we experience to an actual typhoon are a few raindrops as we're pulling into port.

Before I describe what transpires a week later, I have to pause for confession time.

For many years, I've had a horrible, ugly character flaw. It involves customer service, and fortunately it doesn't reveal its hideous self often, but when it does, it usually does so in restaurants. If I receive excellent customer service, all is well! I am a happy, appreciative customer. If I receive mediocre customer service, I can tolerate it. I remain polite. If I receive poor customer service and there's an obvious reason for it, I can tolerate that too. I was a server in my college years; I know what it's like to be running around a packed restaurant taking care of a dozen tables of hungry people.

However—if I receive terrible customer service due to laziness, sheer incompetence, or total disinterest on the part of the server, some switch inside me flips. I am suddenly not a nice person. I never yell or cause a scene (that's not my style), but I become cold, angry, and condescending. I might give the sub-par server a lecture on how they should improve their deplorable behavior, but more likely I will make my low opinion of their sorry self clear via a scathing, condescending voice accompanied by an icy, withering glare.

Even as this is transpiring, I hate what it feels like, and I know I've become ugly. I know because I've seen other people react this way and I know what it looks like, and I feel ashamed, but there is some kind of fury inside me that's taken over, and it's stronger than my conscious mind. Even on the occasions when my self-awareness prevails and I manage not to take out my displeasure on the offending server, I am seething with rage inside and it doesn't feel good. The strength of the emotion mystifies me. I don't understand what triggers it, or why.

Strangely, big things don't bother me as much. For example, my purse being snatched in Vietnam a few years ago with my wallet, phone, and camera inside—I took that in stride. But, take thirty minutes to bring me my beverage at dinner and you unleash my unbridled fury.

I don't remember exactly when this pattern began, but it was sometime during my professional, post-college years. It rears its head occasionally in Bali, where service levels are sometimes wonderful, and sometimes outrageously awful. Try as I might, I haven't been able to find a cure for this irrational knee-jerk anger response.

It's when I'm not thinking about it that the solution finally presents itself.

It's our last morning in Palawan. Helen and I are sitting silently on beautiful Sabang Beach, meditating as the sun rises. The changing light and colors of the sky are so beautiful I can't close my eyes, so I just watch the clouds. Again that sense of awe and wonder fills me. I'm immersed in living beauty.

Finally I let my eyelids slide shut for the last three minutes of the meditation, and that's when it hits me.

As if the Universe had planned this all along, it provided a situation the night before that brought this issue to the forefront of my mind. Helen and I had splurged on a night at the swanky Sheridan Hotel, and we were looking forward to a luxurious five-star stay. But reality didn't quite live up to our expectations. The hotel itself and its beachfront location were gorgeous, and behind them was a breathtaking backdrop of puffy clouds flirting with the mountains below. But our room was warm and humid and had a strange odor that first registered as dank and musty, with lingering notes of dying skunk. As if that wasn't enough, the hotel was experiencing a strange issue with their generators that caused the power to cut off briefly every five minutes throughout our entire stay.

Our dinner experience was the icing on the cake. Half of the items on the menu were unavailable. We waited forty-five minutes for our food and then twenty minutes for our bill while a group of servers stood in a corner chatting with each other.

It was all ridiculous beyond belief and the familiar tidal wave of hot anger swept me up. A devil and an angel argued in my mind. The wise angel managed to keep me from turning on the staff, and I restrained myself to complaining bitterly to Helen. But as usual, the anger didn't feel good and I didn't know why I wasn't capable of keeping that emotion from showing up in the first place.

Sitting on the beach the next morning, faced with the contrast of the immensity of the sky and the smallness of my anger, the explanation suddenly rises to the surface of my mind. It was related to a paraphrased memory of something Eckhart Tolle wrote: *Don't make other people or situations responsible for your happiness.*

I suddenly see the whole big picture clearly. I see the trail of my privileged working-life past, filled with idyllic lunches and dinners at upscale restaurants serviced by well-trained staff. Those meals, during my years of intense work travel, became my reward: my most reliable source of pleasure and relaxation. I got used to that five-star level of customer service. I came to believe that I—and all of us—are entitled to that level of professionalism in the hospitality industry.

Unconsciously, that belief wove itself into my psyche, subtly and subconsciously installing itself as a prerequisite for my happiness; as if my happiness was conditional on my expectation of a five-star dining experience being fulfilled. When the expectation wasn't met, it triggered a primal reaction, as if my fundamental right to happiness was being withheld by this other person who wasn't living up to their obligation to deliver the experience I expected. I allowed my happiness to become dependent on that other person's behavior.

In those situations, I was entirely focused on me and my perspective. I never paused to consider the other person's level of education, training, past experiences, potential other factors going on in their life, possible pain or fatigue or past trauma or any emotional suffering they might be going through. And more importantly, I was letting a small thing be too important. Here on this magnificent beach of white sand and silvery-blue waves under an immense color-streaked sky, I remember how lucky I am. How much I've already been given, how rich my life has been. I already have all I need for happiness.

"Replace expectation with appreciation," one of my yoga teachers used to say. But I had been doing the opposite.

In the big picture of my life, the level of customer service at one restaurant meal is a tiny, inconsequential detail. My happiness doesn't depend on the experience of one meal. My happiness depends on me. It's mine to keep or give away; it's my choice. And it's worth too much to give other people and insignificant situations the power to take it away from me. I have the power to remain happy even in the face of outrageously bad customer service.

Somehow, here on this beach under an enormous sky, that realization clicks into place.

The invisible root in my psyche that triggered my unwanted pattern dissolved that morning, as if it couldn't survive in the presence of the beauty of the sunrise.

It left me a little lighter.

On the flight to Luang Prabang, I begin reading *The Universe Has Your Back* by Gabrielle Bernstein. (Helen recommended it—thank you, Helen.) It's a book that will change my life. In the first chapter, I read: *The presence of fear is a sure sign you're trusting in your own strength.*

I gasp when I read that sentence. It's a quote from *A Course in Miracles*, and it's the recognition of the profound truth of those simple words that catches my breath, along with the realization that I do exactly that on a regular basis.

Then I laugh when I see the next line. "This is a profound message, and I remember gasping out loud when I first read it."

So it's not just me then.

The idea that there's something or someone to trust other than your own strength: Ishvarapranidhana again, in different words. Come to think of it, "the Universe has your back" is a pretty great modern translation of Ishvarapranidhana. I'm running into this concept more and more these days.

My mind diplomatically points out that all I have to do is read a newspaper or a history book and I will quickly be reminded that this world is a brutal place. And yet—I keep finding reasons to believe that there is Something out there looking out for us. In books, in conversations with other people, and most convincingly, in my own life. I'm harboring a growing suspicion that, yes, the Universe really does have our back. That this is actually the way life works—if we let it.

As we're beginning our descent toward Luang Prabang, the captain comes on the loudspeaker to make his landing announcement. "The time is now 2:22," he informs us.

Clearly, it's going to be a magical trip, I think.

And that turns out to be right.

CHAPTER 15

The journey is the reward.
– STEVE JOBS

February 2018

In quiet, mellow Luang Prabang, the sun is shining and life seems to flow with a pace as languid as the Khan and Mekong rivers that serenely wind their way around the city center. An hour drive from the city are the spectacular jade, multi-tiered Kuang Si Falls. I rent a motorbike to visit them early, before the busloads of tourists arrive. For a couple hours, I have the falls almost all to myself, these seven tiers of breathtaking living art.

There's something magical about jade waterfalls. It's as if they are proof of the essential lovingkindness of the Universe.

But Laos' mass transportation system is less impressive than its waterfalls. Three days in advance, I buy a minivan ticket to the village of Nong Khiaw from a respectable travel agency. I arrive at the station shortly before the scheduled departure. Three vans are there waiting. Two are filled with passengers. The third is empty except for the driver.

The man in charge tells me to go to the empty van and he loads my luggage on top. I take a seat inside and wait. Five minutes later, he returns, takes my luggage down from the roof, and moves it over to the roof of the second van. He tells me to sit inside that van. I walk over to the vehicle and peer inside through the open side door. It's completely full of passengers.

"Whose lap am I supposed to sit on?" I ask. He shrugs, like, *take your pick*.

"I can't ride in here, it's full," I tell him.

"It's only three hours," he replies.

He's obviously lost his mind. I tell him no way.

He takes my luggage down and puts it back on the roof of the third van, but for some reason none of the vans depart. During the following twenty minutes, he proceeds to move my luggage from one van roof to another four more times. Eventually, apparently bored of this fun workout, he brings me my luggage and the amount of cash I paid for my ticket and tells me to go buy a ticket at the bus station.

"Absolutely not," I inform him, refusing to take the money. It's clear that he doesn't speak much English so I use a lot of emphatic hand gestures to emphasize my points. He needs to honor my ticket. He has three vans and three drivers here and he needs to stop wasting everyone's time. He can move some other passengers over to the third van and we can all get on our way.

Luckily, my lecture works—combined with the timely arrival of one last passenger, a slim, brown-haired American guy, who probably tipped the scales in favor of sending the three vans on their way instead of keeping all passengers at the station for the rest of the day while the exercise-loving man in charge continued moving luggage from one van rooftop to another. The Transportation Delay Specialist moves two other passengers from one of the full vans into the third van with me and the American guy, and we finally set out. Along the way, the driver stops a few times to pick up locals from the side of the road, so by the time we get to Nong Khiaw our vehicle is almost full.

Anyway, I should thank the Transportation Delay Specialist, because had we left on time the late passenger would have missed the bus. His name is Jarrett and he's from New York. We chat a little during the drive, and I run into him later that afternoon when I'm wandering aimlessly through Nong Khiaw.

Jarrett tells me he's going to do a 5:30 a.m. hike up to Nong

Khiaw Viewpoint tomorrow morning. I've never heard of Nong Khiaw Viewpoint, which is not surprising since my entire Laos travel research consisted of jotting down the recommendations of a German traveler in the Philippines and finding a hotel on booking.com. But I remember the magic of the Rishikesh sunrise hike, so I invite myself along to this one. Jarrett agrees to let me join him.

The one-hour hike up a steep dirt-and-rock path is an excellent cardiovascular workout. It brings us to the top of a tall mountain, where we're greeted by a spectacular, otherworldly sight.

The sun waits below the horizon and the moon hangs in the dimly luminous pale blue sky. We're surrounded on all sides by an ocean of puffy white clouds. Distant mountaintops are islands peeking through the sea of white. It's so beautiful it makes my heart ache.

We stay here for a while, taking pictures and sitting in meditative silence as the sun makes its slow appearance, tinting the sky a shade of pale tangerine.

Imagine, if I didn't run into Jarrett walking through town, I would have missed out on all this.

It turns out that Jarrett's travel plans for the next few days are identical to mine, so he becomes my short-term Laos travel buddy. I don't know it then, but this chance meeting will soon alter the direction of the rest of my Asia journey.

We take the boat to Muang Ngoi ("Muang Noy") the next morning. The seats are narrow wooden boards barely higher than the floor and all passengers are packed in like sardines. I love it. It feels ancient and authentic and the water is liquid green glass between the steep sides of the river that carries us to our destination.

I fall in love with Muang Ngoi as soon as we arrive. It's a tiny village, a quiet, sleepy oasis perched on the sandy riverside, where electricity arrived only a few years ago and where only travelers who relish peace and quiet should go.

One night I meet Jarrett for dinner at a restaurant at the far end of the outrageously rocky main road. It has an open-air bar and tables and hammocks scattered across a big open yard where bonfires are lit when the nightly chill sets in. The red table wine is very drinkable and the food is shockingly delicious: the carrot ginger smoothie and the pumpkin curry are nothing short of phenomenal. I'm amazed that a place like this exists in a tiny village in such a remote corner of the world. Eating here under the stars in the crisp fresh air, enjoying good conversation, is pure delight.

Jarrett talks a lot about Myanmar, where he spent a few weeks before coming to Laos. He tells me I have to go to Kalaw, a charming little town in the mountains with a surprising number of great restaurants. He also suggests my next book: *Steve Jobs,* by Walter Isaacson.

I make a note of Kalaw and download *Steve Jobs* on my Kindle. It's a fascinating biography of the gifted, complicated, extraordinary man who had such a tremendous impact on our daily lives, on the way we work and communicate. As I make my way through its pages, I'm surprised to discover that, while I possess none of Jobs' genius, nor most of his idiosyncrasies (you won't ever find me on a fruitarian diet, going days without showering, or boycotting deodorant), we have a few things in common. Like me, he loved beauty and India and he cried often.

"Every once in a while, I find myself in the presence of purity—purity of spirit and love—and I always cry. It always just reaches in and grabs me," he said once. Because the same thing happens to me, I'm surprised and delighted to read this. I think he would have been an interesting person to talk to—if he happened to be in a good mood at the time.

My last night in Laos, I meet a Canadian man named Johnny. I meet him at a bar in Vientiane that's owned by the two sisters who are my Airbnb hosts. I've come for a drink and a friendly chat with the sister who's bartending. Johnny is sitting at the bar next to me. We start talking. He's from Winnipeg: a big, friendly, good-natured guy. He tells me that a few days ago he woke up on a plane to Hong Kong and had no idea how he got there. He had only gotten himself a one-way ticket, so he decided that since he was here, he might as well see as much of Asia as possible.

"Well, they should make a movie about this," I say. "What's the last thing you remember before waking up on the plane?"

"I was drinking a lot of sake. That's why I ended up in Asia. It's not the first time something like this has happened, but I usually end up somewhere else in Canada, or Paris. I've never been to Asia before."

He's a lot of fun to talk to and he's had an unusual life. He owns a couple bars in Winnipeg and he speaks fluent Arabic. He taught himself Arabic while he was in prison, from age thirteen to twenty-seven. He spent three and a half of those incarcerated years in solitary confinement, aka "the hole," speaking to no one, not even the guards. Food was delivered on a tray through a slot. During that solitary period he studied the major world religions, and Islam was the one that appealed to him the most, because of its inclusiveness. He says one of the first surahs in the Koran says there is no God but Allah, and anyone who worships one God is okay. He liked Taoism and Buddhism as well. He had no use for Christianity—the burning bushes and manna falling from the sky were too much of a stretch for him. He's not Muslim but he really wants to do a pilgrimage to Mecca and Medina.

As for why he was incarcerated, it was because he killed the man who raped his mom when he was thirteen. It was premeditated. He found out who the rapist was and got to him before the police did. His mom had committed suicide after the rape because she couldn't deal with what happened to her. He didn't feel better after killing the perpetrator, but he has no regrets and refuses to let it ruin his life. He's traveling a ton now and enjoying life as much as possible. He says his mom would be proud of the man he became. He loves travel and good pastries and working.

He has a very pleasant, easy-going Canadian personality and a very likable presence. He tells his story matter-of-factly, without emotion or dramatic effect. It's just what happened.

I don't know what I would have done in his shoes so I can't judge him, but he's without a doubt an interesting person. There really are a lot of interesting people in this world.

CHAPTER 16

We see things not as they are, but as we are.
- H.M. TOMLINSON

March 2018

I'm now in Thailand, on Koh Phangan. (The Ph is pronounced "P" and whether the g is pronounced like a hard g or a y is a matter of some debate.) Koh Phangan is an island set on top of a giant bed of quartz, ringed with white sand beaches. If that doesn't sound like another wish-fulfilling enchanted place, I don't know what would.

I came here for another 200-hour yoga teacher training. I chose this one because it focuses specifically on anatomy, to make up for the absence of bona fide instruction in that subject in my first YTT. It also felt right, and one of the accommodation options it offered was the rental of a little house, which was already one wish granted. (Yes, it has a kitchen.) The longest tourist visa I could get for Thailand was sixty days, so that's what I got.

In Koh Phangan, the white sand beaches are powder soft, the sunsets are a spectacular pink, orange, and purple, and Srithanu (pronounced "Sree Tanu"), my home for the duration of this stay, is filled with charming bohemian cafés offering beautiful vegan and non-vegan dishes. A short drive from Srithanu is a secret beach that can be reached by climbing over a swath of large boulders. On the surface of some of the boulders, the quartz that is this island's foundation is exposed, its shades of black and white and gray sparkling in the sun, as if a blatant reminder that this is a magic island.

There are thirty students in the YTT, a mix of mostly Europeans and Americans, with a few from Hong Kong, Australia, and Israel. They're all nice, normal, imperfect people like me. There's plenty of space for all of us in the stunning yoga shala. It's on the second floor, with high ceilings and a jade-green glazed concrete floor. Below, colorful mandalas are painted on the light gray walls of the open-air eating area. Beauty makes me happy and this place sparks joy.

The lead teacher is an Israeli woman named Tal. The first day, she tells us something I'll never forget.

"We're going to contradict each other," she says, smiling, gesturing at the three other teachers seated at the front of the room next to her. "I'm going to tell you sit like this, and Paul's going to tell you to sit like that, and Naami's going to tell you something else. Things like that. We're going to disagree a lot. I designed the course that way on purpose. Different opinions are okay. I want you to understand there isn't just one right way."

There isn't just one right way. This is a powerful message.

The course takes us on a deep dive into the brilliance and complexity of functional human anatomy. We study the way the natural curves of the spine and its cushioning disks are perfectly designed for balance and maximum shock absorption. The way fascia enables everything in our body to function together as a cohesive whole. The complex details of the physiology of breathing, the way every breath is a dance-like exchange with the oxygen-giving air and the carbon dioxide-absorbing plants around us. The way everything in nature, ourselves included, is so intricately and intimately connected.

One day, as we're standing at the front of our mats in mountain pose, Tal talks about gravity. "It works two ways," she points out. "It holds us down to the earth, but it also allows us to stand up. If it happened to be a bit stronger, it would keep us flattened on the ground. As it is, it exerts just the perfect amount of force to keep us grounded, yet also to let us stand and walk and dance and reach for the sky."

That stays with me for a long time. I never stopped to think about it before, because gravity is just part of life. But it's a miracle.

As days turn to weeks, I discover that my first impressions of almost everyone were completely wrong. The German girl who seemed cold with a hint of drill-sergeant vibe turns out to be the most caring, loving person in the class. The Canadian who seemed completely relaxed and totally comfortable in her own skin suffers from anxiety and occasional panic attacks. The Austrian girl who seemed poised, unemotional, and cool as a cucumber melts into tears during one of the sharing circles. Another German student who seemed bold, confident, and outspoken has a panic attack during one class and later tells me she's too terrified of Tal to talk to her, which astonishes me because as far as I can see there is nothing scary about our warmhearted lead teacher.

It reminds me that we never know what's going on under the surface of other people's skin.

"In Tantra, orgasm is one of the key ways to move from a physical solid experience of reality into the lighter more ethereal experience. In other words, orgasm can take us from earth to heaven." (Who can argue with that?)

I read these poetic words in a book I picked up while sipping coffee in an artsy little café. The book, by Shashi Solluna, is titled *TANTRA: Discover the Path from Sex to Spirit.*

I'm not an expert on tantra, but I know the oldest known Hindu tantric texts date back to somewhere between 300–400 AD. Tantra originated in the divergence from the philosophy taught by the Vedic aesthetics, who believed the way to bliss (i.e., union with the divine) was to turn away from the physical pleasures of life and meditate in solitude for lengthy periods of time. The tantric perspective was that life is meant to be enjoyed and that the divine can be found in everything.

There is a lot of tantra on Koh Phangan: tantra schools and practitioners and self-described practitioners of tantra. There are many different schools and lineages of tantra, and not all are highly sexual, but most of the tantra on Koh Phangan is. Some of it makes me raise my eyebrows, like the stories that come out of Sri Thanu's most well-known tantra school (which will close down a year later when a huge scandal breaks out after multiple allegations of sexual abuse) and the yoni massages which are commonly offered as a form of tantric healing. (Yoni means vagina, in case you've forgotten.) It's not for me to say this is not a valid method of healing, but the idea of going to see a total stranger and paying them money to massage my yoni doesn't appeal to me. This treatment is also commonly offered for free by young and old men on the beach who want to "practice," and that doesn't appeal to me either.

A couple girls in my class try it—the paid version, not the practice one. Neither of them experience an orgasm, although the first says the sensations are amazing. The second was less impressed; all her treatment did was leave her extremely horny.

I'm fine with skipping that life experience. But the core idea of tantra—the idea that the world is meant to be enjoyed as part of our spiritual path, that if we look with the right intention, we can find the sacred in everything, that even seemingly mundane things can be a gateway to the divine—that resonates.

The tantra book goes on to say, "Tantra also invites us onto the path of creativity, in which we bring the heavenly vibrations back down into this earthly experience. A lot of music, poetry, and dance are examples of this."

I think that's one of the most beautiful things I've ever read.

While in Koh Phangan, I read *Autobiography of a Yogi*, by Paramahansa Yogananda. (This is a well-known book in yoga circles, but I read it because Steve Jobs' biography mentioned that he read it once a year, every year, which sparked my curiosity.) It's engrossing and highly readable. In the beginning, I'm drawn in by the author's palpable sincerity and strong sense of devotion to God. Then he goes on to relay wildly impossible stories of Indian sages with miraculous superpowers and the book becomes a mind warp. Yogananda convinced me of his sincerity before he started with the stories of sages who can read minds, bring themselves back from the dead, and be in two places at once, so I don't know what to think. There are three possibilities: a) he's making everything up, b) he's psychotic and delusional, or c) he's telling the truth and these things are really possible.

It would have been easy to dismiss him as a liar or a delusional psychotic, except that I had a strong gut feeling that he was writing with absolute sincerity, and he was described by many other respectable people of his day as having an extraordinary aura of radiance, warmth, and authenticity. Also, what he accomplished in his life after coming alone to the United States, barely speaking English, seemed impossible without divine support.

That forces me to consider option c: he's telling the truth, and all these things really happened. And if that's true then … the limits of reality are not what I thought they were.

I like to think I have an open mind, but I also like my mind to stay rational. Up until this point, I have taken it as a fact that there are certain established laws of nature that this world and its residents are subject to, and there are certain things that are impossible. Like for a human being to be in two places at once, for example, which Yogananda describes Swami Pranabananda doing.

I don't know what to think. I don't come to any conclusions right away, but the book stays in my mind for a long time.

I'm eating dinner in a little café one night when Natalie walks in. She's one of my fellow students, a pretty Dutch girl. She joins me at my table and tells me about a gorgeous Spaniard she met on the island. They've started dating and she's glowing with that unmistakable new romance glow. I'm happy for her, and jealous, because I want to be having an island romance with a gorgeous man too. She mentions that three months ago she cut off all communication with her ex-boyfriend and hasn't talked to him since.

In my head I tell myself, *ugh, that's what I need to do with Alex*—and if you think: wait, what, Alex?! Didn't you end the story with him way back in December? Yeah, I did, or so I thought, but he's still texting regularly, if not as frequently as before. He stopped for two days after our December conversation, and then he resumed. He's still following every step of my journey, still flirting sometimes, and still making me laugh. For example, a month earlier:

Alex: *Where are ya off to next?*
Me: *The Philippines. Palawan. I assume you've been there many times.*
Alex: *Yes. I named the island.*

After our December talk his messages didn't have the same effect on me, but I can still feel his presence through them, and now that months have passed with no handsome Frenchman around to distract me, the old attachment is threatening to form. I cut the cord, but it's started to re-braid itself. Once again I have the feeling that this attachment to my ex-lover is blocking any new ones from appearing. His texts are hilarious and they make me laugh and I don't want them to stop. But, even more, I want to not think about him anymore. I want to meet someone who is part of my present and maybe my future, not my past.

I know that cutting off all communication until the emotional connection evaporates completely is a guaranteed cure for this kind of situation, because I've used this strategy before. It's painful, but highly effective. It will dissolve my attachment to Alex once and for all. I've been wondering if it's time to implement this technique again and this serendipitous conversation is confirmation. It's time.

Sitting at the table with the glowing Natalie, I make the decision that tonight, this very night, I will end all communication with my former lover. My one last text will be to let him know, so he doesn't think I'm just being rude. (Ghosting people without explanation is not part of my playbook.) But I can't text him right away because there's a kirtan tonight that I have to rush to get to.

When I get to the kirtan, the room is beautifully set up with cushions in a big circle on the floor. Golden flames of tealights flicker in the center. Spread around the candles is a deck of oracle cards, and surprise, they're my beloved Native Spirit cards. Technically they're not *mine*—mine are back home in storage—but they're the same deck, the deck I've been missing so much, and it's a beautiful surprise to see them here. The shala is filled with a beautiful energy. The kirtan is led by a lovely brunette with a soothing presence and a melodic voice that carries the beauty of ancient forests, other worlds, and many lifetimes. We're singing and she's gently strumming her guitar and I'm looking at the cards. I remember that the last time I saw Alex he pulled one of these cards and it was the Flowing River card, the same card I pulled the night before, the one that said "It's time to let go."

It was true then and it's true again now. I start to cry (which luckily is totally acceptable in this environment. Half the class has been crying this week as one after another, old, buried emotions are dragged up to the surface by yoga, meditation, and Buddhist exercises.)

I go outside to have a full therapeutic cry and then I rejoin the kirtan. We sing and dance, and to be singing and dancing and fully present here is magnificent. That night I write Alex to let him know what I decided, and that's our last communication for a long time.

A few days later, it's a full moon. I walk alone to the beach after dark. The sand is soft under my bare feet. In the quiet silvery moonlight, I sit down to do a short meditation with the intention of manifesting a man into my life—a tall, handsome, kind, athletic, intelligent, sincere man—either the love of my life or just a temporary island romance. I also decide that to attract a decent man, and for the benefit of me and everyone around me, I better do something about my hair stat, because over months of neglect its blond highlights have turned very yellow and I shudder with horror every time I look in the mirror.

Luckily, I find a Swiss hairdresser on the island who knows what a toner is and he works his magic to transform the yellow into a pretty blond. We should never underestimate the power of good hair, I firmly believe. Looking good makes you feel good, and feeling good unleashes magic.

During the midday break of our last day of class, I visit a Japanese coffee shop I've never been to before. While I'm at the front counter placing my order, a tall, tan, blond American with beautiful green eyes walks up next to me. "Is that an American accent?" he asks with a smile.

Conversation follows naturally. He introduces himself: Karl, from San Francisco. He asks if I'd like to sit together; I say yes. We fall into the most refreshing, interesting, intellectually stimulating conversation I've had in a long, long time. It's an exciting breath of fresh air. Karl's an intelligent, spiritual, health-focused nomad with a kind smile, a relaxed sense of humor about everything, and an attractive way of listening intently to every word I speak.

He asks if I want to have dinner tomorrow night. Yes, I do, and with the teacher training ending today, his timing couldn't be better.

He picks a nice restaurant with a coastal view. The salmon and red wine are delicious and so are the slow, sensual kisses in the moonlight afterwards.

The following two weeks—my last two weeks on Koh Phangan—unfold with that same rhythm: slow and sensual. The time with Karl is the perfect island romance, the icing on the cake of my Thailand stay. Like me, he loves good food, good wine, and good movies. He knows the island well. He introduces me to exceptional restaurants and bakeries and an amazing bohemian open-air cinema. Our conversations are spellbinding. He works during the day, so my days are for me and my nights are with him.

We're meant to be short-term lovers, and never anything more, and somehow I know this from the beginning. We never talk about it but he knows it too, I think. And it's perfect just like that.

Over a delicious Italian dinner one night, we're talking about how to know what to do with our lives. After listing a few of the many, many ideas I have for what I could do with my future, I throw up my hands in laughing despair and ask, "How can I know what's the thing I'm supposed to be doing?"

He replies quietly, "It will be the thing you can't not do."

For some reason this silences my playful laughter, leaves me speechless, and brings tears to my eyes. Somewhere deep inside me those simple words resonate as profound truth.

CHAPTER 17

To hear the music of the Soul of the World,
we need silence.

— FRÉDÉRIC LENOIR

May 2018

It's my last week in Thailand. I'm at a meditation center on Koh Samui, and this is Day One of a seven-day silent retreat. It's thanks to my fellow student Julia from Germany that I'm here. I was looking for a Vipassana center somewhere nearby, and she recommended this one—right next door on Koh Samui, a thirty-minute express ferry ride from Koh Phangan. The style of Vipassana practiced at this center is less physically brutal than the Goenka style I experienced in India. Here, the daily schedule includes walking meditation along with the seated meditation, and an hour of yoga every day.

And here, as Julia forewarned me, all meditators take cold showers and sleep in dormitories on wooden beds with wooden pillows and no mattresses. (Yes, wooden pillows.) That sounded like a different form of torture. But Julia said it wasn't bad, so I registered.

The meditation center sits quietly in Koh Samui's thickly forested mountain interior, a steep, winding drive away from all traces of development and tourism. It's a serene, beautiful place, full of grassy walking spaces and stone paths leading through groves of tall trees. There are two meditation halls here: one for the English-speaking meditators and one for the Russians. Both spacious halls have wooden floors and high, angled ceilings, enclosed only with waist-high iron railings through which fresh air and the sounds of nature flow in freely.

The Russian hall is the most beautiful one. Inside, the smooth wooden floors glow in the filtered sunlight. At the front of the room, a gleaming white Buddha sits peacefully in front of a mural of pink lotuses sheltered by a bodhi tree. An aura of tranquility fills the room. But even more beautiful than the room itself is the view from the railing to the left. Beyond and slightly below it, coconut-laden palm trees and leafy mango trees reach toward the sky, and beyond them the lush green hillside slopes down to meet sandy ribbons of beach and sand bars that melt into the vibrant blue sea far below. The sea itself is a work of art, glimmering multi-colored shades of pale aqua and baby blue, only a shade darker at the horizon line than the bright sky above. The view is captivating, breathtaking, sublime.

The lucky Russians. But lucky us too. Even though we English speakers don't get to see this view every day, knowing it's here is enough. In meditation, I can close my eyes and conjure it up.

My pre-registration research revealed that we would all have to volunteer for a daily chore during the retreat. Fair enough. Options included washing dishes, sweeping floors, and cleaning toilets. One previous meditator wrote that she arrived late and got stuck with toilet duty. My nose wrinkled with distaste at the thought. I definitely didn't want the same thing to happen to me.

For some reason, I became mildly obsessed with avoiding that horrible fate. The first day, I made sure to arrive early (not a regular habit of mine) to ensure there would be a wide selection of chores to choose from. My plan worked—but in any case, I needn't have worried, because cleaning the toilets had been crossed off the list. Enormously relieved, I signed up for the pleasant, meditative task of sweeping the floor of the English meditation hall.

The first three days of the retreat, all went fairly well. I was happy to be there, relishing the peace, silence, and beauty. The only problem was my mind, which didn't immediately embrace the idea of intensive meditation. Upon being asked to once again settle into quiet, focused meditation for days on end, my wild rebel of a mind revolted and started racing in all directions like a hyperactive five-year-old. It scoffed at the idea of focusing on the breath. Time seemed to slow down. But I knew this restlessness was part of the process. I just needed to wait, and my chaotic mind would eventually calm down.

At least, that's how it's supposed to work.

When my wild inner rebel hasn't calmed down by day three, doubts start to cross my mind. *Is this a waste of my time?* I wonder. *Should I be out doing something more productive? Because it really feels like nothing is happening here.*

That day at lunchtime, a printed sign is pinned to the bulletin board at the dining hall. The sign informs me: *Even though it feels like nothing is happening right now, a very deep transformation is happening inside you.*

Thank you, Sign. That's reassuring.

That afternoon, the charming nun who is the leader of our retreat makes an announcement. Normally the Russian group takes care of cleaning the women's bathroom, but this time they have a small group and there aren't enough people to do it. Do any of us want to volunteer to take on a second chore and clean the bathroom?

You have got to be kidding me. It's like these toilets are relentlessly pursuing me. Why can't I shake the gut feeling that this task is meant for me?

It also so happens that there are six of us assigned to sweep the floor of the English meditation hall. My presence there is far from essential. Nevertheless, I do not immediately volunteer for the toilets. I wait a day to see if some other gracious soul feels compelled to step up to the task. No one does, and the women's bathroom isn't getting any cleaner.

During seated meditation the next morning, my thoughts wander back over the past nine months of my time in Asia. As the memories replay in my mind, happiness seeps into my heart, intertwined with gratitude for the richness and beauty of those months, for the people

I met along the way, for the magical ways divine timing has worked out perfectly so many times. My mind finally sinks into blissful, contented stillness and I want to sit there in meditation forever.

Somehow, that influx of joy and gratitude is humbling. It melts away my resistance to cleaning the women's bathroom. I've been given so much; it's time for me to give something back. Someone has to clean those toilets; it might as well be me. I'm not above cleaning a toilet, or four. I decide that instead of cleaning them with a reluctant sense of obligation and a wrinkled nose, I will embrace the task wholeheartedly, in a spirit of joyful service and gratitude. Cleaning the toilets will be my thank you to life.

So I clean the women's bathroom every morning for the rest of the week, and the experience is painless. In a nice gesture of solidarity, a couple other girls pitch in to empty the trash cans. After cleaning, I feel lighter, as if some part of my soul has also been cleansed.

As the days pass, the stretches of time where my mind sinks into a wordless state of wonder and happiness grow longer. I sleep like a baby on my wooden bed (padded with my yoga mat) with its funny wooden pillow (padded with a scarf), grateful for the big screened window near the foot of the bed that lets in cooling night breezes. It's somehow liberating to discover that I don't require the cushioned comfort of a mattress to sleep happily. Even though I do look forward to having one in my life again.

The morning of Day Six, the last full day of the retreat, I walk into the meditation hall and pause in surprise, because something is different. A divine fragrance fills the room. I close my eyes and inhale deeply, instantly recognizing the familiar scent. It's jasmine. My favorite—the scent of happiness. There was a jasmine tree at my Florida house, just outside the French doors that opened from the kitchen. That tree only bloomed for two weeks a year but I cherished those two weeks, when I would open the doors every morning to drench my senses in a cloud of heavenly perfume. This scent transports me back there.

Back in the present moment, I walk to the railing and look outside to find the source of this fragrance. An enormous jasmine tree stands next to our building, about two stories tall, covered with prolific white jasmine flowers. On the other side of the hall, another large jasmine tree has also come into full bloom. I didn't know jasmine trees could grow this big. And they chose this day, our last full day of meditation, to bloom. As if Nature is graciously presenting us with a congratulatory reward.

There's a light breeze today, and every waft of fresh air carries the intoxicating scent into the hall, wrapping it around us. This too, feels like a gift. Nature has taken Love and wrapped it in the fragrance of jasmine and, as if blowing kisses, is sending it to me in the breeze. I couldn't imagine a more beautiful gift for this occasion.

Meditation is blissful that day. It's easy to focus on the breath when every inhale is infused with fresh jasmine.

But there is an even bigger gift I will receive from that week of meditation. I'll discover that a few days later.

CHAPTER 18

That is why we are here:
to remember love and allow it to move through us.
— GABRIELLE BERNSTEIN

May 2018

After the retreat, I fly to Yangon, Myanmar's commercial capital. Yangon is a hot, crowded, dusty city, but it is home to three things I love: the Shwedagon Pagoda, Yangon Yoga House, and the delicious mohinga noodle soup at my hotel restaurant. Also, my hotel comes with the luxury of a hot shower, a bed with a mattress, and a real pillow.

I'm relaxing in my hotel room after a hot, dusty day of exploring when Julien calls. He's in Houston, for work. He was in Myanmar last year, he tells me. We're like chess pieces moving over the board of our planet.

He called to hear about my meditation retreat. We've continued texting about once a month, and a few weeks ago we discovered that he had been at a seven-day silent meditation retreat in France just when I was selecting mine in Thailand. Comparing notes, we find that our retreats were very similar, with nearly identical schedules. However, the French retreat didn't offer wooden beds with wooden pillows.

It's nothing momentous, this phone call, but it's nice to talk with him again. He's drinking wine and he's a little flirty. I don't mind but

I'm slightly indifferent because he's on the other side of the world and I'm in my zen post-meditative mental space. But I appreciate the reconnection from across the globe, triggered by the serendipity of seven-day meditation retreats.

The next night, I meet up with my friend Claudia in a quiet riverside bar for a drink. Claudia is one of the German girls from the Thailand YTT and she's spending a month in Myanmar too. As we're chatting, I cheerfully mention that after I finish exploring Myanmar, I'll go to Bangkok for an upper eyelid lift—blepharoplasty—because I've discovered it's only $1,000 to have the procedure done there by a very reputable surgeon.

Claudia looks at me like I've turned into an alien. She's a pretty girl who doesn't wear makeup, isn't fixated on exterior beauty, and speaks her mind with no filter. In no uncertain terms, she shares her opinion: I'm crazy to do such a thing, how could I risk my EYES for something so trivial, what if something goes wrong and I'm messed up for life?

Slightly taken aback by her reaction, I defend my choice. Blepharoplasty is an extremely safe minor procedure. It's been recommended to me by several trusted friends. I have genetically droopy eyelids which are getting droopier with age and this procedure is a simple correction that will make the skin around my eyes look better and tighter. And this is a good time to do it, because I have no job, no commitments, and plenty of time to hide out for a few weeks afterward while the post-operation scars heal.

Claudia remains unconvinced. She wishes me the best, she says, but it makes her feel sad that I would even think of such a thing.

Her vehement reaction puts a small crack in my determination, but I don't admit that to her.

It's later that night when I'm back in my hotel room something very strange happens. I walk into the bathroom, look in the mirror, and there looking back at me I see an unfamiliar face. The features are still my features, but somehow my face looks different. I can't put my finger on exactly what has changed, but the difference is fantastic. The reflection is a strong, beautiful, confident, poised, fearless, magnetic woman. She has some kind of inexplicable glow. Her aura exudes so much calm strength that there can't possibly be any self-doubt or weakness inside her.

I blink, look away, look back at the mirror. The magnificent mirror person is still there. I turn my head from side to side, observing from different angles. What was in that wine? I only had one glass. I'm not drunk.

This is surreal, but fascinating. It feels like I'm in the middle of a plant medicine ceremony, where everything looks the same yet different, and normally unseen layers of existence are rendered visible. It's as if some invisible spirit force has slipped a filter over my eyes and is showing me a vision of a different version of me. Is this a potential me? Me from a parallel universe? Or me on some deeper level, the essence of me, beneath all the layers of ego and fears and self-doubts? My higher self?

I smile at the reflection. She smiles back, a smile that's somehow more captivating than my normal smile. Then I wonder, *is it possible this is how some other people see me?* Because we never know how other people see us.

My mind considers that concept: that I don't know how other people see me, that no one ever knows how other people see them, that much of what everyone sees is their own projection, and lighting also changes the way we look, and beauty is subjective, and why do I care so much what I look like anyway? Maybe there would be nothing wrong with having a simple procedure to make my eyelids look better, but I do have to admit that physical appearance is too important to me. I love all forms of beauty, but I give physical human beauty too much power and I let my physical imperfections become self-created limitations. I've known this for a long time, but I've never been able to free myself of it.

This makes me think of my mother, because she is the opposite of me in this respect. She never gives her looks a second thought. Other than hygiene and basic grooming, she spends no time or effort trying to enhance her outer beauty. She never has as long as I've known her. She also dresses like an Amish person and often wears a tight, disapproving expression, which is not a flattering look.

I'm still staring at the face in the mirror but now my attention is centered on my mother. Thoughts of her are usually accompanied by an uncomfortable sensation. I've never tried to give it a name, but it's something like guilt.

My mother and I clash. She was incredibly strict with me while I was growing up. My father was too, but it was my mother who came up with most of the rules; my father just went along with them. The older I got, the stricter her rules became, and over the years the natural love I felt for her as a little girl hardened into anger and resentment.

By the time I reached adulthood, my heart was chilly toward her. The channel that love is meant to flow through was choked by the icy residue of a decade of hostility. I wanted to love her and I tried to feel love for her, but I couldn't find that emotion inside me. In all honesty, I also never tried very hard. I was free, out of her clutches, and busy living my own life.

Then, five years before this moment in front of the mirror, something happened that started to heal my relationship with my mother.

It was a spring weekend in Orlando, Florida, and I was visiting my dear friend/sister-at-heart Sarah and her firstborn child, a beautiful hazel-eyed baby girl named Alyssa. Alyssa was three months old at the time.

One afternoon that weekend, Alyssa and I were lying on the bed and she fell asleep next to me. I took the opportunity to prop myself up on one elbow and look at her for a minute.

She was so precious, so little, so perfect. Her long eyelashes rested against soft creamy baby skin. Wispy blond hair framed her smooth forehead, rosy cheeks, and tiny delicate features. Her small round belly under her peach-and-white-striped onesie moved up and down as she breathed. She was a beautiful, incredible miracle, and also so innocent and fragile. Watching her, I was enveloped by a wave of love and protectiveness. It was so strong, that feeling.

During my morning meditation the next day, thoughts of the emotions triggered by sleeping baby Alyssa floated through my mind. It was a feeling of such intense love, but I wasn't her mother. The love of a mother for her own child must be even stronger, even though I couldn't imagine one day having my own child and feeling any more love than this. Suddenly I thought of my mother. I was her firstborn child. Is this what she felt when she looked at me as a baby?

That's when it hit me. Everything my mother ever did to me and for me throughout my life, everything from the kisses and cuddles in my earliest years, all the meals she painstakingly cooked from scratch, all of the restrictions she placed on me, all of the things she wouldn't let me do, all of the endless rules she created and forced me to follow, all of the decisions she took out of my hands and gripped tightly in her own, all of the experiences she kept out of my reach—it was all out of love. But it didn't feel like love to me. I suffered because of her. She controlled and imprisoned me when all I wanted to do was be free. She nailed my wings to the earth when all I wanted to do was fly. She kept me locked away from life when all I wanted to do was to live. Her rules made me different and isolated and separate from everyone else when all I wanted to do was fit in. I suffered, but her intention wasn't to make me suffer. She only wanted to protect me, to keep me safe, to keep me on the path she thought was best for me—the path of a good, Christian, God-fearing girl who would be allowed into heaven after she died instead of banished to the lake of fire and brimstone for all eternity.

Her actions came from love, but that love was transmitted through the filter of fear and became distorted so it wasn't recognizable as love by the time it reached me.

The year I turned eighteen, I left for college and was finally free of my mother's control. She handed me the key to the cage and I took it and unlocked the door, and then I sat there in the cage for another decade. I thought I was free because the door was open, but I became a prisoner of my own fear. The cage, although it was a cage, was comfortable and familiar. It was the only thing I knew. At least I was safe in there. Outside was the unknown, and I couldn't see what was out there. There might be no ground. If I stepped outside, I might fall into oblivion.

Years later, I would finally find the courage to step out of the cage, and then I discovered there was solid ground waiting to welcome my feet, and it was soft sand and it led to a new world of beauty, joy, love, and connection. But even after I left the cage, I carried so much resentment towards my mother, and towards my father too, but especially towards my mother because she was the stricter one. She was the one I fought with tooth and nail growing up, with teeth forming words of protest and fingernails attached to hands raised in frustration. I never said the words *I hate you,* because disrespect was not tolerated in our household, but the sentiment vibrated in my heart many times. For a decade afterward I blamed her for stealing years of adolescent happiness from me.

But that quiet morning in Orlando, suddenly I could see something I never saw before: my mother's perspective. All the anguish I must have caused her. To have her adored, precious, firstborn baby daughter grow into a girl who was angry, opinionated, and hateful. I must have been so ugly to her, for so many years. It must have hurt her so much. But she kept going anyway, loving me in her way: cooking for me and making rules to protect me.

Over the years, my anger and resentment had hardened into a thick shell of ice around my heart. That day in Orlando, exposed to the warmth of compassion, it melted. In that instant I forgave her, tears streaming down my face.

We say that ignorance is bliss, but sometimes it causes so much pain.

After that Orlando morning, I wrote to my mother and asked her to forgive me for the hurt I had unknowingly caused her. It meant a lot to her, and it made my heart lighter, but it didn't make our relationship perfect. Her beliefs and inner wiring remained starkly different than mine and our interactions remained challenging, but they were at least more loving.

Now, five years later, I still haven't learned how to love my mother perfectly. I don't know how to love and accept all the qualities I perceive in her as ugly or judgmental, often so prevalent in her state of being and in her pinched, disapproving aura.

It happens in a flash. As I'm looking at the reflection in the mirror with my thoughts focused on my mother, it's as if a veil is pulled away from my eyes. I'm no longer seeing my face in the mirror. I'm picturing my mother and I'm finally able to look past her skin-deep layer, through the judgmental tightness of her personality, and see all the way to her core, where there is a soul who is fragile and exhausted, who thinks the world is a scary place and who is starving for love. I don't think she knows what unconditional love feels like. She lost her mother when she was a little girl and she often used to say that she made lots of mistakes with me because she didn't have a mother to love her. Maybe I'm wrong; maybe she feels unconditional love from my dad, because he's very loyal to her, but he's not a demonstrative person and I don't know if she feels enough from him. Either way, she needs to feel it from other sources too.

At this moment, the hard shell around my heart that had prevented me from feeling genuine love for my mother cracks and falls away, and all of a sudden I'm filled with so much love for her. It's Universal Love that she needs, and it's me who's supposed to give it to her. It was meant to flow through me to her and this unconscious shell around my heart had been blocking it.

She's a soul who was divinely put in this life as my mother. She was the first human to ever give me love. All of a sudden I deeply wish for her to feel truly loved and supported. Something within me says that's her missing piece for healing—and even if it's not, I just want her to feel the love and support I've felt from Life. I want her to know that enormous love and support are actually all around us.

An idea comes to me, the seed of which was planted several months ago, after my three weeks at the Ayurvedic retreat in India. I want her to experience being lovingly, thoroughly taken care of, as I did there. I had suggested it to her and offered to pay for her plane ticket, but she's never been outside North America and she was scared of going to India. Now I realize that she doesn't need Indian strangers giving her love and support. I can give that to her myself. Instead of giving myself a month to recover from eyelid surgery I can give my mom a beautiful one-month retreat in her own home. She's the hardest-working person I've ever known. I've never seen her rest. In recent years, her health has been getting progressively worse and I've been worried about her. So, I'll go and take all the work off her shoulders and let her feel rested and cared for, for once. I'll cook beautiful, nourishing meals for her, do all the cleaning, teach her restorative, rejuvenating yoga classes, and give her one month of lovingly supported rest and relaxation.

Maybe there wouldn't be anything wrong with getting eyelid surgery, but to offer love to my mother is more important right now. I leave the mirror and immediately sit down to write her a long email proposing the idea.

As I start typing, I realize that tomorrow is Mother's Day.

What perfect timing.

My mother replies two days later. She was touched and appreciative of the offer. *Perhaps your expression of love is the reason I did so well yesterday,* she writes. *It is the first Sunday in three weeks that I was not totally exhausted.* She adds that she'll have to work out a few things regarding the timing before she can say yes or no.

For her sake I hope she'll say yes, but on some level it doesn't matter, because what happened that night in front of the mirror healed something inside me. It was all connected … the Asian journey, the stillness of meditation to let it sink in, the toilet cleaning to crack the shell of my ego and create a space for more love to flow in, the mirror vision to show me how to see in a different way, and the love melting the icy barrier that was blocking love from flowing towards my mom. Not being able to truly love her was in some way also preventing me from truly loving myself, and I suspect also on some level from being able to receive true love.

A few days later I reach the end of *The Universe Has Your Back,* and find these synchronistic words:

> *There is no greater experience than allowing the presence of love to move through you. As you heal your own life through your connection to love, you will be guided to help others do the same. Sometimes that guidance will lead you in directions you never could have imagined.*

I haven't seen that unfamiliar reflection in the mirror since. I think she just came to deliver a message I really needed.

CHAPTER 19

Let yourself be silently drawn by the strange pull
of what you really love.
- RUMI

May 2018

The best thing about Bagan is the mornings. They're a dreamlike interlude where I have the world to myself, in the dark quietness just before dawn. My electric scooter and I are alone on the smooth deserted roads. Tall, silent trees surround us. The wind strokes my skin and only muted sounds of nature break the absolute stillness.

The paved roads give way to slim sandy paths and these paths lead to secret temples tucked away among the trees. I park my scooter outside one of them, slip through the unlocked door and make my way up a narrow, crumbling, low-ceilinged staircase onto the roof, where I sit to wait for the sun to send its first rays across the horizon. The sky lightens into pale pastel shades, foretelling the sun's pending arrival, silhouetting the dome-shaped tops of the hundreds of pagodas that peek above the trees. I sit, and wait, and watch. A little after 6 a.m., glimmers of orange light start to appear behind cracks in the clouds. The sun begins his slow journey upward, drawing his paintbrush of light across the sky, illuminating a green landscape below, bejeweled with ancient orange brick pagodas.

It was a young friendly local who showed me where these secret temples are. They are secret in the sense that it's still possible to climb up onto their roofs. The Burmese government has sealed off access to the rooftops of all the others. We watched the sunset from one of them yesterday, a sunset that lit the sky with fiery streaks of red and orange. Afterwards the young local showed me some of his paintings. He has talent; some were really beautiful. I would have bought one if I wasn't a wandering homeless gypsy without a square millimeter of spare space in my luggage. (Being obligated to cart all of your possessions with you everywhere you go is an extremely effective way to transform yourself into a minimalist.)

After the sun rises, Bagan becomes a giant sauna. The intense dry heat makes me crave the cool freshness of the mountains, and that's perfect, because my next destination is the little mountain town of Kalaw, the place my Laos travel buddy Jarrett recommended. And that's not the only reason I'm going to Kalaw. For one thing, an Israeli girl in Koh Phangan told me Kalaw was her favorite place in Myanmar. Also, as it so happens, I've applied for a job there.

Back in Koh Phangan, halfway through the YTT, I had started thinking about where to go next. As much as I love learning and as tempting as it was to continue doing yoga teacher trainings forever, what I really needed to do was put all this learning to use and find somewhere to teach. I had no idea where I wanted to do that or where to start looking. All I knew was that I didn't want to teach in a place that was already inundated with yoga. Ideally, I wanted to bring yoga to a place where yoga had never gone before. Somewhere it would make a difference.

Luckily, just after I got this clear in my head, a fellow student told me about Yoga Trade, a website where yoga teaching jobs around the world are posted. I checked it out right away, and the first post that caught my eye was one in Kalaw, Myanmar. According to the post, a small NGO was looking for a certified yoga teacher to start a yoga program at their vegetarian café. The NGO was also in the process of building a farm and a natural building and permaculture training center. The yoga teacher would have the opportunity to help with the café and farm if they wished, supporting the project with any other skills they could bring to the table.

The teaching position was volunteer and would require a

minimum commitment of three months. Volunteers would be offered delicious vegetarian meals from the café kitchen. Accommodation could be provided but there were also many affordable options in town if the volunteer preferred to find their own lodging.

My heart lit up. Myanmar is where I wanted to go next, and this opportunity encompassed so many of my interests, it looked suspiciously like it had been custom designed just for me. As far as Google could find, there was currently no other yoga in Kalaw, so it checked that box. I love creating things, and the chance to create a yoga program from scratch would be ideal. And as a novice teacher and lover of all things delicious, I would be delighted to teach in exchange for delicious meals for a few months.

I promptly applied for the position. A few weeks went by and I didn't hear back, so I wrote to the café via Facebook Messenger. Still no reply. After more weeks passed, I gave up expecting a response and applied for a posting in Siem Reap, Cambodia. This second opportunity was similar but less exciting: teaching yoga at an outdoor jungle shala in exchange for meals and housing. No café, eco-shop, permaculture, or sustainable building involved. However, the shala owner responded to my email right away. We spoke on the phone and connected well. She already had teachers lined up for the next few months, so we agreed I would teach there in September. It was the end of April when we talked, so that left me four more free months. Enough time to visit Myanmar, visit my mother, and then some.

My mother, however, hasn't yet accepted my offer. She's found some obstacles and is trying to sort them out so we can agree on a date. Meanwhile, I continue my exploration of Myanmar.

I open my eyes and find myself in an enchanted land.

I didn't know it was enchanted when I arrived because I arrived at 5 a.m. and everything was dark. It was an overnight bus that brought me here to Kalaw, and I was groggy and semi-delirious from the bumpy eight-hour ride from Bagan. It's not the bus's fault I couldn't sleep—the VIP buses in Myanmar are surprisingly plush and luxurious, with wide cushy velvet seats, movies to watch, and attendants who offer you beverages and refreshments as if you were on a plane—but they're no match for the road conditions, which leave you shaken like a caipirinha. Thank the Lord, my hotel let me check in right away. I fell immediately into a sound, grateful sleep in a comfortable bed. When I open my eyes a few hours later, daylight has arrived and now I can see where I am.

The hotel is a European dream; a small cluster of elegant British colonial buildings set on a property of lush green lawns and vibrant gardens. Inside and out, every square inch is immaculate. Along the walkway to the front entrance, rows of bright roses bloom profusely in shades of red and pink and cream and pale yellow. Their perfume is intoxicating.

I booked the most economical room at this dreamy hotel, but the base of the toilet in my bathroom is leaking water, so they upgrade me to a spacious, beautiful suite with gleaming dark wood floors, big windows and a Pinterest-worthy bathroom. It's Room Number 111—clearly a gift from the great and generous Universe Genie, who knows that beautiful hotel rooms spark pure joy in my heart, and for which I'm deeply grateful.

But there is plenty to explore in Kalaw, so I don't spend much time in my beautiful room. With a rented bicycle as my mode of transportation, I start to get acquainted with the town and its surroundings. Nestled in the mountains of Shan State, quiet little Kalaw is all cool, pine-scented air and green hills and trees and bright flowers and sweet smiles and peacefulness and no traffic. After months of intense tropical heat, Kalaw's cool freshness is heaven, and everywhere I look my eyes feast on beauty. Delicious, diverse food options are plentiful. There are, of course, plenty of Burmese restaurants, the best of which serves an addictive dish of steamed ground fish blended with savory herbs in banana leaf packets, accompanied with a spicy sauce. There's a restaurant run by a charming Burmese woman trained in a French culinary school, who unpretentiously prepares simple but elegant sandwiches, salads, pastas, and beautiful desserts. There's an Italian restaurant with a brick pizza oven and a sophisticated ambience owned by an Italian man and his Burmese wife. (They make homemade limoncello and fantastic tiramisu—cue the celestial music.) There's an Indian restaurant inside a high-ceilinged former theater which serves irresistible butter chicken and masala chai. There's a self-described Mexican restaurant owned by a friendly Burmese man named Min who previously worked as a chef in Dubai. None of his tacos or quesadillas even remotely resemble anything ever seen on any Mexican table, but he makes an excellent pan-grilled fish served beautifully with an herbed tomato compote and fresh salad for the equivalent of $3 US. Min also serves up instant solutions to anything I'm looking for. No good motorbike rental options in Kalaw? I can rent his for 10,000 kyat ($7 US). I want to visit a spectacular waterfall I saw a picture of that hasn't made it onto Google Maps? He'll drive me there. (He doesn't know exactly where it is either, but he's fully confident we'll find it.) Am I looking for lodging? No, but in case I ever am, he just opened a hostel next door. Min becomes my first friend in Kalaw.

There's no such thing as a supermarket in this town. All produce, fish, meats, rice, beans, flowers, kitchen tools, shoes, clothing, and pretty much anything else you might be looking for are sold at the outdoor market. All the fruits and vegetables are fresh and seasonal, and right now the seasonal offerings include edible flowers with ombréed stalks of lime green and magenta, local white mushrooms shaped like flowers and—*mangos*. Heaping baskets of sweet, juicy, yellow-orange mangos. I'm told thirteen varieties of mangos are grown in this country. I never know which variety I'm eating, only that I never found one I didn't like.

This being Myanmar, there are pagodas everywhere. Sitting casually in the center of town is a sparkling silver one. Every square inch of its elegant exterior is covered with tiny shimmering silver glass tiles, like oversized glass confetti. Just down the street from this festive pagoda is the vegetarian café in search of a yoga teacher, and after a few days of getting my bearings, I pay them a visit.

The café is simple and rustic, but cozy. Peaceful afternoon light streams in through the open windows and the air is filled with the rare and wonderful scent of freshly baked bread. A pretty Burmese teenager greets me in perfect English and offers me a menu. The options are appealing, although the menu could use a design update, in my opinion.

I order the Burmese garden salad and an iced ginger lemonade. They're both delicious—*really* delicious. With that incomparably satisfying full-flavoredness of food that's been prepared entirely from scratch with just the right proportions of everything and served immediately. I'm impressed. The slices of homemade bread that accompany the salad taste as heavenly as they smell.

Steve Mitchell is the person who posted the Yoga Trade announcement. He isn't around at the moment, but the young waitress tells me he's at the farm and should be back after six.

When I come back after six, a man is behind the counter talking to three Burmese teenagers. He's a nice-looking fair-skinned American with a trimmed goatee, thin, probably in his early forties. He looks like he just came in from a day of farm work.

His conversation with the girls finishes just as I walk up to the counter. "Hi, are you Steve?" I ask.

"I am," he replies, a little warily, as if bracing himself for whatever I'm about to throw at him.

I compliment him on the incredible homemade bread and explain that I responded to his post on Yoga Trade a while ago but didn't hear back. Since I happened to be traveling through Kalaw, I thought I would stop in and check if they were still looking for someone.

A guilty look spreads across his face. "I'm sorry about that. We've been so busy … we bought fourteen acres of land a little while ago and are starting a farm and there has been so much going on. I've been terrible about getting back to people. But yes … we are still looking to start a yoga program. Um … I'd like to tell you more about it but it's kind of a bad time right now. Do you have time to come back tomorrow?"

My agenda is quite open. We exchange phone numbers and arrange to meet the following evening.

The next morning, while reading *Ayurveda and Panchakarma: The Science of Healing and Rejuvenation* by Sunil V. Joshi, I come across a life-changing paragraph. The book has just explained that dharma is the word Ayurveda uses to describe the idea of the soul's special purpose and path. It goes on to say:

The most obvious sign that life is being lived in accord with dharma is the joy that comes from doing those things are most closely aligned with our soul's purpose. Because increasing joy informs us of our proximity to our dharma or life's purpose, the soul is ever discriminating among experiences—choosing those experiences that give more happiness, knowledge and satisfaction, and avoiding those that give pain and a feeling of lack.

I stop to think about that. So …. in other words, my purpose here on this planet is just to consistently do what makes me happiest? Meaning that …. not only is it okay to do what makes me happy, not only do I not have to feel guilty or selfish about doing what makes me happy, but I'm actually *meant* to do what makes me happy? That's what all of us are meant to be doing?

This is the best thing I've ever heard! It also aligns with what I've been experiencing lately in my own life and noticing in the stories of others, and what I read in *The Universe Has Your Back,* but to receive the corroboration of India's five-thousand-year-old "science of life" is an impressive stamp of validation.

Why doesn't everyone know this?? Why don't they teach this in kindergarten? It's too good to be kept a secret.

A couple years later, I'll hear Jack Canfield phrase this concept more succinctly as: "joy is your internal guidance system."

Brilliant.

That night, I bike over to the café to meet Steve. Outside, it's raining gently. A Spanish guy with disheveled hair is sitting at a table by the wall when I walk in. He turns out to be Luis, Steve's partner in the farm project. Luis is good-looking under the messy hair but he looks like he neither showers nor smiles often and doesn't speak much. We exchange a few words about Spain while waiting for Steve to come down. Apparently I'm a bigger fan than Luis is; he seems ambivalent about his motherland.

Steve arrives a couple minutes later. We sit down at an empty table and he fills me in on his background and the details of his many projects, both ongoing and planned. He's American and has lived in Asia for seventeen years. He spent twelve of those years in Thailand and speaks fluent Thai. He speaks and writes Burmese pretty well too. He was a monk for a little while, and he used to run an orphanage along the Thailand-Myanmar border. He has four adopted Burmese kids, two girls and two boys ranging in age from twelve to twenty-one. Later I find out they were the four kids at the orphanage with the most serious health problems and he adopted them when it closed down. He used to have a partner, a British woman, but they separated a little while ago. He and the kids have been in Kalaw for five years.

Starting yoga here is an idea he's had in mind for a while now. They have space for a shala on the second floor above the café and they have fifteen yoga mats already. The target market is both tourists and locals, but mainly tourists, because that's who their customers are. A small but steady flow of tourists pass through Kalaw, many of them to do the famous trek from Kalaw to Inle Lake. The proceeds from yoga would support the NGO that the café is part of, which pays the salaries of the girls who work at the café and also will support the construction of the farm and the permaculture/sustainable building training center. Extra proceeds would be very helpful right now because low season is always tough, and this low season is tougher than others, thanks to the atrocities reportedly being committed by the Burmese army against the Rohingya in the north of the country along the Bangladesh border. Sometimes the café has just one or two customers a day.

They could also use help with managing the café. Steve's oldest daughter currently holds the role of café manager, but she's ready for a change. She's planning to look for a job at a hotel soon. And their social media could use some attention—it's essentially non-existent.

The list of their other ongoing projects and opportunities is long, and exciting. They make all kinds of natural products, including beautiful, fragrant soaps and lip balms, and they need new packaging and new label designs for all of them. Locally, they're famous for their homemade, all-natural ice cream, which they make the old-fashioned way, with a churning machine and ice and salt. Steve gives me a few samples and I immediately understand why it's famous. The salted caramel, the chocolate, and the masala chai are next level. We're talking Best Ice Cream in the World here. Like, you've never really lived until you've tasted this ice cream. It's mind-blowing how delicious it is. All other ice creams I've tasted in my life up until this moment have been nothing but cheap imitations. With the exception of a few gelatos—but I digress. A few people have suggested they should start distributing their ice creams to other hotels and restaurants and Steve wants to move forward with that.

I support that plan wholeheartedly. The more people who have access to this deliciousness, the happier the world will be.

On the yoga side, they have a couple other projects in the works already. In January, they'll be hosting a yoga charity retreat for a group of physicians with an organization called Yoga Moore. Moore is my mother's maiden name and I use it occasionally, so that name sticks in my head.

Everything involving the farm and permaculture training center will happen on fourteen acres of land they bought a few months ago. The land is a twenty-minute drive out of town and Steve and Luis are in the initial stages of planting and building. Steve shows me photos of other buildings they built during their years in Thailand. They're made of adobo and bamboo and they're all curvy and gorgeous, inside and out. One has a spectacular round reciprocal bamboo roof that involves no joints. It's a masterpiece of art and engineering.

These projects and their potential are tremendously exciting, and they're also going to require a tremendous amount of time and follow-up to make them into reality. Steve needs help, that's for sure.

I explain the situation with my mother, who's promised to give me her definitive answer by Monday. If her answer is affirmative, I won't be available to start until July. That's okay with Steve; it's low season until October and they're not in a rush.

He explains the lodging they can offer. "We have another house a few minutes away, where Luis stays. It's a cute house, but it has no indoor plumbing, just an outhouse. There's no shower and no hot water, but a cold bucket shower is an option. Or you could shower at the café, but there's no hot water here either."

There are hardcore, super cool people in this world who would be totally fine with those ascetic living conditions. I am not one of them. I tell Steve I'll arrange my own lodging.

If we go forward, they'll write a letter of invitation so I can get the seventy-day business visa. It's easy to renew for another seventy days when that runs out; I'll just need to make a visa run outside the country.

We agree to talk again on Monday when I know my dates.

On the ride back to my hotel after our discussion, I feel a mixture of excitement and nervousness. Doubts have snuck in, born of the dampness in the air and the rain that's still falling and the knowledge that rainy season will last for four more months; the thought of the house without hot water or indoor plumbing, the grumpiness of Luis, the vibration of lack that subtly wrapped itself throughout our conversation. Is this really the path I'm meant to go down? How does this fit in with what I just read about dharma and increasing joy? Rain and grouchiness and cold showers don't increase my joy.

I'm still wondering about this when I get to my room and turn on the computer. The screen shows 11:11.

The next morning I wake up before my alarm. I reach for my phone to check the time and the screen shows 5:55.

Another sandwich of my faithful signs. It seems that this project is part of my path. And anyway, magical signs aside, I couldn't not take this on. They need me—that is, they need someone, and it seems unlikely Steve will ever get around to replying to any other applicants—and this is exactly what I was looking for. A place and a project where I'm needed and can make a difference, and where I can learn, and get experience teaching yoga. So what if it includes challenges? I like challenges. I intentionally seek challenges. Besides, I'm already starting to fall in love with Kalaw, rain and all.

Decision made, the apprehension alchemizes into excitement and ideas start flowing. Joy dances in my veins once again. This is where I'm supposed to be, I can feel it.

In the days and weeks that follow, the rain continues but it feels like the sun is shining. More beautiful surprises keep appearing and everything seems to be unfolding in perfect alignment.

My reservation at the idyllic European hotel is reaching its end. While scouting others, I find one that confirms beyond any doubt that I have in fact arrived in a living fairy tale. It's comprised of three flawlessly picturesque Tudor-style houses with sloping gable roofs and big porches. The main building is an ivy-covered gem, complete with a black and white dog curled up on the front stoop. I expect Hansel and Gretl to walk around the corner at any moment. The front lawn is perfectly manicured, framed with palm trees and bushes and flowers everywhere. It looks like a dream.

The woman at the front desk, a good-natured Burmese woman with a twinkle in her eye and an easy laugh, shows me a couple of the rooms. She giggles when we get to room number eight and informs me that eight in Burmese is "shit."

I make a reservation for the next few days, for the cozy attic room number fourteen, of which the Burmese translation is less memorable. I check in the next day, and although my new room is less five-star than my luxurious suite, I love it. It's immaculate. Not a wrinkle is to be seen anywhere on the pristine white duvet cover, and the wood-paneled walls remind me of my Ayurvedic retreat cabin.

Breakfast is included with the room, and the next morning I am served a phenomenal breakfast that covers the entire table for four. The Shan noodles are served with a pitcher of Burmese tea (Burmese tea is exceptional, by the way), a plate of sweet, juicy sliced mango, a plate of banana bread, a plate of samosas, and several small plates of tofu and other garnishes for the noodles.

The breakfasts in Kalaw rival each other in their deliciousness. I've already discovered the incredible banana bread French toast and coconut sesame crepes at the yoga café, and now this. Who could have imagined little Kalaw would turn out to be such a foodie heaven? Even Jarrett's recommendation didn't fully prepare me.

CHAPTER 20

After all, life is the ultimate mystery.
- DEEPAK CHOPRA

May 2018

The day after I check in to my new hotel happens to be Alex's birthday. As a general rule, I never remember anyone's birthday, but I can't not remember his because it's the same day as my baby sister's. This poses a dilemma, because I'm committed to upholding my vow of abstinence from communication with him, but birthdays are sacred and I want him to know that I wish him well.

To resolve this conundrum, I decide to test out something I read in *Autobiography of a Yogi*. In that book, Yogananda wrote that telepathic communication—specifically, the ability to read minds and send thoughts into the minds of others—works like radio signals. "Thoughts are no more than very subtle vibrations moving in the ether," he explained. To send a thought into someone else's mind, one simply needs to focus intently and use the force of powerful individual will to function like a broadcasting radio.

He went on to say that this concept is not as farfetched as it may sound, quoting Nobel prize-winning physiologist Charles Robert Richet to make his point:

Very strange, very wonderful, seemingly very improbable phenomena may yet appear which, when once established, will not astonish us more than we are now astonished at all that science has taught us during the last century. … The phenomena which are already known to us only don't surprise us not because they are not incredible, but because they are familiar.

The last line is definitely true. We do, in general, take radios and TVs and cell phones and video conferencing for granted, although whenever I stop to think about how they work, they leave me astounded. If I can communicate instantaneously with friends and family on the other side of the planet via video chat on a small wireless handheld device, why shouldn't I be able to telepathically send a simple birthday wish into Alex's mind? It sounds wild, but also perfectly logical.

I conduct my experiment via a small birthday-wish meditation ceremony inside my hotel room. I sit cross-legged on my yoga mat, arrange the travel-size crystals Alex gave me as my goodbye present in a half circle in front of me, close my eyes, and begin with a little prayer. I respectfully let the Unseen Powers of the Universe know that I would like these wishes to reach Alex, and if it's possible I would like him to somehow feel that they come from me. I would like my spirit to reach his. Not wanting to be too demanding, I add, *but if not, that's okay.* Next, I shift into meditation. For about five minutes, I visualize myself silently sending Alex love, happiness, and birthday wishes of well-being. I visualize the energy of my thoughts traveling from my consciousness to his. My intention and attention are focused like a laser.

As the meditation continues, unexpectedly, from some hidden place deep in my psyche, a strong, warm wave of love for him rises up. It surprises me to discover that such depth of feeling for him is still there. But there is no pain or wanting or attachment in this love. It's beautiful and pure and free. It doesn't want anything in return.

The love for him was a gift to experience, but it's no longer for me to carry. I visualize all the love I feel shapeshifting into a glowing cord emanating from my center, and I unplug it from me. I let him go, with one final wish for him to be happy and well.

And then I feel something that I've only ever experienced twice in my life: a physical and energetic sensation like a sonic boom of energy reverberating from my heart and radiating out into the world. This makes me suspect the experiment may have worked. But given my self-imposed communication ban, I probably won't find out anytime soon.

That evening, my mind wanders into a daydream. Will I contact Alex when I go back to Florida, whenever that is? I don't know. I'll want to see him, but maybe it's not a good idea. Maybe I'll leave it to fate. Maybe we'll accidentally run into each other at Target or something.

An hour or so later, my cell phone dings. There's a text from Alex. *Hey! Are u back in West Palm? Cause I swear I saw you or your body double at Costco!*

For a moment I sit frozen, rereading the words on the screen, and then some emotion I can't define begins to dance in my cells and I start to laugh. Not Target, but Costco. Not the same big box store, but pretty darn close. Does this count as a successful telepathic experiment? I'm only a sample of one, so this can't be considered scientifically conclusive, but it's enough to convince me that this is some kind of magic. Life is full of all kinds of magic and my skeptical mind should just get used to it.

Equally marvelous is that his text didn't trigger that annoying achy, longing, emotional response that his messages used to. I just feel happy. Happy and free. I feel like dancing. I briefly debate if I should reply, since my vow of noncommunication was meant to last until I was over him, and now it feels like I'm over him. And it's his birthday. And what time is it in Florida? It's earlier there so I can wait and reply later. I look at my computer because it's still on Florida time, and the screen says 11:11 a.m.

That is the icing on the metaphysical cake. And a clear sign that it's okay to reply, so I text back. *I'm in Myanmar; no Costco's here! But I was thinking of you and sent you bday wishes in a meditation, so maybe my spirit temporarily materialized over there. And I hope you had a very happy birthday.*

We text a little bit back and forth—he's as goofy and funny as ever—and then we go back to non-communication. And my attachment to him is really gone, once and for all.

Two days later, my mother gives me her answer. She really wants me to come, but she still has so many things to figure out and she doesn't know when she'll be ready.

I trust that if I'm meant to go look after her, there will be a better time in the future. And for now, I can dive wholeheartedly into the Kalaw projects without further delay.

I walk over to the café and find that they're closed because the power is out, but Steve and some of the kids are in the backyard. Since the café is closed, we have plenty of time to talk. Steve reveals new information he didn't get around to mentioning before, including the minor detail that, thanks to a grant they won last year, they are receiving $14,000 from a British NGO and they need to spend those funds by July 1st or they'll lose them. Among other things, this money can be used to fund yoga classes and cooking classes, locally-made products and packaging, and the farm/sustainable building project. It can be used for yoga props (hurrah!!!), and interior decoration and updated menus. Our last conversation left me under the impression they had No Money Whatsoever, so the news of this windfall is a complete surprise. I have the impression that if left to his own devices, distracted by everything else on his plate, Steve wouldn't find the time to spend this $14k in the next 33 days. Lucky for him, spending money happens to be one of my natural talents.

He unveils more exciting plans, including a book corner he wants to set up in the café, Friday movie nights he wants to start hosting, and a four-week natural building course for foreigners he plans to offer in January. It's pretty much everything I'm interested in, all rolled into one. With money to fund it. If I had wished for a dream project for this phase of my life, I couldn't have designed a better one. I feel like a wide-eyed little kid being presented with an enormous pile of festively wrapped Christmas presents.

And it's all happening in this magical place where it feels like I am exactly where I'm meant to be right now—even with the daily drizzle that has started and the terrible Wi-Fi that's nonexistent half the time.

When I get home and turn on the computer, it's 10:10.

I've negotiated a long-term stay at the cozy fairytale hotel with its sweet and beautiful owner, Ohmar. Ohmar is delighted that we'll be starting yoga in Kalaw, and she agreed to my discounted rate proposal. On top of that, she generously offered free laundry service for the duration of my stay. I'm overjoyed that this dream place with sweet staff and amazing breakfasts is going to be my long-term home—for less than one-third the cost of my former monthly mortgage. With this phenomenal Asian cost-of-living, my house-sale proceeds could last me for a decade.

That evening, I take a cooking class with Steve's oldest daughter, Hayma. This girl was born to cook and teach cooking classes. Indian food is one of her specialties, so we prepare Indian dumplings with peanut sauce and a few side dishes.

As we're rolling the dumpling dough, the family's adopted grandparents arrive—a kind, well-to-do Burmese couple who don't speak English. With big smiles, Adopted Grandfather joins in the stuffing of the dough, the rolling of them into nice circles between our palms, and the ladling of them into the hot oil. When all is done, we have a feast big enough for a family of ten.

The grandparents, Steve, Hayma, and I sit down at the table and I produce a bottle of Burmese wine to go with the meal. (Yes, Burmese wine exists, and surprise: it's excellent! Some not-so-excellent Burmese wine exists as well, but the good stuff is called Aythaya and tonight we're drinking the 2016 Shiraz & Dornfelder. It comes from a vineyard in Shan state, about two hours away, which was founded twenty years ago by a German winemaker.)

It feels like a big family dinner. The lights of the café are warm and soothing, and then Luna the cat crawls up on my lap to cuddle and now everything's really perfect. It so happens that this is May

31st, the one-year anniversary of the last day of my corporate job. I'm full of warm fuzzy feelings of contentment and well-being, and also awe at the way Life has guided me, with impeccable timing, to this place that somehow feels like home and a fairy tale at the same time, and an incredible project to dive into.

Just before my 28-day visa is up, Kalaw hosts a series of tourism conferences. This is really great timing because I meet a lot of people here—mostly hotel owners and managers and trekking guides—and do a lot of yoga promoting. I also start to learn about the fascinating tribal realities of current day Myanmar.

Of Myanmar's population of 53 million people, only about 68 percent are ethnically Burmese. The rest belong to different ethnic groups, of which 135 are officially recognized by the Burmese government. Those 135 groups are clustered into 8 major national ethnic races, more commonly known as tribes. It's because of all this that Burma's name was changed to Myanmar in 1989. The name was supposed to be more inclusive of non-Burmese ethnic groups, but the ethnic groups found the change to be merely symbolic and weren't impressed. Many believe their ethnic interests aren't represented by the current government, and because of that, internal fighting continues across large swaths of the country between armed ethnic groups and the Burmese army. Exactly what their ethnic interests are, I haven't learned. The issue is quite complicated and deeply rooted in Myanmar's long history. The warring ethnic groups are called EAO's (ethnic armed organizations) and there are three EAO's fighting here in Shan State: the RCSS (Restoration Council of Shan State), the TNLA (Ta'ang National Liberation Army), and the KIA (Kachin Independence Army). Because of the tribal fighting, many areas of the country are off-limits to foreigners.

It's hard to imagine, because the Myanmar that I've seen is so peaceful. But it is the reality of this rich, beautiful, complex country.

I never learn the details of the historical grievances and cultural differences between each tribe, except that they've been fighting each other for a long time and they each have different textile patterns (each more colorful and intricate than the last), different culinary and craft specialties, and some have different wines and liquors. (*Khaung yae,* a sweet, caramel-colored Kayan traditional rice wine, is exceptional, FYI.)

As someone who loves variety and who finds repetitive sameness extremely boring, it bewilders me that they fight each other over their differences instead of embracing and celebrating them; instead of understanding that they all contribute to the rich, diverse beauty and appeal of their one shared country. It makes as much sense as if individual M&Ms were to get mad at each other because they're different colors and they all have to share the same bag.

Maybe someday it will change.

CHAPTER 21

Was it a coincidence, or were you guided?
– TONY ROBBINS

June 2018

I choose Chiang Mai for my visa run because it's not far and because Karl from Koh Phangan told me it's a beautiful city. Little do I know that not long afterward, this choice will alter the course of my life.

In Chiang Mai, I'm on a mission to find yoga props for the shala. Serendipitously, I've already found bolsters and straps in Yangon, because Yangon Yoga House just closed their second location and they sold me all the bolsters and straps I needed. They didn't have any spare blocks though and didn't know where I could get any. There are plenty of options online, but the shipping to Myanmar is astronomical from everywhere, even from China next door.

There are many wonderful things to be found in Chiang Mai, including delightful restaurants, an excellent and unbelievably affordable dentist, and fifteen yoga studios. The website of one studio in the Old City grabs my attention with its eloquent class descriptions, especially one in particular: a kriya fusion flow that weaves breathwork and postures together, combining kundalini and hatha yoga. That sounds incredible. I bike to the studio for that class.

The studio is warm and inviting, with teak chairs and colorful Thai cushions in the entryway and incense wafting through the air. At the front counter, a brochure catches my eye. It's a brochure for Yogamour.

Ohhhhh …. not Yoga Moore, *Yogamour*. Yoga + love in French. This must be the group Steve told me about; the ones hosting a retreat with him in January. What a surprise to find their brochure here. I take a picture of it to show Steve.

The kriya fusion flow is taught by a radiant blonde named Rebecca with blue eyes and a bright smile. Her aura is comfortable, open, and fun-loving. She exudes light and she's an excellent teacher. At the end of class, she makes a couple announcements. One is about Yogamour and their next project.

Afterwards, I ask if she was talking about the same Yogamour who'll be doing a project in January with Steve Mitchell in Myanmar.

"Yes!" she exclaims. "You know Steve?"

I explain how I know Steve. It turns out Rebecca is the founder of Yogamour, and she's the one coordinating the Kalaw retreat, along with another teacher in Yangon.

"I had no idea you were in Chiang Mai! Steve didn't tell me."

"He may not know I live here," she replies. "I've never met Steve in person. It was Imogen who connected us."

We marvel at what an amazing coincidence this is and arrange to have lunch the next day. And I ask if the studio sells yoga blocks. "I need to buy twenty for Kalaw."

"No, but I know where you can get them!" she says happily. "Decathlon! They're really good and cheap!"

The next morning I rent a motorbike and drive to the retail wonderland that is Decathlon. Sure enough, I find all the blocks I need, nice foamy sturdy light ones for a mere $4 each. (I also buy a lot of other things for myself, and this is the beginning of my enduring love affair with Decathlon.)

At lunch, Rebecca tells me where to get the remaining items on my list: incense and metal straws for the café. Thank goodness I ran into Rebecca. She's lived in Thailand for ten years and has been to

Myanmar often. She shares valuable insights on life in both countries. Once again, with no planning by me, I was guided to the right place and the right person.

It isn't the first time I've serendipitously run into someone like this, by the way. Most recently there was the airport reunion with Helen in Bali. Seven years ago, the week after I moved to Miami, my new roommate invited me to come with her to a networking event. A few minutes after we arrived, a petite brunette with sparkling brown eyes walked up to me and asked, "Have you ever been to Morocco, Sonya?"

It was my friend Elaine from New Jersey, who I met in 2002 during a semester abroad in Spain. We had spent an unforgettable spring break week in Morocco that year with three other friends. We hadn't seen or spoken to each other in nine years.

As it turned out, Elaine was meant to be in my life. She was an encyclopedia of everything worth discovering in Miami, and more importantly, it's because of her that I discovered plant medicine— which now, in retrospect, I consider the beginning of my personal spiritual journey. After this rekindling of our connection, she would become one of my closest friends.

There was also my first overseas work trip. I was twenty-five and it was to Costa Rica. I arranged to go early to spend the weekend on a Costa Rican beach. My friend Josh was in Costa Rica for the summer and I thought it would be fun to meet up with him, but I had lost his phone number and didn't know where exactly he was. (Those were archaic pre-social media days; I didn't have the option to open Facebook and track him down instantly.)

My trip plans were shaken up because the first leg of the journey, the short Tampa-Miami flight, was cancelled due to engine problems. The next flight wasn't until the following day. Because of that, I scrapped my plan to take the six-hour bus ride to renowned Tamarindo beach and went to Jacó Beach instead, which was only a two hour bus ride from the airport. Walking down a small sandy street in Jacó, I spotted a guy who looked like Josh.

"Josh?" I asked.

It was him.

We couldn't believe it. What are the chances??

Nothing life-changing came from that encounter, as far as I can tell. Josh and I never had any romantic connection, in case you were wondering, and he was with another girl that weekend, but the three of us had a great time, and that surprising meetup made us really happy. I think sometimes the Universe arranges little miracles for no other reason than to give us extra happiness. Maybe it just likes sprinkling magic around to make life a little more festive.

CHAPTER 22

No rain, no flowers.
- ANONYMOUS

June 2018

Back in Kalaw, the days go by fast. After a week of deep cleaning, painting, and decorating, the transformation of the yoga space is complete and the shala is ready.

Classes officially begin July 3rd. The first class has a diverse mix of five students: a Swiss girl, the Burmese grandparents, Steve's oldest daughter Hayma, and Luna the cat, who participates at the end by curling up on top of Hayma's legs during the resting supported bridge and supine spinal twist poses.

From then on, the shala slowly but steadily attracts a trickling stream of students, both locals and foreigners. There is the lovely Muslim Burmese woman who lives around the corner and speaks no English, who negotiates a monthly rate and from then on comes to every single class, morning and evening. On Saturdays, she brings her ten-year-old daughter. There are no men in the room, so she takes her hijab off while we practice and puts it back on at the end of class. All our communication is through smiles, hand gestures, and my twelve-word Burmese vocabulary.

After a couple weeks, my loyal student tells Hayma she can't come anymore because she's moving to Yangon. I'm not sure if this is true or she just got burnt out after her sudden burst of intensive yoga.

The café girls come to classes sometimes when the café isn't too busy. These girls are sweet and adorable, by the way, and to know them is to love them. There are three of them and they're all around eighteen. Mya Mya is the most talented cook of the three: smart, capable, and efficient. Thandar Myo is the playful, soft-spoken, outdoor-loving one who loves to bake. Shwe Yi is small, shy, and doesn't speak much English.

Then there are the Western students, like Jessie from Australia, who gives the studio its best compliment: "This is so beautiful! It looks like heaven." There is ashtanga-loving Melanie from North Carolina who shows up just when I'm craving a student who wants a strong, athletic class. There are the six lovely Burmese girls in their early twenties from all around Myanmar who have come to Kalaw for a weekend reunion. I chat with them while they're eating ice cream in the café. They tell me they would love to do yoga tomorrow, but they don't have yoga clothes. They're all about the same size as me.

"Well, I have plenty of yoga pants and shirts if you want to borrow some," I tell them.

Yes! They would love that.

So I bring my supply of yoga clothes to the shala the next day. The girls each find something that fits and I teach a class to six beautiful Burmese girls all wearing my pants. Afterwards they buy friendship bracelets for each other from the eco-shop and they buy an extra one for me.

There are the Portuguese girls from Porto who are full of light, and other Europeans, mostly French, Spanish, British, and German. There are a lot of Israelis, because a lot of Israelis travel to Myanmar when they're not traveling to India. And many other assorted nationalities. It turns out that a great way to meet lots of wonderful people is to start teaching yoga in a remote tourist town.

There's also a lot of interest in yoga among the local population. That is to say, I'm told everyone's talking about it, but it seems people are more interested in talking about it than actually coming to classes, even though I offer everyone a free trial class. But after a few weeks, a group of three ladies from KBZ Bank negotiate a monthly rate to come twice a week. Two ladies from a local spa start coming too, occasionally. There are also some days with no students, because it's low season. That's okay, because I always have other things to do with my time.

I bring the café's social media back to life. I start responding to all Facebook messages. I create an Instagram account for the café and begin regularly posting droolworthy photos on both pages. The following starts to grow, especially on Facebook, which is huge in Myanmar. Occasionally the café gets mentioned by a blogger with a huge following, which makes Steve happy.

The packaging design and sourcing doesn't progress very fast, because Steve doesn't have much time for it and he's indecisive about my proposed designs. I suspect he's indecisive because he doesn't love any of them, although he never overtly says that. I personally think they look great, but we have different styles. He does get more incredible lip balms made and repackaged, and none of the grant money is lost.

I don't get the chance to absorb much permaculture and sustainable building knowledge. My only contribution to the farm is helping with the planting of hundreds of mulberry tree cuttings. On that day, Luis presents his completed masterpiece of a water filtration system made from a special kind of red clay. He breaks out a rare smile on this occasion.

After a couple weeks with a bicycle as my mode of transportation, I realize I need a motorbike. Biking the hilly roads of Kalaw is an excellent workout, but it's exhausting, and slow. Steve helps me find a motorbike, a beautiful little black and red TVS Dazz. From then on, Kalaw and its surroundings are my oyster.

With Steve's blessing, I begin teaching occasionally at a little nearby paradise; a gorgeous retreat center nestled among forested hills half an hour drive from town, with exquisite villas, organic gardens, a beautiful spa, and a gorgeous yoga room with polished wood floors and a wall of floor to ceiling glass windows. They offer yoga and meditation retreats and private classes. They don't get many yoga/meditation bookings, but when they do, they're a lovely experience every time. It's nice to be earning a little money, of course, and the early morning thirty-minute drives to the hotel are beautiful, with mist hovering over the land and water buffalo lounging quietly in the fields.

I start trying to learn Burmese, and notice I said *trying*. Burmese belongs to the family of Most Frustrating Languages in the World, right up there with Chinese. It's a tonal language, and that's the main problem. I can't hear the subtle differences in the sounds that to Burmese people are as unmistakable as the difference between a cat's meow and a dog's bark. Fortunately, I master some important phrases, like one taught to me by my friend Min at the Mexican restaurant. *"Zeh chideh! Kalaw mah nee bah-deh; neh neh sho pi bah!"* "Too expensive! I live in Kalaw; discount for me please!" This phrase is extremely useful at the market; it makes all the vendors laugh and give me a lower price.

Another bewildering feature of the Burmese language is that sometimes it doesn't have one universally accepted word for very basic things, like for example, a hand, or an arm. When I ask three different Burmese people from the same small town how to say "hand" in Burmese, I get three different answers.

"Leh mow(n)," one tells me.

"No, that means arm," the next person says. *"Leh chow(n)* is hand."

"No," says the third person, *"leh chow(n)* means fingers, hand is *leh* and arm is *leh teh(n)."*

With this lack of consensus on what to call human body parts, what disparity must there be on more complex words? Does this linguistic individuality ever lead to catastrophic consequences, like for example, if someone needs to go to the hospital for a hand amputation? Imagine how wrong this could go if the patient thinks *leh* means hand and the doctor thinks it means arm. Let's face it, horrible mistakes like this occasionally happen even in American hospitals where hand universally means hand.

Fortunately, I never actually hear any reports of amputations gone wrong in Myanmar.

My favorite letter in the Burmese alphabet is *za-gwe*, or as I prefer to call it, the curly squiggle:

At first I like it just because it's cute. Then I notice that it looks like the way I travel through life. Not the fastest way from Point A to Point B, but the slow, winding, scenic route. So it takes longer to get to the destination, but I get to see and experience so much more along the way.

In late July, Luis goes back to Spain and Steve goes back to the US for a month. When Steve gets back, it'll be my turn to leave, because my visa expires September 1st, and also I've had enough of rainy season. Steve doesn't mind if I leave for a while because I'm going to post an ad on Yoga Trade to find another teacher to cover classes while I'm gone. My heart is missing India, so that's where I'm going to go.

My Indian friend Nesha (of the Dharamsala YTT and unforgettable Rishikesh adventures) and I have come up with a brilliant plan for an epic three-week zigzagging trip across most of India, starting in Bangalore where she lives, visiting Pondicherry, Auroville, Ajanta and Ellora, Manali, remote Spiti Valley, and finishing back in Dharamsala.

You might think that would be enough for one visa run, but ... Cambodia is also calling me.

For several reasons. Many little signs have seemed to point in its direction over the past year, the most intriguing of which was last year's reading of my astrological map by a British astrologer named Debbie at the Ayurvedic center in India. Her reading revealed that, according to the stars and planets, the southern coast of Cambodia is the most auspicious place on planet Earth for me. It's the place on my chart where all the main lines of good fortune intersect.

This seems like something I should check out.

Debbie also did a reading of my birth chart, which revealed that September of this year is the month everything would be starting. Exactly what "everything" will be is unclear, but it seems to refer to some project or man that I will love and have lots of energy for. Maybe this man or project is waiting for me in auspicious Cambodia?

As if all that wasn't enough, I keep hearing about this incredible little island named Koh Rong Sanloem off Cambodia's southern coast. Quiet, unspoiled, white sand beaches and crystal-clear water. I miss beaches and this place sounds like heaven.

But ... it seems maybe a little excessive to try to squeeze both most of India and the whole southern coast of Cambodia into one visa run. *Less is more* is one of my mantras, and I don't want to wear myself out zipping all over the place. Since I can't make up my mind, I ask the Universe out loud if it could please give me a sign to let me know whether I should go to both countries or just India.

The day goes by and by late afternoon, the Universe has revealed no signs. I decide I should go ahead and make this decision based on logic. Better to keep it simple and save Cambodia for later. Besides, September is still the rainy season there.

That evening I start to book an August 31st flight to Bangalore. I have to pause to fill out the lengthy India visa application before completing the booking. I've just finished the application when Helen calls—a nice, unexpected surprise—and we spend an hour excitedly catching up on the events of the past six months.

I hang up with her and start over with the booking process, and then my phone dings. It's a voice note from Nesha. Her message says that, actually, it would be better if I arrive around September 10th or 11th because she won't be able to take off work until then. As I'm listening, my eyes wander to the bottom right corner of my computer screen and I see that it's 11:11 (Miami time, because my laptop is still on Miami time).

Since I have to leave Myanmar by September 1st, this makes it crystal clear I should go to Cambodia before India. And then the significance of the 11:11 hits me: there's the sign I asked for.

Thank you, Universe!

As always, I'm intrigued by the details of how this magic works. If Helen hadn't called, I would have already booked the Bangalore flight for August 31st and skipped Cambodia. Did one of my guardian angels ring up Helen's higher self and nudge her to call me, to delay me as long as needed? Or was Helen going to call me regardless, and the Mystical Powers That Be just worked around that?

However it works, the appearance of my requested sign makes me even more excited about my upcoming epic visa run than I already was. I promptly book my ticket to Phnom Penh and start researching destinations along Cambodia's southern coast. I find enchanting things like a blog post titled, "Kep, Cambodia: Asia meets France by the seaside," and a gorgeous $30/night hotel on Agoda with jaw-dropping sunset ocean views. (I book that hotel immediately.)

Those hotel and sunset photos are a sugar fix for my soul. I love Kalaw, but—I miss the tropics. I want to walk barefoot on a beach, and wear little sundresses and sunbathe and drink coconuts that came from a tree ten feet away. And also, I miss romantic male connection. It's been three months since Koh Phangan. A little tropical romance with a nice attractive man would be really great. A little rejuvenating fling, or the love of my life could appear. Either way. That's the wish I send out, trip-planning and daydreaming.

One Friday night the week before my Cambodia/India getaway, two beautiful, cosmopolitan Burmese girls from Yangon come for the evening yoga class. They're around my age, speak perfect English, and are in Kalaw for the weekend.

After yoga, we chat over dinner in the café. Their names are Ingyin (pronounced "In-jin") and Pon, and they're staying at my fairytale hotel home. Ingyin has the high cheekbones and slender curves of a model, with bright, expressive eyes. She wears a serious expression, but her laugh is genuine and escapes easily. Pon laughs easily too. She's down-to-earth and distracted by her phone, probably because she owns a large restaurant in Yangon and has a lot on her plate. They sometimes argue briefly in Burmese, then laugh and are instantly back on good terms. According to Ingyin, they've been friends forever. They argue a lot, but they're still best friends.

Ingyin tells me they've hired a driver to take them to see waterfalls around Kalaw tomorrow.

My eyes widen. "I love waterfalls."

"You should come with us," Ingyin says.

So the next morning I join them for the two-hour drive and short hike to the spectacular Taw Kyal waterfall (pronounced "Taw Chall"). It's magnificent. It's my favorite kind of waterfall: a frothy, multi-tiered cascade that forms connecting layers of small pools, like twenty-nine waterfalls in one.

Ingyin is less impressed. She loves waterfalls as much as I do but she prefers the tall, skinny ones, and she's seen more amazing falls than this one. She loves the hidden, off the map ones that no one knows about except some locals in nearby villages.

Pon agrees that it's beautiful but she doesn't have strong feelings about waterfalls.

In the afternoon, rain starts pouring down and foils our plan to hunt for more hidden falls. On the way back, we stop for delicious Shan noodles at a tarp-covered roadside café and Pon teaches me how to order them without MSG. In the backseat of the car, Ingyin and I talk nonstop. We share the same curiosity for life, depth of emotion, and love of books, nature, meditation, and massages.

And this is the beginning of a beautiful friendship, born of a shared love of chasing waterfalls.

My last scheduled class at the studio is Tuesday night. It hits me during the class, while looking around at the warm, welcoming studio, that this is exactly what I was wishing for in Thailand four months ago: a cozy, quiet little place to become comfortable with teaching. And as I'm listening to myself talk, feeling comfortable and confident and enjoying the smiles on the faces of my three students, I realize that I also got something I was looking for when I left the US. I found my voice.

In years past, I would listen with admiration as confident yoga teachers fluidly guided their classes, convinced that I could never have that ability. I'm clumsy with spoken words. I trip over them. I could never guide a class so beautifully with the pressure of a classful of students focusing on my every word, I thought.

My issue with words extended beyond yoga classes to many forms of spoken communication. Not so much at work, because professional communication came naturally most of the time, but on the personal level it was different. Often, when speaking, I would experience a feeling of disconnection—especially if I was talking about something that mattered deeply to me or anything uncomfortable. It was a feeling of two different wavelengths searching for each other but not connecting—the wavelength of what I felt and the wavelength of what I was expressing out loud. In between the two was a mysterious current of discomfort and uncertainty. My own voice was a mystery to me.

When I set off on this Asian journey, this is one of the things I wanted most: to find my own voice.

Now, I listen to myself as I'm leading the class and I realize this is a voice I didn't have before. This voice is calm and relaxed and confident and full of light. It's not too sweet, too nice, too serious, too gentle, or too bossy. It sounds natural to my ears and feels natural to my heart, and it's mine.

I love this voice.

In this moment of realization, I'm filled with immense gratitude, to life for bringing me here, to Steve for having this space available for me, to every student who came to my classes to give me the opportunity to practice teaching.

There wasn't supposed to be a class the next day, but that morning Ohmar tells me one of her guests has requested one. I'm busy with packing and quite honestly, I don't feel like teaching. I thought I was done for now and I've already switched into pre-vacation mode, but I don't want to withhold yoga from someone who wants it. I decide to teach out of gratitude to life for all it's given me.

The student is Esther, a Dutch woman living in Hong Kong. Before we begin, I ask her if she has any special requests, or anything she wants to focus on. "Just inner peace," she replies.

The class style is yin yang—part hatha, part yin. The dynamic hatha comes first, followed by a relaxing yin second half. The hatha part of the class flows nicely, as far as I can tell. The music playing is my Before Class Spotify playlist, which has only three songs on it. After the third song, Spotify continues selecting new songs on its own and they're beautiful, so I let it keep going.

When we transition into the yin part of the class, that's when the magic begins. It's something about the soft ethereal music, and the sound and feel of nature outside. The wind is blowing gently, and the sounds of the summer evening are a low humming melody. Usually I close the windows at the start of yin because it coincides with the beginning of mosquito prime time, but tonight I leave them open to let the magic waft in. There are no mosquitos tonight. Something about the magic in the air is amplified by the stillness of the long-hold yin postures. The peace soaks into my muscles, my veins, my mind, my entire being. I feel transported and present at the same time. I'm still aware that as the teacher, I have the responsibility to hold space during this class, and I hope Esther is feeling the magic too.

Evidently, she was. After class she says, simply and sincerely, "Wow—yin is powerful. That was a gift. Thank you."

It was a gift—from life, to both of us. And also a gift from her to me, for asking for what she wanted and creating this opportunity, and a gift from me to her for saying yes and showing up to teach. The magic wasn't caused by anything I did or anything amazing about my teaching. I didn't even pre-plan the music that night. We both just showed up and then life swept in with the magic. We don't have to control the details; they are in more capable hands than ours. Ishvarapranidhana.

And that is how my first chapter of yoga teaching wrapped up. I am forever grateful to Esther for wanting a class that night, and to Life for the magic.

CHAPTER 23

Beauty is the passionate and positive expression
of the complete self.
— VIDAL SASSOON

September 2018

My first week in Cambodia is spent in Phnom Penh, Kep, and Kampot. It's enjoyable but uneventful, except that in Phnom Penh I get my hair trimmed and balayaged at Kate Korpi Salon by a sweet, adorable Cambodian hair savior named Lucy. I found Lucy by searching for photos of balayage on Instagram. It's been four months since I've been inside a salon and my hair is crying for attention like a drowning man for a lifeline.

We chat while Lucy applies strokes of color to my hair with confident, experienced hands. She loves her job and the salon, she tells me. She's really grateful for the opportunity. The owner and managers train all the employees very professionally and they treat everyone really well. She's never been on a plane before, but in a couple months she's going to fly to Siem Reap with a team from the salon to do hair for a wedding. She's really excited about that. She exudes an aura of sweet happiness and a quiet sparkle. I leave the salon feeling brighter than when I went in, because my hair's been transformed and because of the contagious presence of Lucy.

As the ferry from Sihanoukville draws close to the sandy white shores of Koh Rong Sanloem, the sea air is soft on my skin and a strange feeling spreads through me. There is magic here; I can feel it. It's waiting on this island, hidden inside peace and stillness. The shimmering pale aqua water around us is as still as a calm lake.

As I walk down the long wooden dock to the beach, I have the surreal feeling that I'm walking into a dream. I've seen many beautiful beaches, but something about this one feels different.

The first person I see on the magic island is a tall, ruggedly attractive Eastern European-looking man leaning against the railing at the end of the pier. He's built like a soccer player. The moment I see him I feel a jolt of sudden attraction.

Attraction is sometimes such a primal thing. Of course I can feel my own attraction to this stranger, but in the split second that our eyes meet, I can also feel his towards me, even before he speaks a word.

When he speaks, it's to ask, "Do you need accommodation?" I like the way he says it, softly and politely, in a pleasant masculine voice.

"No thank you," I reply.

"If you change your mind, come see us at Blue Ocean Villas."

"Okay, thanks," I say, and then I spot the boat taxi driver from Serena Resort who's here to pick me up.

My beachfront resort is lovely and modern. I check in and settle into my room, which is not beachfront because I'm sticking to my long-term travel budget, but it's cute.

That evening I go for a walk down the beach in search of rum and a coconut. There's an outdoor bar about fifty yards from my hotel. As I walk up to it, I see the guy from the pier sitting at the end of the bar closest to me. I might have been surprised except that this is a magic island, so of course he would be there.

We exchange hellos and I ask the bartender if they have rum and fresh coconuts. They have rum but no coconuts.

"But they sell coconuts at a little stand about 200 meters that way," the bartender adds, gesturing down the beach. So I walk to get my coconut and bring it back to the bar.

The guy from the pier is still there when I return. "Mind if I join you?" I ask.

"Of course not," he says and slides over on the bench to make room for me.

I order a shot of rum and a lime to accompany my coconut and chat with the guy. He's from Serbia and his name is Andrej. He's been on the island for a year. He has the vibe of somebody who's made a few bad decisions in his life, but he's genuine. There's no pretense about him. I like him.

He's been in jail a few times; for selling drugs when he was a teenager, and more recently for two months here in Cambodia, for getting into a bar fight, which causes visions of *Brokedown Palace* to flicker in my head. I ask him what Cambodian prison was like; he says it wasn't bad.

Under the surface roughness, his vibe has a sweetness, honesty, and a kind of innocent vulnerability. His smile has a charming crookedness—the left corner raises more than the right. He talks about his boss, the resort owner, like he's his guru. "He taught me so much. He taught me to not react to situations, to not be affected by other people, and he taught me about self-love, which I didn't used to have before, at all."

I love that I'm sitting in a bar in paradise drinking a rum-spiked coconut listening to a Serbian ex-convict discuss self-love. And it feels so good to be in the presence of rugged masculine energy. I missed this. I'm suddenly feeling more fully alive.

Andrej tells me his resort is looking for a yoga teacher and he would like to show me the resort and introduce me to the owner. He invites me to lunch there the next day, and we agree he'll pick me up in the boat taxi at 1 p.m.

When I'm ready to leave, he politely insists on paying for my rum. He insists sweetly, by bringing his palms together in front of his heart, leaning towards me and saying, "Please, I want to pay for this. Please let me."

Who could say no to that?

The next day Andrej picks me up in the boat as planned. It's drizzling when we leave the shore and it's raining harder by the time we arrive at his resort on the other side of the bay. We run to the restaurant through the raindrops. The look and the vibe of the resort don't wow me, but lunch is delicious.

Afterwards, Andrej gives me a tour. The rooms are free-standing villas built on the side of the hill with plenty of space between each; they look nicer than the restaurant. "Can I see one?" I ask.

"Of course," he says, and leads me inside one of them. The white-walled interior is nice, spacious, with vaulted ceilings and an enormous bathroom. After the quick tour, he shuts the door, places his hands on my shoulders, and looks into my eyes. "So, you're here for a few days and then you're leaving…" he says.

"Yes…"

"Is this okay?" He kisses me.

I kiss him back. "Yes." This is exactly what I wanted.

He walks me toward the bed, his arms still around me, and I ask, "Are you going to get in trouble?"

"We'll find out," he says.

He's a kind, sensual, giving lover. Outside, the sky is still thick with clouds and rain falls occasionally—it's a day to be indoors. We stay in our clandestine villa all afternoon. By late afternoon, I'm hungry. Andrej asks if I want anything. He had raved about a delicious chocolate dessert the restaurant makes, so I request chocolate.

He returns ten minutes later with a beautifully plated slice of chocolate mousse on a thick chocolate crust. I take a bite. It's divine. Possibly the world's most delicious chocolate dessert. That settles it: this is beyond any doubt a magic island.

Andrej leaves once more to run an errand and comes back five minutes later. "There's someone I want you to meet," he announces abruptly. "The boss is back and he's in a mood. He's kicking us out. But I want you to meet him before we go."

Okayyy … awkward time for an introduction, but—I fall back on the motto I developed after years of perennial corporate insanity: whatever. We're all adults here, and anyway, I was wanting to meet this guru-boss Andrej had spoken so highly of. However, my first concern is the unfinished dessert.

"Okay, but can we take the chocolate?"

Andrej assures me he'll pack the chocolate and escorts me over to a neighboring villa. The guru-boss comes out to the porch to meet us. He's blond, also Eastern European, named Matis. He's probably a few years older than me.

Andrej introduces me, and Matis and I exchange a few polite words. He asks how long am I on the island, where am I staying. He's a little abrupt but his annoyance is directed at Andrej, not at me. He informs me that Andrej "exceeded his authority by giving you a room here."

I start to reply: "I apologize for ... any inconvenience" but he doesn't let me finish.

"You have nothing to apologize for; it's him who needs to apologize."

There are a couple awkward moments of silence. Andrej doesn't apologize for anything. When he speaks, it's to tell Matis, "She's a yoga teacher."

"We're about to have lots of yoga teachers over here," Matis tells me.

"I would imagine so, it's a perfect place for it," I reply.

We say polite goodbyes and Andrej leads me down to the restaurant. I sit at a table to wait while he goes to take care of something. A few minutes later, Matis walks over with a bowl of soup. "Mind if I join you?" he asks.

"Please."

He sits down across from me and we start talking. I learn he's from Lithuania and he lived in Florida for a while, on Anna Maria Island, a beautiful little place where I used to go to the beach every weekend during my Tampa college years. Small world. He asks about my background. We talk about how this island is magic, and how you feel it from the moment you arrive. He tells me they may have an opportunity in a few months that could use both my yoga and business background. He explains some of the details. They want to start targeting guests with niche offerings including yoga, tennis, and dance. He asks about the timing of my availability and asks if we can exchange contact details. I give him my Whatsapp number.

Andrej comes over intermittently, first to bring me a glass of red wine, then to take Matis's bowl when he's finished with it, then to ask if he'd like anything else.

Matis replies to him brusquely, not looking at him, making it clear he's not back in his good graces.

After a while I politely excuse myself and go over to Andrej, who's waiting by the bar. He kisses me on the cheek. "Ready to go?" he asks.

Yes, I am. After we leave, he squeezes me in a hug. "I'm so proud of you," he said. "You stayed cool. I wanted him to see that you were a lady."

It was a unique experience, I'll say that.

And so Andrej becomes my island romance for these few days on the magic island. My fulfilled wish—exactly what I had been craving. Some loving, connection, sincerity, and masculine energy. We're comfortable together. He's sweet, and affectionate, and the connection with him feels natural and honest—but not deep or meant to be long-lasting. Although my deepest wish is still for true love, I know it isn't going to be that with Andrej. We don't match, not that way. And that's fine. I'm enjoying this so much for what it is; for the here and now. Knowing there's no future takes all the pressure away.

One day he tells me more about his Cambodian prison time. He's quite calm about it. "Foreigners are treated quite well. It's a little worse for the Cambodians. There were about 150 of us there. There are two floors, and the foreigners are on the top floor, which is a little nicer. Not just Western foreigners, there were some Chinese guys in there too. We were only separate for sleeping, other than that everyone was together. It was peaceful, there was no fighting. You have a lot of free time; I got to work out."

Me silently in my head: *Oh, maybe that's why he has such a nice body. No, I think he's one of those guys who will always have a good body because he's just naturally energetic and athletic. Because, he does have a really nice body….*

Oh, back to the story. He mentions something about being in prison because he tried to burn down a bar.

"Bar fight," is what he had said before. My eyebrows raise. "Burn down a bar?"

He explains. "I was at this bar one night. It was late and I was hungry. They had closed the kitchen, but I saw them take some food to the owner. I asked if they could just make me a sandwich or something. The owner's wife was sitting there, and she said, 'There are a lot of buffalo around here and they shit a lot. You can go look for some of that.'"

He pauses for a moment, and then continues. His tone is nonchalant. "I stayed cool. I controlled myself. I told myself: *She's a woman, I'm not gonna hit her.* I left the bar. I ran to my boat, grabbed the fuel canister, ran back to the bar with it, poured it on the bar, and took out my lighter. But I saw I had spilled some of the gasoline on my arm, so I couldn't light it."

Well. This adds a whole new literal dimension to the expression "fiery temper." His story is a little unnerving, but my intuition doesn't sense any personal threat to me in my next two days on the island.

He says the jail time was good for him, and he's grateful that Matis gave him another chance after that.

I admire Matis for that.

The third day we see each other, Andrej surprises me by announcing that he's quit his job; he's leaving the island in a week and going back to Europe. To Stockholm. He's not sure exactly what he'll do, but he has friends there he'll stay with until he figures it out. "It was good here, but it's been enough time," he says.

I get that.

For my last night on the island, I move to a different hotel, one that I discovered walking past. Its beachfront cabins are set on a beautiful wide stretch of beach dotted with palm trees and foliage. The cabins have front walls of floor-to-ceiling glass that are mirrored on the outside and transparent on the inside. It's absolute design genius. Really, why would anyone build a beachfront cabin and *not* use one-sided glass for the front walls?

I'm looking forward to a romantic last night there. (Although it's important to know, in case you ever find yourself in such a place, that the exterior glass is only mirrored during daylight. After dark, with the lights on inside, they're totally see-through. So don't forget to pull the shades.)

Andrej comes over that afternoon, and he's in a strange, restless mood. He can't stay still and his mind is somewhere else. His energy is grating. As we're sitting on the gorgeous beach, I think to myself how much happier I would be at this moment if it was Nesha here instead of him. Nesha, with her bright effervescent energy, who would be spinning in circles of joy on the sand with me in the presence of all this beauty. Nesha comes to mind first because I'll see her in two days, but I would happily temporarily trade Andrej for any of my likeminded, joyful, beauty-loving close girlfriends.

We've walked into the ocean and are sitting chest deep in the clear, tranquil water, and I catch Andrej gazing off into the distance, looking angry at someone who's not there.

"What are you thinking about?" I ask him.

"Nothing smart," he replies with narrowed eyes.

Is he contemplating setting some other establishment on fire, I wonder.

He shakes off his faraway thoughts and brings himself back to the present. He says, "Make sure I get your number before you leave."

He doesn't have my number because he doesn't have a phone. Our plans have always been made in the old-fashioned, pre-cell phone verbal format of "see you tomorrow at one" … "bbq tomorrow at seven," etc.

"Of course."

"When I get settled in Stockholm and see how my crib is I'll let you know, and you can come and stay with me."

"Okay, yeah, let's see," I reply noncommittally.

"Do you want to go inside?" he asks, looking toward my cabin.

I smile. "Sure."

Making love, he's as fully present as ever. Afterwards, he has to leave to do some boat driving for the hotel. We have a date that night, to take a boat to see bioluminescent plankton in the water a little ways away from the island. He's supposed to pick me up here at 7:15. But he doesn't show.

I never see him again.

I'm surprised, confused, and I don't want to admit this, but a little sad. Even though I didn't expect to see him again after the next morning, I was looking forward to one more night, and more than anything, the strangeness of his disappearance bothers me. Plus, I'm disappointed to miss the bioluminescent plankton.

But that night, the hotel manager tells me you can see the bioluminescence just by walking out into the ocean from the beach, if you wait until after midnight when all the hotels turn their lights off.

Waiting for midnight, I go for a walk down the beach. The night is quietly sublime. The sand is soft powder under my feet and the stars overhead are bright against the dark gray sky and the glassy surface of the water glows in the dim light. It feels otherworldly. Just me alone in the quiet beauty of this enchanted island.

Maybe it's better that Andrej left me to the luxury of my own company. Maybe his timing was perfect.

Back at the hotel, no one is around except one of the Ukrainian waiters, who's sitting at one of the tables. We talk a little. I tell him I'm waiting for the lights to go off to see the plankton.

"Maybe you want some company?" he asks.

"Sure."

Eventually most of the lights on the beach go dark and we wade out into the ocean. Sure enough, once we're far enough from shore, the glowing plankton is there, sparkling in the water like underwater fireflies. They're huge compared to the ones I've seen in Florida and Puerto Rico, glowing with brilliant white light. It's so fun swimming with them, watching the ephemeral lights appear as our limbs and bodies move the water around. This is so much better than taking a boat out to see them.

The Ukrainian guy comes close to me. "Can I kiss you?"

"No!"

One man per day is enough, thank you.

The next day, I wake up to soft morning light and the idyllic sight of the beach, palm trees, and aqua-pastel ocean through the floor-to-ceiling windows. It's quite decadent to be here alone.

But I want to be sure nothing happened to Andrej. For all I know he lost his temper again and is back in Cambodian jail. I text Matis.

Hi, is Andrej ok? We were supposed to meet yesterday and he didn't show up. I just wanted to make sure nothing happened.

I saw him this morning, looked ok to me, he texts back.

I'm glad to know he's alive and unincarcerated. Still, his mysterious ghosting has left me mildly unsettled, because I don't understand the reason for it. I don't know why, and I always want to know why.

At breakfast, I notice the book *Origin* by Dan Brown on a bookshelf in the hotel restaurant. I start reading it while I eat. The story begins at the Guggenheim museum in Bilbao. The author goes into great detail describing two of the works there—so much vivid, intriguing detail that I google the Guggenheim Bilbao to see images of the thirty-foot bronze, steel, and marble spider sculpture *Maman* by Louise Bourgeois and the ensemble of curving, spiraling steel sheets that form *The Matter of Time* by Richard Serra.

The book is engrossing, like all of Dan Brown's books, and I wish I had found it yesterday. I take it with me to a beachside lounge chair and keep reading. I don't make it past the first few chapters before I have to check out.

The following afternoon, I'm in Phnom Penh when I receive a Whatsapp text from Julien.

Hi beautiful Sonya, how are you? Where are you now? I'm in Paris and was thinking of you.

It always gives me a little spark of happiness to receive a message from him, with the associated memories of sensual Balinese bliss they trigger.

Hi Julien! I reply. *Today I'm in Phnom Penh but yesterday I was here …* (I attach a few pictures) *… Koh Rong Sanloem … villa with glass walls that are mirrors from the outside, brilliant!* 😎 *Ça va bien?*

He replies: *Ouaouuuuu nice pictures!!* 😎 *I'm good, thanks. I worked all summer except for one week when I went to visit Spain: less glamorous than Cambodia.* He attaches three pictures: one thirty-foot-tall spider statue, one curving steel installation, and one statue of shiny, brightly colored metallic balls. Along with the pictures, he writes "Bilbao Guggenheim."

My jaw drops. The Bilbao Guggenheim?? And the giant spider *Maman* and *The Matter of Time?* He just sent me pictures of exactly what I spent hours reading about yesterday morning. This is so weird.

I tell him why it's crazy that he's sending me pictures of the Guggenheim.

He doesn't comment on the wild coincidence, he just replies that the Guggenheim needs to be seen one day. Then his messages get flirty. I flirt back.

CHAPTER 24

The best and most beautiful things in the world cannot be
seen nor even touched, but just felt in the heart.
— HELEN KELLER

September 2018

Nesha picks me up at Bangalore airport. We have a wildly joyful reunion involving a lot of screaming and laughing and jumping up and down. That night, we light incense and pull an oracle card each from her Gaia Oracle deck. The card that comes up for me is *Lost Love*.

The heading is a little dramatic for my current situation. But the card's explanation is perfect:

> *It is normal to feel sad when a relationship or a friendship ends. Yet,*
> *this healing card has shown up in your reading today to let you know*
> *that everything truly does happen for a reason. Trust and accept that*
> *higher forces are at work in your life at the moment and that your soul*
> *is guiding you towards ever greater love. There is little point in searching*
> *for answers. Accept things as they are. All is part of a higher plan for*
> *your life.*

That settles it. Andrej appeared at the perfect time and he disappeared at the perfect time. The card's consoling words wash away the last of my lingering fixation with the unknown *why* of his unexplained disappearance.

Our zigzagging grand tour of India begins in Bangalore with a celebration of the Festival of Ganesha—the annual holiday of joy, abundance, and prosperity. In Pondicherry, we savor the beauty of French colonial architecture and the sweetness of melt-in-your-mouth banana Nutella crepes. Auroville fails to impress us, although the center is pretty and the concept behind it sounds utopian. The people who work at the center don't seem happy with life. They never smile. A strange vibe hangs in the air. Our greatest happiness is when we stop along our drive away from Auroville at a small roadside stand to buy a drink from a woman in a pink and gold sari. She smiles at us, a genuine human smile, and we feel that we've come back to the land of real, living humans.

On the other side of India, we discover the magnificent caves of Ajanta and Ellora, exquisitely carved into ancient stone. Here, Hindu, Buddhist, and Jain temples peacefully coexist side by side. In the walls of the Hindu temples, stone men and women embrace each other passionately. Because what is life without passion?

But what is life without serenity, the Buddhists would respond. Their temples, next door to the Hindus, are all about stillness and contemplation. As if passion got out of hand and humanity reacted by reverting back to peaceful, passionless meditation.

I don't want to have to choose between peace and passion. I want both.

In Ellora's Cave Twelve, one of the Buddhist temples, Nesha spontaneously snaps a photo while I'm walking slowly down a stone hallway, admiring the row of peaceful stone gray Buddhas seated side by side along the wall to my right. Filtered light flows in from the left, highlighting every feature of the aging statues. The details of their faces have eroded over time, but the curves of their bodies remain crisp. They've been sitting here in motionless meditation for thirteen centuries, their hands resting peacefully in cosmic mudra. A Buddha in the middle catches my eye. He's half-dark, half-light, divided perfectly in half by a vertical white line down his center. He reminds me instantly of yin and yang. Maybe he represents all of us, with our light and our dark sides, with our conflicting desires for peace and pleasure.

Nesha happens to click the shutter just when the thin line of my shadow lines up perfectly along Buddha's center, where his light and dark sides meet. The camera catches me looking up at him, my long red skirt swaying gracefully mid-stride. The picture couldn't have been more perfect if we had meticulously planned every detail.

The photo strikes me somewhere deep in my soul. It reminds me of the lesson that is still ongoing for me in this classroom that is life: learning to love and accept the whole being, both the light and the shadows, of others and myself. It's so easy to love light and beauty, but learning not to dismiss someone entirely when their shadow-side emerges, learning not to close my eyes or run from the darkness—I haven't learned this yet. And I haven't mastered the art of dealing with my own shadows either.

"A world within a world ... a place where the gods live."

This is how Rudyard Kipling described the remote section of the Himalayas where we would spend the second half of our journey: Spiti Valley. It was Nesha's idea to come here—I'd never heard of this place.

Spiti Valley is not a great place to be driving around by yourself, especially at the onset of winter—precisely the time of our visit. It's notorious for frequent road closures caused by rockslides and snowfall. Cell service is next to nonexistent. Wi-Fi? Not a chance. During winter, entire sections of the valley are cut off from the rest of the world for months at a time.

So we found a tour company who let us arrange a customized itinerary. Our planned route was to take us in a wide half circle northwest from Shimla, passing close to the Tibetan border and onward through Kalpa, Tabo, Kaza, the stunning moon lake of Chandratal, and finally back east to Manali.

We spend a day and a half in Shimla before meeting our driver and the rest of the tour group. Shimla is a picturesque mountain town surrounded by rows of green mountains and light misty clouds that hover above and between them. It's bigger and more beautiful than I expected. It drizzles all day, but rain can't disguise the enchantment that flourishes here. When night falls and the city lights come on and a touch of crisp chilliness descends, an aura of Christmastime fills the air.

The incredible buffet breakfast at our hotel is worthy of the gods: flaky na'an and feathery light chola bhatura with its creamy and savory sauces, the potato-stuffed aloo parathas, colorful sooji upma, and of course, soothing masala chai. It's my first experience with sooji upma, a melt-in-your-mouth creation of semolina, finely chopped veggies, cashews, and a savory blend of God knows how many spices. I could happily have stayed at that table eating breakfast for the rest of my life.

But, Spiti Valley is waiting.

The three other travelers in our tour group are from Mumbai: two women and a guy. Our driver is named Bunty. He's a likeable, easygoing Shimla native who's been driving the distant roads of Kinnaur and Spiti Valley for over ten years, and, most importantly, he knows all the best places to eat in these parts. Mostly little mom and pop hole-in-the-wall places, often without so much as a sign out front, where we would never have dared to stop on our own and where the most incredible, flavorful, bliss-inducing curries and homemade chapatis I've ever tasted in my life are served.

The days are beautiful and the nights are freezing. The roads are often blocked by large piles of fallen rocks, so our route changes frequently. One day we find ourselves trapped for six hours behind a giant fallen pine tree, which for unknown reasons chose that afternoon to uproot itself and sprawl squarely across the only road to our campsite. We're eventually rescued by a Caterpillar JRC from a neighboring village (and by "neighboring," I mean four hours away), which hacks the trunk into pieces and removes them from the road.

We spend two nights in the small town of Kalpa. One morning Bunty drives us from Kalpa to the spectacular but morbidly-named Suicide Point, where a slender road wraps along the edge of a light beige and gray-hued cliff of solid rock that plummets nine thousand feet straight down into a valley far below. There are no guardrails.

The height is both dizzying and exhilarating. We spend a little time here, admiring and taking pictures, and then go on to visit the nearby village of Roghi. Nesha and I want more time in nature, so we tell Bunty and the others to drive back without us. We'll walk. It should take us about three hours.

The road through Suicide Point is deserted now; we have it to ourselves. Our feet land lightly on the gravel-covered road. The pine-scented mountain air is cool on our skin. The soft hum of birds singing floats around us. We walk mostly in silence. Before, with people and voices around us, there wasn't enough stillness to feel the presence of this place. Now that we're alone and it's quiet, we can feel it.

The Himalayan landscape stretches out before us. The vastness of it and the immensity of the space around us overwhelms our senses. It's so big and we are so small. It's too much to take in. Every time we glance to the right at the towering range of snow-frosted, cloud-haloed mountains, sharply contrasted against a brilliant cornflower blue sky, they seem more beautiful than our last glimpse. Even time seems to slow down in the stillness of this place.

Through Suicide Point, we follow the thin road that carves along the edge of the cliff face. On our left, a wall of solid rock rises up toward the heavens. On our right, that same rock drops down into the void. As we walk, we fixate on more details. Somehow, in the steep solid rock of the mountainside, whimsical pine trees with curvy trunks have taken root and grown to maturity. Not just one or two, but many.

How does that happen? How does a seed sprout in solid stone and develop into a full-grown tree? If this can happen, what else is possible?

We pass a tree with two long exposed roots that look like arms. His root-arms are wrapped around a large boulder beneath him, as if in a cherishing, protective hug, keeping that boulder from tumbling down into the abyss. As if to say, *I love you. I got you. You're safe.*

There is something deeply touching about this living, loving sculpture.

They say life is measured by the moments that take your breath away. Every step of this hike is one of those moments. It's stunningly beautiful, but it's more than that. There is a Presence here, an indescribable Presence that fills us, awes and humbles us, seeps into our pores, filling our hearts and minds and every cell in our bodies. I'm not sure if this Presence always resides in this valley, or if It simply chose this time and place to reveal itself to us. All I know is that It shocks our conscious minds into stillness beyond words and something deeper, something primal within us, connects to something indescribably majestic.

Everything else pales in comparison to this present moment. We stop walking and stand still, absorbing this, speechless and overwhelmed. We don't know what to do with the emotions filling us; we feel that our hearts might burst. We want to somehow offer something back, but what do we have to give?

We finally do the only thing that feels natural: we come to our knees and bow our hands and foreheads to the ground in reverence.

I'm grateful to be experiencing this with Nesha, because not everyone would feel this, but Nesha feels deeply, the way I do. We're silent and awed together.

There is something about the enormous splendor of this Presence that dissolves human pettiness. We arrive back at the hotel quieter, more peaceful, our hearts feeling a little more pure.

That night at 4 a.m., I wake up and can't go back to sleep, so I reread the Gaia oracle card I pulled before bed: Purification.

It begins: *What is it that your heart truly desires? What do you perceive is missing in your life?*

God knows there are many things my heart truly desires, but my greatest, deepest wish is to find true love with the man of my dreams. To get to share this life with him. That's the thing I feel is missing.

The card goes on:

In order to find the answers, you must look inside your heart. Close your eyes and relax. Imagine a beautiful flame, warming your heart and soul. Feel its purifying and healing light burning away your fears and doubts, healing your body and mind and clearing away all obstacles either imagined or real. Feel your heart center as an endless space full of only love and light. Feel the peace. Now, what is your heart saying? When it brings a tear to your eye you will know that it is your truth. Your soul will guide you towards happiness; all you need to do is follow. Trust!

That's beautiful … but for some reason I don't feel like meditating. I feel like listening to the next segment of the ten-episode "How To Attract Love Into Your Life" meditation course I signed up for a few weeks ago on Insight Timer.

Now, just so you know, I'm not really the kind of person to sign up for any course called How To Attract Love Into Your Life. My ego thinks it's a little too cool for something like that. However, in a moment of total honesty with myself, I had to acknowledge that attracting love into my life was, in fact, the thing I most wanted to do. The woman offering this course— Christina Sian McMahon, Ph.D.— had managed to successfully do that, while I had not, so it was possible I might learn a thing or two from her. I also knew that the Universe likes to see us take a step of action toward what we want before handing it to us on a silver platter. Maybe this could be considered my requisite step of action.

So I paid the $4.99 to register and told my friend Anisha about it so I would have a witness if it worked.

I sit up in bed, put my headphones on, and play the next episode. It's Episode Four. In it, Christina tells the story of meeting her husband. On her thirty-nineth birthday, she made a wish to meet him before her fortieth birthday, and she ended up meeting him three weeks before that deadline. She added, "I would have preferred to meet him a lot sooner, but he wasn't available because he was in another relationship."

She goes on to say, "When you're manifesting, keep in mind that there are two people involved here, so when he's ready for you, that's when you'll meet him. You can't control when he's ready to meet you, but what you can control in the meantime is your preparation for meeting him."

At that point, unexpectedly, I start to cry.

When it brings a tear to your eye you will know that it is your truth, the card said.

"Just keep trusting," she continues. "The Universe loves you, and the Universe is going to give you the deepest wish of your heart. Maybe the time isn't right yet, maybe it's right for you but it's not yet for him. Just keep working on yourself so you'll be ready when you meet him, and just keep trusting."

They were the perfect words for me at that moment, and after hearing them, I need time to let the message sink in. I pause the meditation and do my own silent one, following the script on the oracle card. It's a beautiful meditation, profound, loving, consoling, healing.

And then I'm able to fall asleep.

CHAPTER 25

Remember this, that very little is needed
to make a happy life.
-MARCUS AURELIUS

October 2018

I'm back in Kalaw. The rains have ended and perfect weather has arrived. It feels like heaven. My fairytale hotel home is more fairytale-like than ever, lush and green with new flowers blooming, and the staff welcome me back with warm hugs and sparkling eyes. As if breakfast needed to get any better, they've started making their crepes with butter and they're irresistible.

The smiles of the café girls and Steve's kids are as sweet as ever. Luis has gone through a transformation; he smiles now too, says nice things, and comes to yoga regularly. He now has a girlfriend in Yangon, who might deserve the credit for this dramatic personality shift. High season is beginning, and although everyone says it's quieter than last year, there are a lot of people around. The café is often full, yoga classes are often full, and cooking classes are in full swing almost daily. Lima beans are in season at the market, which is really exciting to me because I have a strange love for lima beans, and also there are leafy greens, some sort of spinach variety, with edible curly green ribbons attached to every stalk. Like every stalk comes individually gift-wrapped by Nature.

The café now has a second yoga teacher. She's Emily, a blond, blue-eyed Scottish girl. She's in her mid-twenties, smart and motivated, with a charming, charismatic personality, and she's really excited about being here. She's been hired (by Steve, with me doing all the communicating) to share the yoga teaching and help manage the café (because Hayma is planning to start working at a hotel). We hit it off well on the phone before I left for India and we've been in touch by Whatsapp ever since. Steve's very impressed by her. She's already created a great new logo for the café by the time I get back.

As much as I love my fairytale hotel, I'm craving a place of my own, with a kitchen. Emily wants a kitchen too, so we decide to rent a house together. Kalaw isn't exactly a hotspot of great rental options, but with the help of my friend Ruby, we find a four-bedroom, two-story house with a lot of potential.

Ruby and her sister own a small convenience store in town, and I met Ruby one day during Project Yoga Shala Creation when I was in town looking for a mop. Ruby greeted me at the entrance with a warm, knowing smile and excellent English. She's Burmese, in her early sixties I think, with bobbed hair, twinkling eyes, and a quietly sparkling aura.

There was something about her. She felt familiar. During that first conversation, the odd thought came into my head that she might have been my mother in another lifetime. I thought I saw recognition in her eyes, but that could have been my imagination. Maybe we just recognized each other's vibe. I never asked her about that, but she became a good friend. I always think of her as "Ruby from the mop store." She's well-traveled; she was a flight attendant for many years. According to Steve, she's well-connected and knows everyone in this town.

Maybe that's why she's able to find us a house so fast. It's cute on the outside, and on the inside, it has potential for cuteness. Every room is painted the standard interior color of most Kalaw buildings: lime green. The downstairs floor is concrete and the wood floors upstairs are covered with lime green paint splatters. It has a squat toilet and no hot water, but the landlady agrees to put in a Western toilet and hot water for us. She—the landlady—is a slender Burmese woman with a quiet, natural elegance and a beautiful smile. She doesn't speak English, so Ruby translates for us.

We draw up a six-month lease, with a move-in date of November 1st. The rent is $240 a month. That's $120 each. (In case you don't feel like doing the math, that's less than one Starbucks latte per day.) The house is unfurnished, but at that price I can afford to buy paint and furniture and everything else necessary to transform this into a cozy little sanctuary.

Emily, who's on a tighter budget, is happy to leave the decorating to me. Steve has put me in touch with a local carpenter who will build anything I design and his hourly rate is so low it makes my jaw drop and my heart dance for joy. I go hog-wild designing furniture. Okay, not that wild. I design a box frame for my bed, two nightstands, a clothing rack, and shelves for the kitchen. Emily orders a clothing rack too. I have other ideas in mind for living room and rooftop lounge furniture but I'll hold off until the essentials are finished. The carpenter has no power tools, so it will take him a few weeks to complete my order.

Besides the lease, many other documents are required to rent a house as a foreigner in Myanmar. Steve makes a list of everything we need, complete with attached photocopied examples. The list includes a guarantee letter, a request letter, some form called Details, approval from the village head, an invitation letter (from Hayma), a copy of Hayma's company registration, a copy of our passports, a copy of our visa, a copy of the entrance stamp in our passport, a copy of the rental contract, and a completed immigration Form C, as well as copies of identity paperwork from the landlady and her husband.

Once we've assembled all the documents, Hayma and I take them over to the village quartermaster for his official stamp of approval. A Burmese person has to cosign the lease for us, and the plan is that Hayma will. But the village quartermaster isn't around that day, and for several days afterward Hayma is always either busy or not feeling well, so finally Ruby comes with me to meet the quartermaster and she cosigns for me instead. I pay the first and last month's rent with a big stack of kyat (pronounced "chaht"), because everything is done in cash here.

I move into the new house November 1st. Emily decides to wait until our mattresses arrive, as for now she's quite comfortable at the little hotel where her rate is $5 a day. I sleep on my bedroom floor on a thick pile of blankets those first mattress-less nights and I'm happy as a clam. It feels so good to have my own place and my own kitchen, and the shower is steaming hot, thanks to that brand new water heater.

My first night in the house, I walk up to the rooftop. Just as I open the door and step outside, a shooting star flashes brightly across the sky overhead—a sudden brilliant flash of ephemeral light. This is either a well-timed, meaningless coincidence or an auspicious cosmic welcome—a benevolent blessing from the cosmos on my arrival in the house, a wink of celestial confirmation that I'm meant to be here. I take it as the latter.

As soon as I'm moved in, I devote all my free time to painting, beginning with my bedroom. It feels fantastic to have this agent of dramatic change in my hand again: a paint roller! The grungy lime green of the walls is soon buried under fresh coats of lavender-tinted taupe. Once the bedroom is finished, I move on to the kitchen, transforming the walls with a joy-sparking shade of light teal.

And then, three days after I move in, Steve says to me, "You know you're staying in that house illegally, right?"

I raise my eyebrows. No, I don't know that. What is he talking about?

It turns out that besides that big stack of documents that we took to the village quartermaster, there's *another* big stack of documents that he and Hayma have to gather and submit to the local immigration office before Emily and I can legally move in. Steve says he told me this before. Because human memory is notoriously unreliable and there were so many documents and it's all fuzzy in my head by now, I can't categorically deny that he did, but I have no recollection of such a thing. He definitely had said something about immigration, but we already submitted Immigration Form C and I was under the impression that the approval from the village quartermaster covered everything. But it's entirely possible that Steve explained everything clearly and I wasn't listening closely enough. My mind may have wandered off to visualize paint colors and furniture while he was talking about Immigration approval.

The word *illegal* makes me nervous, but my Kalaw friends tell me that most expats don't bother to submit those documents to Immigration. Technically yes, they're required, and if someone wanted to make trouble for you they could come and ask for them, but in all likelihood that's never going to happen here. In the bigger cities maybe, but not in little Kalaw.

With this consensus, and because the entire town has been nothing but warm, welcoming, and supportive to me since the day I arrived, and because I'm used to Steve constantly expecting the worst, I'm not worried. Steve and Hayma will take the stack of documents to Immigration soon enough. Anyway, I don't have much time to dwell on it, because Life has gotten very busy, between shopping for the house, designing furniture, painting, running (because the Kalaw Half-Marathon is six weeks away), helping wait tables and wash dishes at the café when it gets crazy busy, taking the bus back and forth to Yangon twice to get a new passport because I've run out of pages (which is a great excuse to do more shopping for the house and get massages and eat Mandalay noodles and Thai food with Ingyin), and teaching yoga classes for the studio, and yoga and meditation retreats at the retreat center, and meeting interesting people.

Even with all the busyness of high season, I get a lot of stillness and alone time because of half-marathon training and painting the house, and it's in these moments that I am most aware of my happiness.

It surprises me how happy I am, in this simple town, in this simple house, living this simple life, teaching yoga and running through the mountains and spending hours painting walls. In my whole life, I've never been happier than this. When I'm alone in the house painting, the sensation of happiness intensifies under the lens of my awareness and grows bigger, expanding until it's too much to contain in my body and I feel it blasting out of me into the ether. I don't even know why I'm this ridiculously happy, but the mysterious happiness persists regardless.

CHAPTER 26

You can't connect the dots looking forward.
You can only connect them looking backwards.
- STEVE JOBS

November 2018

One day not long after moving into the house, I'm eating lunch at one of my regular cafés when I get a text from my ex-boyfriend Ryan.

I should explain a little about Ryan. He was the longest-lasting relationship of my life thus far: a whole three years. Although technically, our years together weren't whole, because we broke up five times. But if you subtract the intermissions and add up all our time together, it comes to about three years.

Ryan was a great guy, a really great guy. Being with him was like winning the boyfriend lottery. He treated me like a princess, and I could write a whole page about all his wonderful qualities. But I'll skip that and get to the point. The problem was that he was deeply in love with me, which was a beautiful thing, and I loved him but I couldn't love him back the same way, and that made me feel like a horrible monster.

I tried to make myself be in love with him though, I really tried, and that made everything messy and confusing, and there was a point in time where I thought we would never speak again. In the end, we made up, and we were on friendly terms again by the time I left the

US. He met someone else, too, before I left, and they're now happily engaged.

The reason he texted is that he's in Saigon for business. It's his first time in Asia and he's loving it. *Honestly I get why you want to just travel,* he writes. *Anytime I experience something new like this it makes me want to quit it all and see what else there is to see!*

That makes me smile. I send him a picture of my Kalaw house and tell him about my new home transformation project. I add that I've mentally sent him enormous gratitude many times for talking me into buying the Florida house and introducing me to the magic of home renovation—which ended up being my bridge to freedom and adventure.

He replies that he's glad he could help facilitate my freedom bridge, and he's working on his own. Then he tells me some big news: he almost sold his company a couple months ago. He got an incredible offer that would have left him set for life.

As I read the details of the offer, my eyes fill with tears of happiness for him. Financial success is one of his big goals. And in no way is that a bad thing—he's created for it. He has the brain, the drive, and the personality. I know the tremendous amount of work and passion he put into launching his company, and the obstacles he had to overcome to get to this point. I know what that offer must have meant to him. I also know I can take partial credit for the existence of that company, because its inception was inspired by break-up #2— our healthiest and most transformative break-up (after which he became a kinder, fitter, more compassionate person). Ryan has a highly intelligent business mind and he used to constantly come up with brilliant business ideas, sketch them out, talk about them excitedly, and then never do anything more about them. It was the same with the idea for this company until one day I finally told him what somebody needed to tell him.

"Look, you have all these great multi-million-dollar ideas but you never do anything with them. What kind of world would this be if everyone just sat around talking about great ideas and never did anything about them? This is a really great idea. Why don't you go make it happen?"

So he did. It was a lot of work in the beginning and he faced an onslaught of challenges that would have crushed a lesser man. But he didn't give up, and his sales and distribution have grown slowly but steadily over the years.

I remember all that and I'm full of happiness for him now upon hearing what his efforts led to, but all I text back is, *Wow!!! That's a pretty nice offer! What made you turn it down?*

It's too long of a story to text, so he calls to explain the eleventh hour twist of fate that prevented the sale from going through. It must have been a dizzying blow, but he took it in stride. "It may work out better in the long run," he says. "Most importantly, it was such a great validation that we've got a good thing going here."

The news stays in my mind, along with my happiness for him. Later, I'm at home painting the bedroom, and in the quietness and solitude the dots connect in my mind and I suddenly understand our whole story.

I know he suffered a lot of heartache because of me, and I suffered a lot of guilt for that, but I came to believe in the end that our paths were meant to cross and also that they were meant to diverge, and I knew things would work out for him. And they have. He's now engaged to a woman he loves, a beautiful brunette who's cool and supportive and perfect for him, and he got his business success too. And I got my freedom and adventure and my chance to experience life. Without him, I wouldn't have bought and fixed up the house that would end up financing this magnificent adventure. And without me he wouldn't have started his company and he very possibly wouldn't have transformed into the kind of man who would attract his fiancée. We both needed each other for that phase of transition and transformation.

Everything about our convoluted relationship makes sense now.

I start to cry. Not just little baby tears, but full-on shoulder-shaking, heart-jerking sobbing. I'm sobbing so hard I have to set the paint roller down. These aren't tears of sadness streaming down my face. I'm sobbing away all the guilt I felt for not being able to make myself be in love with him, the guilt I felt for hurting him when I ended it, the guilt I felt for disappointing other people who wanted us to be together because they thought we were the perfect couple. And I'm sobbing because of the shocking beauty of the way life works. Because I can see that we were absolutely meant to be together for a little while, and we were absolutely meant not to stay together forever. Because neither one of us would have gotten where we are now without the other. And because I can see now that love was there through all of it, even through the messiest parts when we lost sight of it, and over the years it's become a purer kind of selfless, unentangled, unconditional love. And that is beautiful beyond words, and I'm crying for all of that.

CHAPTER 27

Your heart knows the way.
- RUMI

November 2018

One of the best things about my new house is that it's located on Market Street. The street has a different official name, but everyone calls it Market Street because it is where, once every five days, the Five-Day Market materializes. This means that one out of every five days I can't get my motorbike out of the driveway, but that is absolutely fine because in exchange I have the world's most convenient shopping set up on my doorstep starting at 5 a.m. I wake up and look out the window to see orderly piles of cabbage and tomatoes and mushrooms and lima beans and the artistic gift-wrapped ribboned spinach and ginger and limes and carrots and white onions and spring onions and gourds and cobs of corn stretching down the street as far as the eye can see, attended by women seated behind each pile. I walk outside with my basket and because it's early, I get the best pickings of everything. It's a produce-shopping dream come true.

Of all the streets in Kalaw, only mine got the name Market Street, but the Five-Day Market actually wraps around multiple streets. Mine is the longest and that's probably why it got the name. There's an entire street full of flowers (maybe known as Flower Street?) and I wouldn't have minded being there either, although having all the produce right out front is definitely more practical. And I'm happy not to be on the smelly fish street, with all the fresh and dried fish.

The air is full of creative energy. Thadingyut ("Todd-in-jute") Festival, the Burmese Festival of Lights, is the last week of October, and in its honor I plan a week of light-themed yoga classes. Midway through the week, a bearded young Israeli comes to class. He tells me he wanted to do a yoga retreat in Myanmar and couldn't find one so he's going to make this his own personal yoga retreat. He comes to all of the rest of the Light classes.

He's the only student for the last class, a Sunday-morning energizing vinyasa flow with the theme Illuminate Your Day. *Awaken your muscles and brighten your day with this invigorating vinyasa flow,* is the description I gave it.

After the final Om, the Israeli opens his eyes and gives me a huge smile. "Thank you. I do feel awake and brighter. Thank you for this whole retreat. I'm feeling how I wanted to be feeling." And that is a gift to me because it's a reminder that I'm not here for nothing. I was able to pass along the gift that I wanted to: the gift of feeling good.

And then there are the days where I feel off and the tribe of critics in my head come out of hibernation. They resurface during one evening yoga class. My words aren't flowing tonight. They sound forced and awkward to my ears. Through the whole class, the inner critics whisper that I sound unnatural, repetitive, and uninspiring, and the sense of clumsiness must be palpable in the room. But after the class, a lovely French brunette tells me that I have really nice energy, she really liked the class, and she's looking forward to tomorrow morning, and her words are a gift that reminds me that the tribe of inner critics are best ignored.

In November, I start thinking about Christmas, for two reasons. One, my visa expires December 23rd, so I will need to go somewhere outside Myanmar. And two, I definitely do not want to spend another Christmas in Asia. I want to go back to Florida and spend Christmas with Sarah, my sister by heart, and her daughters (aka, my beloved little nieces), and her parents, who always make me feel like part of the family. Sarah invited me months ago and she's excited that I'm coming.

I start looking at plane tickets. I have enough award miles left for a one-way ticket to Miami, and there are plenty of award flight options available. I select one, go through all the additional steps of selecting seats on each flight, etc, and click the Purchase button.

A message appears in the middle of the screen. *We're sorry, the flight you selected is no longer available.*

Darn. One of the flights must have just sold out. I go back to the beginning and try again with a different combination of flights. When I click "Purchase," the same message appears.

That's weird.

I try again. And again, and again, and again. The same message appears every time. *We're sorry, the flight you selected is no longer available.*

There must be a glitch in their system. I wait until the next day and try again. It's a repeat of yesterday.

I try to login to Skype to call American Airlines. I'm locked out because I forgot my password, and trying to reset your Skype password is like trying to break into the Pentagon. Their security questions are impenetrable. I set up a new Skype account and call the airline. I'm on hold for ten minutes and then get disconnected.

Frustrated, I go back to the website. Thinking maybe the Yangon outbound flight is the issue, I try other cities as the departure. Bangkok. Hong Kong. Singapore. Same message every time. *We're sorry, the flight you selected is no longer available.*

I try flights to New York and Chicago instead of Miami. Same failure message.

After many days and God only knows how many hours of this, I'm about to lose my mind. This is unbelievable. It's like giant garage doors have slammed shut on all four sides of me, barring my way in every direction. I look at non-award flights on all airlines. They're all over a thousand dollars for a one-way flight, and there's no way I'm going to pay that when I have award miles sitting in my account waiting to be used.

My poor laptop (once again) narrowly escapes being hurled across the room. I'm seething in anger and frustration like a kettle about to boil.

And then, it finally registers that maybe Life is trying to tell me something. Maybe I'm not meant to go back to the US in December.

But *whhyyyyyy*, Life? I really, *really* don't want to spend this Christmas in Asia. Besides, I need to go somewhere for my visa run. If not Florida, where am I supposed to go instead?

That night, at home in my quiet bedroom, I decide to reframe the question. Not where *should* I go, where do I *want* to go? What does my heart want?

To that question, the answer comes immediately. My heart wants to feel warm and loved and cozy at Christmas. My heart wants to spend Christmas in a place that feels like Christmas, with people who feel like family, with Christmas decorations all around and Christmas music in the air and stockings hung by the chimney with care and, ideally, since I'm listing everything, snow on the ground.

With this vision in my head, the perfect solution presents itself immediately. A few weeks ago, my French-Italian friend Sebastien happened to mention that he's going back to France to spend the holidays with his family, and he casually told me I'm welcome to come. We've been friends for years and I stayed with his family for a few days when I was twenty-three. (That's now fifteen years ago, yikes.) His family was so nice, especially his mom, and throughout the years she and I still ask Seb about each other from time to time. Besides, I love France. I hadn't given the invitation a second thought when he brought it up because I thought I was going to Florida, but the idea of Christmas with Seb and his family suddenly seems incredibly appealing.

I message him, explain the situation, and tell him I was thinking of going to France…is his invitation still open?

He replies immediately, *FRANCE! Come to our place, I'll be there mid-December to end of Jan.*

Me: *Are you sure your parents won't mind? As it's Christmas and all, maybe they want to be just with family.*

He writes back, *You are family!*

His unhesitant reply makes my heart happy. We work out the

details. I find a cheap Yangon–Lyon flight, so I book it with cash. American Airlines' system won't let me book the return flight with miles, so I give up. It's better anyway leaving it open-ended. I have other friends in France I could maybe visit afterwards, or maybe I should go back to Spain … or maybe somewhere in Europe I haven't been before. Who knows, everything in Europe is so close, I can figure that out later. The important thing is, my Christmas plans are booked!

It occurs to me that Julien is in France, so I should let him know I'm going there. But it's late and I'm tired; that can wait till tomorrow. I curl up happily in bed and drift off into a sound sleep.

When I wake up the next morning, there's a text waiting from none other than Julien. Our texts had gotten fun and flirty for a while, but it's been over a month since I last heard from him.

Hello jolie Sonya. How are you?

Nice timing! I write back: *I'm good, how are you? Yesterday I bought a ticket to France for Christmas!*

Him: *Noooooooooo you'll be in France for Christmas! Good news!! You know, it would be a beautiful chance to see you!!! I would be delighted.* 😊

I write that I'd love to see him again too, if he has time, and that I'm going to spend Christmas with friends near Lyon and after that, play it by ear and explore a little.

He writes that Lyon is wonderful at Christmastime, and he'll make time to see me again, with pleasure. He lives in the southwest of France in a town called Pau. But he can come see me pretty much anywhere. And I am welcome anytime.

He adds: *Very nice coincidence that you're coming to France.*

Me: *And very nice coincidence that you wrote me just a couple hours after I bought the ticket. I was going to write you today but you beat me.*

Him: *Spiritual connection.* 😊

Over the next few days we put a plan together to meet the end of December and spend New Year's together, and he'll take the first week of January off to show me the region. And I'm no longer disappointed that I couldn't get a ticket to Florida.

CHAPTER 28

Life is not what you expect.
-ILAIYARAAJA

By the middle of November, the kitchen transformation is finished. The walls are a gorgeous pale teal, the custom wood and iron shelves I commissioned from the carpenter have been installed, a vase of fresh flowers sits on the table in front of the window, and I've bought two cute gas burners and nice cookware and dishes. It's absolutely delightful to cook in here, and to eat breakfast up on the rooftop, looking out over the pine-tree-covered hills that rise up into the morning mist.

My bedframe is finished, my clothes are hanging happily on their custom wood rack, and I've started painting the bathroom. The mattresses have arrived but Emily still hasn't moved in. She says Steve asked her to wait until they get the approval from immigration. She's waiting quite patiently, because it's now almost three weeks since the start of the lease and Steve and Hayma still haven't managed to assemble all the documents for immigration. At least her hotel is only costing her $5 a day.

It's late November. Everything is flowing along beautifully and I'm existing in a state of idyllic happiness, feeling perfectly aligned and blissfully in love with my house. And then, BOOM! Life hurls a curveball.

Ingyin, Pon, and another friend of theirs are in town for Ingyin's birthday weekend. We're all in the car on our way to lunch when Steve calls to give me the news: the Burmese government has decided Emily and I can't live in our house. Steve and Hayma finally took our documents to the Immigration office this morning and unfortunately, their timing wasn't great. The day prior, two regrettable events transpired in Kalaw: a foreign tourist was hit by a car and seriously injured. And Mark, the Belgian owner of a local hotel, suffered a heart attack while riding a bike and passed away. He was sixty-two.

These unusual events have set the immigration officers on edge. They're skittish now and don't want to take responsibility for signing off on the approval for us foreigners to take up residence here. They've decreed that we can't stay at the house until we get the approval from the immigration office in Taunggyi, Shan State's capital, and the Taunggyi office is closed this week for the holiday. If I were to ignore them and they were to catch me staying at the house, there would be serious repercussions not only for me but also for Hayma, who as my official sponsor is responsible for me while I'm in the country.

The news of sudden temporary eviction comes as quite a shock, but it pales next to the news of Mark's passing. I knew Mark because I stayed at his hotel for a few days my first month in Kalaw. He was a nice man, serious but friendly, married to a Burmese woman, spoke fluent Burmese, owned two goats, made amazing crepes and homemade jams.

As for the news of sudden homelessness, it would be unwelcome at any point, but this moment seems to be precisely the absolute worst possible time for it. This week is the Firework Festival in Kalaw and almost every hotel is fully booked. On top of that, Ingyin is supposed to stay with me this week after her friends leave.

Luckily, there are a handful of rooms remaining here and there. The dreamy bed and breakfast Kalaw Vista has a room available for the next two nights. Gloria Hotel has a room for the two nights after that, and Natureland Two has a room for the following two nights. Ingyin and I decide this is a new adventure. Hotel hopping!

Our hotel-hopping adventure turns out to be a great experience. Our three hotels are all comfortable and beautiful; each charming in their own ways. We have a great time discovering these new places, getting acquainted with the nice staff, and of course I take the opportunity to promote Kalaw Yoga to all of them and hang up yoga posters everywhere. So far, the temporary eviction has turned out to be not so bad at all.

This same week, Ingyin and I discover a place of magic. I found out about it a couple weeks earlier thanks to Emily's jaw-dropping Instagram photos of stunning views of clouds and mountains from a pagoda high above Kalaw. She hiked there with Steve and the kids while I was out of town. The pagoda is called Ma Naw Hla, (pronounced "Manola," which is how I'll henceforth be referring to it because that's how I spell it in my mind).

"Where is this place?" I asked Emily.

She showed me on Google Maps, explaining that the map doesn't actually have the right location, and it's a long hike from the location on the map, just follow this trail...

So one afternoon, Ingyin and I set out to find Manola. We take my motorbike as far as it will go, along a winding path up the mountain that begins as smooth concrete and farther along becomes a bumpy dirt road filled with big motorbike-jostling rocks. When we reach the point where the path angles into a steep uphill incline, we park the bike and continue by foot. The trek to our destination takes about twenty minutes.

There are no other humans around. The late afternoon sun bathes everything in soft golden light. Spread out around the mountaintop are assorted statues and spires of white and gold and seafoam green. A regal white Buddha in a gold cloak stands facing four seafoam green nagas (snakes) with bared teeth and outstretched tongues. Off on his own, a slim golden Buddha sits in meditation facing the mountain vista with a serene smile, framed by pink bougainvillea and sheltered by his own personal roof. There's a meditation platform for humans too, also sheltered by a roof. Around us and the Buddhas and the nagas, for 360 degrees, are endless mountains and clouds, a calm blue sky, and a sense of deep peace. It's a place where dreams come to be born.

I wander around exploring, silently intoxicated by the beauty and serenity. When I find Ingyin, I see on her face that she feels the same. Her eyes glow.

"I love it here," she says.

Manola becomes my mountain sanctuary. I come back many times afterwards, and never once do I see another soul here. I learn that the real magic is at sunrise, when the mountains are bathed in an ocean of clouds and celestial rays reach down to meet them.

The morning after Ingyin leaves, I meet a sweet Burmese woman at breakfast. Her name is Mwae and she and her husband own the Natureland Two hotel. She has an adorable chubby-cheeked one-year-old baby boy. I tell her everything I love about the room and the property, and about my struggles in trying to add Burmese text to the yoga flyer. She generously offers to help me with the Burmese font and says they'll move me to another bigger room for the same price.

At noon, one of the staff comes to take me and my luggage to the new room. It turns out to be not just a room; it's a small two-story villa. It's amazing. A small flight of stairs leads to the sitting area downstairs, and another flight of stairs leads up to the spacious bedroom with a sloped ceiling, and the bathroom has both a bathtub and a separate shower. The villa is decorated with potted ZZ plants and cute umbrellas, and the floor is beautiful polished wide-plank wood. Again I feel like I've come home. It makes me feel so happy, tears of gratitude come to my eyes. I send Ingyin pictures and she wants to come back.

After the holiday week, Steve and Hayma go to the Taunggyi Immigration Office. I plan to go with them but Steve says no, that would make it worse, I should definitely not go. I can't imagine why, but he's the one who's lived here six years, so I stay home and hope for the best.

But they come back with bad news. Taunggyi isn't willing to issue the authorization either. They've referred the matter to the head of immigration for all of Shan State, and he's out of office for the entire month of December. They said absolutely no one can stay in the house right now. "They were pissed that you signed the lease," Steve adds, the inference being that, *if you hadn't signed the lease they might have approved it, and this is all your fault.* "And Hayma may be in trouble now, and probably even Luis can't stay at the farm or at the other house."

Apparently Steve had told me not to sign the lease—another detail I don't remember hearing—but I signed it because when I went to see the village quartermaster for his stamp of approval on said lease, he told me to sign it. Being that he's the local authority and it was his stamp of approval we were asking for, signing it seemed a reasonable thing to do. It seems like an odd detail for the Burmese authorities to be upset about, but if I had gone to Taunggyi, I could have humbly apologized for my ignorant mistake and possibly talked them out of their anger and into approval for me to reside in the house I'm already paying for. I don't bother saying that aloud, because Steve is a tight ball of stress and exhaustion, and not only because of this news. He's suddenly facing a similar situation of his own, because his landlord has just sold the café/house—breaking their lease—and he and his kids have to be out by the end of February. That's in less than three months, smack in the middle of high season.

This new development is unsettling, and confusing, because my house gave me so much pure joy, and I still can't shake that feeling of inner knowing that I was supposed to be there. And what about the auspicious shooting star? Was I wrong about everything? Was it all a mistake? I thought I would save money moving into the house, and now I have to pay for a house and a hotel, but that's the not the worst of it. The most unsettling factor is that Steve, Emily, and Hayma blame me for this situation. They never say so outright, but from that day on I feel the subtle undercurrent.

It makes me uncomfortable. Do I deserve the blame? Maybe I do. Maybe I didn't listen closely enough. But would it have changed anything if I hadn't signed the lease, if I hadn't moved in? We could also blame Steve for not being more clear, we could blame Steve and Hayma for taking so long to assemble the documents for immigration, or we could blame the Shan immigration officials. Or we could blame no one, and accept that it is what it is.

That's what I decide to do. And I don't stop loving my house. I keep painting, because I don't want to leave this project unfinished and because it's giving me joy to paint, even if I'm not allowed to live here. Maybe I'm just supposed to make the house beautiful for someone else.

Chapter 29

We travel the endless corridors of our mind
until one day we find a pathway that leads us to our heart.
— Toni Carmine Salerno

November 2018

When the Universe jerks the rug out from under you, it usually sends other forms of consolation to make up for it, and this time, it sends consolation from all sides. There is Julien, who's texting me with vacation plans and saying he's looking forward to spending those days with me. To get to him, I'll be taking the train from Lyon, which is on the opposite side of France from where he lives. I'm going to stop and visit friends in Albi on the way, and he volunteers to come pick me up there. That will mean a three-hour drive for him each way, and thus it's a very chivalrous offer. His messages fill me with happiness and excitement, but a kind of calm excitement. I'm looking forward to seeing him again too.

Another consolation is Natureland's sweet owner Mwae, who becomes a dear friend. I might have stayed there for the next month in my little two-story villa if not for the fact that the shower wasn't hot enough. So I continue my hotel hopping, but when I check out, instead of charging me the $20/night she had quoted me, she charges me $14/night, and I recognize this as love.

And another is from my soul twin Nesha, who a few days later feels inspired to pull an oracle card for me. She sends me photos of the card and its corresponding interpretation. It's from the Gaia oracle deck and the card is called *Sacred Earth Mother: A Message of Love.* The first line says: *We travel the endless corridors of our mind until one day we find a pathway that leads us to our heart.*

I read that just before falling asleep. At 4 a.m., I wake up with the sense that my soul has a message to relay. My soul rarely speaks to me directly, but when it decides there's something I need to know, it follows a ritual of waking me up between 3 and 4 a.m. It keeps sleep out of reach, so I'm left with the options of lying in bed tossing and turning, or getting up, sitting in meditation, and waiting for the message. As usual, I don't feel like getting out of my comfortable bed at this inconvenient hour, but eventually I give in, find a seated position on the floor, and wait.

Nesha's message of love floats back into my mind. Other thoughts float along with it. I think of how often I've thought of love recently because I notice it around me so often, in big and small ways, all the time. I think of this deep desire I've had for so long to find the man of my dreams, my true romantic love, and how I've always wished for my story to have a perfect fairy-tale ending … and new beginning … him arriving to sweep me off my feet and us starting the next beautiful chapter of our lives together. And I see that even though that I didn't find love in that way yet, I did find Love.

I found Love everywhere. I notice it around me every day. It's in the sweetness of the smiles of the people in Kalaw I pass on the street, in the moments their smiling eyes meet mine and a spark of loving goodwill travels felt but unseen from their hearts to mine. It's in the aura of the girls at the café who greet me every day with warm hugs and bright smiles. It's in the hearts and voices and messages of my friends, physically on the other side of the world but always present in my heart. It's in the gestures of the hotel staff at breakfast, who bring me avocados as treats just because they know I love avocados. It's in the stunning flowers that unfurl as beautiful surprises as the seasons pass. It's in the trees in India that grow in the solid rockface of steep ravines, their sturdy roots wrapping giant boulders in a tight embrace. It's in the chorus of birds chirping outside my window. It's in every sunrise and sunset. It's in the way everything always works out perfectly. It's all around, always, all the time. I'm surrounded by Love. And this Love is so much bigger than the love I wished to find.

I'm sitting here in stillness and a warm glow starts in my heart and spreads through me, and I'm basking in happiness and awareness of all the love around me and a sense of being filled, of nothing missing, and somewhere in some deep level of my being there's a shift. All of a sudden, the idea of finding the man of my dreams seems unimportant. If he comes along, that will be wonderful I'm sure, but only if he makes me happier than I am already. And I'm already very happy right now here alone, surrounded by love all the time and just getting to do whatever I want. I really love all this time to myself to do whatever I want, actually.

I sit basking in love and contentment a while longer, and my soul shows me that if the love of my life does come along, I won't have to be tortured by a fear of losing him. Because if he ever does leave, it will be okay. Even if he leaves, I'll still be surrounded by love; this Love that will always be here. This immense Universal Love.

The next day, my little sister posts this on Facebook:

> "To love and be loved is the greatest happiness of existence." —Sydney Smith
> Don't think for an instant that if you're single you can't have this happiness. I had one of those "aha" moments today. For years, one of my greatest fears has been of losing people that I love. This has caused me to sometimes show excessive anxiety, neediness, even desperation sometimes. But I see that it doesn't have to be this way, because I already have everything I need. I am loved more than I can ever comprehend by the only One who will ever love me perfectly. The One who will truly give me a happy ever after—the only One who can make those imaginary fairy tale endings reality. Because He loved me with *everything* He has, and I want to love Him with everything I have. THAT is the greatest happiness of existence—for now and eternity!

Her words are describing the same message delivered to me in my meditation, but hers is from a Christian viewpoint, because she is a devout Christian. She's on the other side of the world, in Florida. This Love, it's whispering to both of us, offering us both the same gift, not prejudiced by our different religious/spiritual beliefs.

God is Love, the Bible says. I think that says it all.

Now that I've decided that finding the man of my dreams isn't that important, Nesha sends me a link to a soulmate tarot card reading. This reading is a recorded video online, which in my skeptical opinion seems a highly unlikely way to deliver an accurate reading to God-knows-how-many diverse strangers who choose to watch said video, but Nesha says it was eerily spot-on for her and she wants me to try it. So I try it.

It's a Pick-a-Card reading, so the reading isn't the same for everyone. There are three cards to choose from. You pick one and then watch the interpretation for that card. I click the middle card, and that sends me to a new video where a dark-haired woman with a charismatic presence and an attractive accent pulls more cards and interprets them. She says my soulmate and I are both doing a lot of inner work and we both made a decision to trust our intuition more. (I can't speak for my soulmate, but that's true for me.) She continues in her calm, resonant voice.

"There is a need for you to surrender something, for a realization of some truth about yourself, some deeper truth that's below your ego. There's a need to search for deeper truths. You might be able to connect to this other person psychically, and you need to communicate with your own soul better to understand it more. You need to stand in your own power, develop your creativity. You're a strong, creative person and you need to develop that more. You're looking for an equal, someone who can match you in strength. You're at peace with someone else's imperfections because you're at peace with your own." (This feels true now. It wouldn't have not so long ago. It reminds me of the half-light, half-dark Buddha from India.)

"When you no longer settle, when you decide 'this is what I want,' it's gonna come. You'll only attract someone when your energies match. There's a very strong spiritual/psychic link between the two of you. You're open to commitment. The other person is facing some karma. Maybe it's a person you already know. Looking forward, there's going to be some ending that will make you stronger. You might be facing some patterns that aren't healthy. They want you as much as you want them. There's going to be some transformation that makes you much stronger. When you come together, there's going to be a sense of peace and calm and you'll be to one another like a refuge. Your meeting will be fated and you are asked to develop as much equilibrium and calm as possible."

I can't deny that her words about me and my soul resonate as truth. But we'll see about all the soulmate parts.

December 9th is the Kalaw Half-Marathon and Nature gives us a gorgeous day for it. The course takes us on an adventurous, wildly scenic route up hills, over rocks, past buffalos, and through six-foot-tall grasses. My training pays off. I feel good and the hills don't destroy me. The best part of the race is somewhere around halfway where thirty smiling grade school kids in green and white uniforms are lined up along the side of the road, cheering enthusiastically and handing out high fives. The second-best part of the race is that I teach post-run recovery yoga afterward, a sequence I designed after extensive research specifically to diminish post-run soreness, and it's so effective that I experience no muscle pain at all after this race. In my opinion, that qualifies as a small miracle. Yoga rocks.

After the race, I'm finally tired of hotel hopping and so I come home to my fairytale hotel. They give me a new room, a spacious second floor one with a vaulted ceiling, which becomes my new favorite. There's now fresh guava juice in the morning and an outdoor fire at night. Because Ohmar knows I'm also paying the rent for the house I can't live in, she gives me an even more discounted rate which is so far below their regular rates that I won't disclose it publicly, and again I feel the presence of love.

After weeks of feeling the unspoken tension under the surface, I have a heart-to-heart with Steve and Hayma. It clears the air and I think we all feel lighter afterward. Nonetheless, I sense that maybe the time has come for our paths to separate. With Emily there, I'm not really needed anymore. They can easily find a second yoga teacher. I love Kalaw, and I want to stay in Kalaw. But I only want to stay in Kalaw if I can live in my house.

I also don't want the responsibility for all of my actions falling on Hayma anymore, so I brainstorm other ways of obtaining my next business visa and other options for putting down long-term roots. I consider coming back on a long-term meditation visa. I propose a partnership to Ingyin: I'll buy a house in her name, remodel and resell it, and pay her commission. She tells me I'm too eager and optimistic and maybe later this could be a good option, but it's not the time yet.

This is all true. *Slowly, slowly,* as they say in India and Myanmar.

So this phase of my time in Kalaw draws to a close with an uncertain future.

A few days before I leave for France, I go back up to Manola for the sunrise. This time, it's pure unfiltered magic. The entrance gate is enveloped in mist. The clouds are an ocean beyond the roaring nagas. Cherry blossoms are blooming near the Buddha statues. When I'm driving back down the mountain, the narrow winding path rounds a corner and suddenly before me is a perfect view of Kalaw far below, nestled in the valley between the mountains. The white hazy clouds hover between the town's hills, tall buildings and trees peeking up between them. I park the bike to stop and stare. It looks unreal. It looks like a scene from a fairy tale. It's the most beautiful thing I've ever seen. The beauty flows into my heart, mingles with my love for this place, and wells up as tears in my eyes. I'll carry this memory with me forever.

The day before I leave, I finish painting. I didn't paint the entire house, but I finished what I started: my bedroom, the kitchen, the bathroom, and the first-floor living area. The sense of completion and immense satisfaction is my reward. It looks fresh and bright and renewed. It's ready for something, for someone.

CHAPTER 30

There are deeper workings of the spirit at play
than the ones that appear on the surface.
- SRI SRI SHUDDHAANANDAA BRACHMACHARI

December 2018

I arrive at the home of Sebastien's family December 23rd and waiting for me is exactly what my heart was craving. Outside, the ground is covered with snow and inside, the Christmas tree sparkles with lights. His family welcomes me with warm hospitality and I sink into instant comfort. His mother, Nicole, is as sweet as I remember, and his Italian father, Renato, has a wonderful chill, happy vibe. Renato drinks wine every day and I drink wine with him. Nicole prepares copious, delicious meals and steadfastly refuses to ever let me help with food preparation or wash a single dish.

Seb's little brother Gilles, who was sixteen years old the last time I saw him—the time he, Seb, and I took a high-speed road trip through France, Italy, and Monaco (high-speed because that's the only speed at which Seb knows how to drive)—is now grown up and married, with an adorable one-year-old daughter named Lana whose playful, fun-loving smile can melt hearts.

For this holiday week, I become the laziest person in the world. I spend my days eating, drinking, and binge-watching Netflix with Seb. The only non-lazy thing I do is go running with Seb every day, even though it's freezing and the ground is covered with snow. He graciously matches his pace to mine even though he could easily have left me in the dust. At the end he always sprints off for the last few hundred meters, taking off with the graceful, effortless power of a gazelle.

And here, I will pause and explain the background story of Sebastien and me, because as life would have it, he played an important role in my spiritual journey.

Along the winding path of the sixteen years since we met, we were sometimes just friends and he was sometimes in love with me and I was sometimes in love with him, but only for a very short time were we in love with each other at the same time. I don't know what I was for him, but he for me was the one who broke my heart open so more light could get in. The reason I know this beyond any doubt is another wildly magic "coincidence."

It was January 2016. I hadn't seen Seb in many years, but we reconnected one weekend when he was living in Toronto and I was there for work. He had changed since I last saw him. His aura was different. He was calmer, happier, more relaxed, more mature. And funnier. Physically, he had always been cute and athletic, but sometime during the years since we last saw each other he had become an elite triathlete and his body was now six feet of hard, graceful muscle. I felt good around him. And attracted to him, like one magnet to another.

That weekend, all the stars were aligned. Everything sparkled: the city, my work event, the time with Seb and his charming friend Cristina, who I met that day and who was destined to become a good friend. All weekend, everything felt perfect.

That was the start of our four-month long-distance romance. It was lovely, and he was sweet, wonderful, and loving. I felt loved and free at the same time, which was something no man had ever made me feel before, and it felt amazing. But one day, I just wasn't into it anymore.

The shift wasn't completely out of the blue. There had been a few occasions where we didn't connect, where we were on different wavelengths. But it was sudden.

We were in different countries, so I broke it off over the phone.

I prefaced this ending by, "The most important thing is our friendship, right?" and then announced that I just wanted to be friends.

He reacted very coolly and calmly. He said of course he understood, and it was totally fine, and yes, we would still be friends.

And that would have been perfect, except a couple weeks later I changed my mind and decided that in fact, I didn't want to just be friends. But now, he didn't want more than friendship. I had assumed I could get him back, since I thought I knew how he felt about me. He had told me the most beautiful things. It had felt like real, rare, unconditional love, and I took it for granted that his love would always be there waiting if I wanted it.

But, to my shock, it wasn't. After I ended it, his heart had changed. Or maybe it froze. This, of course, made me want him more. But I couldn't get him back. As the weeks stretched on and he remained unavailable, I tried everything I could think of, including kicking my ego to the curb, baring my soul, and telling him my true feelings. He wavered and gave me mixed signals for a while, but in the end it was clear that it was over for him, and that shattered me.

My heart has been broken before, more than once, and I know my pattern. I cry nonstop for a day or two, thinking I might die from the pain, and then I pick myself up and get on with life. But this time it was different. I cried nonstop for a couple days, but when the tears let up, I found myself trapped in a strange pit of heartbreak and desolation. All the joy in life seemed to have evaporated along with his love.

Even at the time, this made no sense to me. My brain repeatedly told my heart that it was ridiculous to carry on like this over a man, especially a man you broke up with a few weeks ago and might very well break up with again if he gave you another chance. But my heart had become convinced that Sebastien's love was essential to my happiness and my brain couldn't talk my heart out of it.

My heart's certainty was cemented by a reading I got from Rose the psychic medium a few weeks later. Rose and I became friends later, but this was only the second time I'd seen her. I don't get readings often and I didn't seek this one out; it was at a charity event and to get a reading was the polite thing to do. When Rose asked me what I wanted to know, I said, "I don't know. Do you notice anything?"

She said, "Is there a man in your life?"

I laughed, "Uhh, no, not really."

She replied, "Is he blond?"

I was very surprised. First of all, I just said no. Second, Sebastien is blond (rare for a man outside Scandinavia these days), and so am I, and it's something we joke about all the time because we're both constantly doing ditzy things.

"Yes," I admitted.

"His energy is here," she told me. (That was funny too, because one unusual thing while we were dating is that even when we were separated by thousands of miles, I often felt that his energy was there with me. He told me once, "I'm always with you," and strangely it felt like he was.)

She continued, "He looks a little like you. You look like you could be brother and sister." (Even more eerily spot-on, because in one of the last photos we had taken together, I thought we looked like brother and sister, which was mildly disturbing.)

Rose told me, "This is going to sound cheesy, but it feels like you are twin flames. I see that you have three chapters together. I don't know which chapter you're in, if all three are in this life, or past or future lives, but there are three."

When we were younger, Sebastien once told me that I was the female version of him, and so Rose's words convinced me that he was my twin flame and we were meant to be together. I didn't actually know much about twin flames, but I assumed they were like soul mates who were a lot alike, like twin soul mates, between whom love would burn brightly and passionately, destined to last forever. It seemed very mystical and beautiful and fated.

So, fueled by the certainty that we were meant to be together and I had messed it up, my sadness went on. I was usually okay during the day because work and life kept me busy, but in the stillness of nighttime, the grief would resurface. At night, the sadness was a huge gaping hole of emptiness inside me and I had nothing to fill it with. For three months straight, I woke up in the middle of almost every night and sobbed like my heart was broken.

One night, when I was home alone crying for approximately the 87th night in a row, I finally decided to seek an answer from the Universe. I wanted a clear and specific answer in writing, so I chose to select a book to open to a random page. I went and got *Eat Pray Love* off the bookshelf. I'd read the book once several years earlier and although I'd forgotten the details of its contents, I remembered that it was full of remarkable insights and spiritual wisdom. (In case you've never read the book, for a quick background, our real-life protagonist Elizabeth gets out of an unhappy marriage, has an intense love affair that ends painfully and leaves her very depressed and stressed out, and then takes off to spend a year in Italy, India, and Indonesia exploring different sides of herself. Also, FYI, the book is much better than the movie.)

With *Eat Pray Love* in my hands, I sat down on my living room floor and asked out loud, "Why is it so hard for me to get over this guy?" and opened the book somewhere towards the middle.

The random page my fingers opened to is when Elizabeth is in India at an ashram and she's been in a horrible mood for days, unable to meditate, angry at the world, and can't stop obsessing about her ex-boyfriend. She's having a conversation with her friend Richard.

Richard tells Elizabeth something beautiful, and she starts crying and tells him, "I think the reason it's so hard for me to get over this guy is because I seriously believed David was my soul mate."

And Richard replies, "He probably was. Your problem is you don't understand what that word means. People think a soul mate is your perfect fit, and that's what everyone wants. But a true soul mate is a mirror, the person that shows you everything that's holding you back ... they tear down your walls and smack you awake. But to live with a soul mate forever? Nah. Too painful. Soul mates, they come into your life just to reveal another layer of yourself to you, and then they leave. And thank God for it. Your problem is, you just can't let this one go."

And then a little farther down on the page, Richard tells Elizabeth the beautiful line about how David's purpose was to break her heart open so new light could get in.

There were 334 pages in the book, and I opened to that one. To the perfect, specific answer to my question.

I reread the page a few times to let the words sink in. I had thought Sebastien was my soulmate, my twin flame, the man of my life, but maybe we weren't meant to be together. Maybe he was my soulmate, destined to play an important role in my life, just not the role I thought.

When I read the sentence about her heart being broken so new light could get in, I understood that this is what my heartbreak did for me. But first it let new light get out. After Seb didn't want me back, I found inside my heart the kind of love that feels unconditional, the kind of love that makes you selfless without even trying, that makes you want to give without caring what you get back. It felt good to have that inside, even though it hurt that I couldn't give it to him because he didn't want it. But the hurt softened me, and made me look beyond my own busy life, and I started noticing people around me who needed love in little ways, and since I had all this love to give, I started giving little pieces of it away whenever I could. I saw that the little pieces of love turned into happiness when I gave them away. They made the receiver happier and they made me happier too. The light that seeped out through the cracks brought more light back in.

I went on to research twin flames, and I learned that they weren't exactly what I had thought. Twin flame love, according to some sources, isn't necessarily romantic love, although romance is often involved. It's not necessarily a strong physical attraction, although that's often part of the connection. The most important feature of a twin flame encounter is that it is likely to lead to a massive and probably very uncomfortable internal shake-up, which can be the catalyst for a deeper understanding of yourself and the meaning of divine love. It is said that the greatest gift offered by a twin flame relationship is the opportunity to experience and express unconditional Love.

My sadness and heartache disappeared that night, replaced with awe and wonder that the great mysterious unseen Powers Beyond our Comprehension out there in the universe would take the time to pay attention to little me and my question and guide me to a crystal clear, detailed, perfect answer. And the clarity of that answer shifted me into a place of acceptance that I wasn't meant to be with Sebastien forever. My pain and sadness over losing him was gone.

It was from that night that I started to really suspect that there is a clear and present unseen Force of benevolence operating in this world, and because I don't understand what it is or how it works, I call it magic.

Exactly one week later I met Alex.

And if you're wondering, was it awkward for you to see Sebastien after that? No, it wasn't. I saw him many times afterwards, since I was often back in Toronto for work. We had closed the door to a romantic future, but our friendship remained a beautiful thing.

It's Sebastien who puts the idea of Portugal in my mind, during this Christmas holiday. We're talking about my plans to start a retreat center. I'm tired of just thinking and talking about it. I want to take action. I don't feel ready—or financially equipped—to start something big, but I like the idea of starting with a small bed and breakfast. I had thought Myanmar could be the place for this, until this recent issue with my house. So now I need to find a new place.

"Portugal is a good place to buy property as a foreigner right now," Sebastien tells me. "It's really cheap, and they have some crazy tax incentives. Cristina moved there a few months ago and she's working as a realtor. You might want to talk to her."

Cristina is the friend I met that memorable 2016 day in Toronto. She's a remarkable person and an enchanting human being. Portuguese by blood and raised in France, she's fluent in French, Portuguese, English, and Spanish. She's warm, vibrant, intelligent, capable, professional, energetic, fun-loving, and full of joy. She is the ideal realtor.

I don't reach out to her immediately, but I start researching Portugal and its property investment laws.

CHAPTER 31

Don't move the way fear makes you move.
Move the way love makes you move.
Move the way joy makes you move.
- OSHO

After a week of holiday decadence with Sebastien and his family, I take the train to the other side of France to meet two girlfriends in Albi, because that's where they live and it's conveniently on the way to Pau. Julien has arranged to meet us that evening at the main plaza in front of the cathedral. And by the way, I don't know if you've noticed, but if the B in Albi jumped out of line and parked itself in front of the A, it would spell Bali. As if Albi is Bali, revisited. I like that funny little synchronicity.

Now that the day has arrived, I'm nervous. I haven't seen this man in a year. What if we don't have the same connection? What if he's not attracted to me anymore? What if we have nothing to say to each other?

We accidentally run into each other earlier than expected, inside the Albi cathedral. I've just walked in with my girlfriends Cloe and Eyenie, and we see that a wedding is going on, far up at the front of the large cathedral. Then Eyenie nudges me and says, "Is that your guy?"

I look to my left to see a salt-and-pepper-haired man in a gray coat walking towards us, smiling. It takes me a second to be sure it's Julien. In winter clothes and the cathedral lighting and without the

Balinese tan, he looks a little different than I remembered. Still handsome, but a little older. I probably look older too. We *are* older. But his smile hasn't changed, and there's no awkwardness in our reunion. I introduce him and the girls, and when he steps away to take pictures of the cathedral's gleaming interior Eyenie whispers to me with raised eyebrows and a sparkle in her eye that maybe this wedding is a sign.

Outside, we watch the Christmas sound and light show that's projected on the side of the cathedral. The show is spectacular and I'm excited that this Frenchman is here, right next to me. I'm also secretly a little tense, even in spite of the mulled wine I'm sipping. Outwardly we're all acting normal and smiling and laughing, but I wonder if he feels the same secret tension I do.

After a little more socializing, Julien and I say goodbye to the girls. It's time to head to our next destination: the Chinese lantern festival in Gaillac.

Inside his car, a gorgeous bouquet of coral-tipped yellow roses is waiting for me, and now that we're alone in the car and talking easily, my tension starts to melt away. When he takes my hand in his, a current of energy travels up my arm into the rest of my body and I feel the connection; that connection we had in Bali. He must feel it too, because he pauses to look me in the eye. Then he kisses me, and the bubble of Balinese happiness reforms itself and shimmers around us, and that's when I completely relax.

At the festival, our comfortable happiness is enhanced by delicious food and fantastic local Gaillac wines, served to us at booths sheltered by white tents. The night is chilly; I hold onto Julien's arm for warmth. The lanterns turn out to be an entire imperial Chinese city constructed of glowing fabric sculptures, bright with light and color, spread out over four hectares. We walk past multi-tiered pagodas, forests of pandas, peacocks with blazing capes of blue and turquoise, stately Chinese women striding through markets, an enormous red snake with teeth bared and intense eyes, and a statuesque Chinese dancer who captivates us with her elegance as she spins slowly, a rippling violet scarf swirling gracefully around her. On the souvenir wine glasses our wine was served in, the name of the festival is written. It's *Féeries de Chine*; Enchanted China.

I love being inside the enchanted China with this Frenchman whose energy is calm, open, and positive and who comfortably expresses his genuine admiration of everything. His presence feels good. He makes me feel good.

We stay in Cordes-sur-Ciel that night. Cordes-sur-Ciel is ancient, a fortified city on a hill built 800 years ago, and our bed and breakfast is almost as ancient. We walk through the thick wooden entrance doors and are transported back to the 14th century. A winding stone staircase leads us up to our room. In a tall hollow in the staircase wall, a medieval knight in full body armor and a red cape stands at attention. The walls of our suite are thick solid stone, but it's furnished with modern comforts, and the bathroom with its luxurious Italian fixtures is worthy of any self-respecting spa. The king-sized bed is soft and inviting.

We discover that the physical connection between us is as intense as it was a year ago. Our lips and skin and bodies come together and the world dissolves and my consciousness splinters into a thousand bright glittering pieces that shoot out into the cosmos, and when the world resolidifies and I come back to this realm, every cell in my body is lighter. I'm as light as a cloud and my mind is as light as a cloud and when I open my eyes, everything in the room has become subtly more beautiful, and there are no problems left in the world.

Eventually we fall asleep, snuggled together like two spoons, my back against his belly and his arm wrapped around me.

The next day we drive to Biarritz. In all the times I've been to France, I've never been here—in fact, somehow I'd never even heard of this idyllic place until Julien mentioned it, but everyone in France knows of Biarritz. It's a city on the Basque coast, half an hour from the Spanish border, where the Atlantic ocean meets the southwest corner of France and the central north of Spain. Everything here is classy but charming, without trying too hard, and the waves along its coast are dotted with surfers. Basque-style houses are prevalent, with signature half-timbering and colorful shutters and gable roofs. Picture-perfect sidewalk cafés are everywhere and smiling, well-dressed people fill the tables and mingle in the streets. It's the day before New Year's Eve and the air is festive.

We arrive just as the sun is about to set. We walk straight to the beach and watch as the sun sinks slowly from a pink and orange sky into the silky pale blue sea, its reflection painting a stripe of pink gold across the water that stretches directly towards us like a celestial spotlight. To our left, the mountains along the coast wrap around the sea, forming a cove in the distance. To our right, the smooth caramel sand forms a wide, spectacular beach and the ocean beyond it is a silvery pale aqua. Surfers coast on long white tipped waves toward the shore. Behind them an ivory-colored castle sits on a stretch of rock overlay above the ocean.

Okay, technically it's not a castle. It's a large mansion built in the late 1800s which very much resembles a castle. Close enough for me. I have the surreal feeling that I've walked into a European fairytale. We've seen the enchanted China and now we're in the enchanted France. Or maybe this is heaven.

After sunset, the Christmas lights come on all over town. Julien has a holiday apartment in the center of everything, a seven-minute walk from the beach and right next to Les Halles, the world's most beautiful place to buy groceries. Inside a warehouse-sized building with vaulted ceilings, large stands laden with picture-perfect fresh produce, fresh flowers, croissants, baguettes, quiches, cheese (so many different kinds of cheese!), meats, fresh pasta, spices, and desserts are manned by friendly independent vendors. Along one wall are little bars offering crepes and galettes and coffees and *vin chaud* and all kinds of other deliciousness, and a smaller building next door houses the seafood market. The vendors are friendly and cheerful, with the air of loving life.

This is definitely heaven.

I learn that Julien cooks, effortlessly and very well. He flambees scallops and serves them accompanied with champagne, raspberries and foie gras. In the morning he wakes up before me and by the time I get out of bed, a tantalizing breakfast of fruits and fresh croissants, pastries, and crepes from the bakery around the corner is waiting on the dining room table. During the day, the streets are filled with the music of live bands in cafés and we join the crowds milling and sipping mulled wine. At night, the front of the cathedral becomes a canvas for the nightly sound and light show, like the one we saw in Albi, equally spectacular.

We spend our New Year's Eve together, in his apartment, and there's nowhere else I want to be.

It's 2019. From Biarritz, it's only a two-hour drive to Bilbao, so one day we visit the Guggenheim Bilbao. (After that odd serendipity of four months ago, we must.) I walk through the steel curves of *A Matter of Time* and take photos of Julien under the giant spider. We visit tapas bars and marvel at the inexpensiveness of Spanish wine and savor delicious tapas.

One day he says something about himself being old.

"How old are you?" I ask.

"Fifty-three," he answers promptly. "I'm with a girl who's fifteen years younger than me. That held me back in Bali, and that's holding me back now. I have standards…"

I raise my eyebrows in brief surprise because I thought he was younger, and then laugh at his consternation. In Bali, I thought he was probably in his early-to-mid forties; the past couple days I thought maybe forty-seven, forty-eight. But it's just a number. Forty-eight, fifty-three, what does it matter. And considering that we're here spending this ultra-romantic holiday together, I don't know what he means by "holding back." I also don't know what he means by "standards." That sounds like reverse age discrimination, but there's something endearing about the fact that he's worried about it. I tell him I always like to be the younger one. I don't mind being fifteen years younger.

Julien was married before, for twenty-five years. He and his ex-wife separated three years ago and have been divorced for two. He has two sons, who are both in their twenties. From the way he talks about his sons, it's clear that he loves them. Both of his parents have passed away, and he has one brother. I meet his brother and one of his sons. They're nice people with good energy; open, friendly, easy to talk to.

After a few days in Biarritz, we relocate to his apartment in Pau (pronounced "Poe," as in Edgar Allen). Pau is beautiful too, with wide cobblestone streets and Christmas lights everywhere and a river and a castle and views of the snow-capped Pyrenees.

A person's home tells so much about them, and I like what his apartment tells me about him. It's relaxed and classy, like him, with a tall wooden bookshelf filled with books by Thich Naht Han, the Dalai Lama, Paulo Coelho, Matthieu Ricard, and Khalil Gibran. A big wooden Buddha sits in one corner, and he has four Koshi wooden sound chimes. It's very zen, clean, and comfortable.

Here, our days change rhythm, become more like real life. After the first week of January, Julien resumes his normal work schedule. We meditate in the mornings before he leaves, and when he comes home, we cook dinner. Sometimes we go running. It feels good.

We spend a lot of time cuddling. He's a world-class cuddler. I assume that he is, like me, a lifelong cuddle fiend, but no. It's a recently acquired skill for him. One day he tells me, "Never in my life have I done so much cuddling. I think if you take all of cuddling I've done before in my entire life, it's less than this week."

I adore Julien. I don't use the word love because for me, love in the context of a romantic relationship is a serious, deep level of emotion that requires a lot of time and a thorough understanding of the other person, but I adore him. For his kindness, his open energy, his affection, his handsomeness, his passion and intensity, his cultured and sometimes adorable French accent, his habit of spontaneously planning fun things to do, the way he puts his glasses on and gets very serious and focused when he's reading something, his way of being, for the way I feel around him. When I'm around him, it's just happiness. My mind becomes quieter and doesn't look for words to explain anything. It just feels good.

Most of the time, that is. I can tell he adores me too, from the way he looks at me and how he is with me and because he occasionally tells me so. But sometimes he is distant. Sometimes his energy feels far off or distracted, and it makes me afraid he doesn't adore me enough. He'll get tired of me. This won't go on to become something more, and I want it to become something more. I don't want it to be over in a few days. I want this fairytale to last.

One day I notice a book on the bookshelf by Thich Nhat Hanh. Its title is *La Peur*. Fear.

That's the name of the emotion I'm feeling deep down, under the current of the pleasure of these beautiful vacation days. Fear, because my future is uncertain, and I can't sense the next step. For some reason I don't understand, I'm feeling a strong internal resistance to the idea of going back to Kalaw. But nothing else is calling me, except that I feel so good right here, I don't want to leave. Specifically, I want to remain on this comfortable brown leather couch, curled up against Julien with my head on his chest. I wish I could just stay right here, forever.

I know the fear hiding in the pit of my stomach is more than just uncertainty. It's fear that all this happiness won't last. It's fear that maybe I'm not strong enough to handle whatever the future will bring. It's a ridiculous fear. I have so many options, so many choices. The world is my oyster—except for Kalaw, maybe, where I'm not allowed to live in my house. But I don't know which way to go from here, and that's scary. And this couch with Julien is comfortable and safe, and I'd rather just stay here.

But he doesn't invite me to stay, so I buy a plane ticket to Portugal. We say our goodbyes a couple days early, lounging on the couch one night, because he wants to say what needs to be said at that moment. The feeling that the end is coming makes me cry, a few silent tears that slide down my cheeks. In response, one tear rolls down from his left eye. Enough to let me know that he felt something too.

The day before I leave France, I sit alone and think about Myanmar. That inner resistance to going back is still there. Immigration hasn't issued the approval for Emily and me to live in our house. If I listen to my heart, I will only go back to Kalaw on a tourist visa. But my sense of duty tells me I should go back to resume teaching for Steve. So, I do something very simple and obvious that I should have thought of sooner. I email Steve and tell him that I'm going to stay in Europe a little while longer. But, I ask, does he need me there to teach, or will he be okay with just Emily? If he needs me to come back and teach, I can. Otherwise, I will come back on a tourist visa.

I hit send, glance at my phone, and see that it's 12:12. Relief spreads through me, and at that moment I know I was supposed to be there, in Kalaw, and now I'm supposed to move on.

Steve writes me back a very warm email thanking me for the offer, but assuring me they will be okay. Emily can cover the classes, and he's excited for my opportunities in Europe, and I should please let him know if I need them to do anything with the bike or the house. And so all is well and I am free to move on to the next chapter, wherever it may be.

Julien never brings up the future, except that our last night together he brings out his deck of oracle cards and does a six-card pull to find out about his future for the next six months. His last card is *Amor.* The deck is in French, so I don't know why that word is spelled the Spanish way. He looks at it and with exaggerated emotion and gesturing dramatically like an Italian starts repeating *"Amore, amore!"* The Italian way, with the accent on the e.

Meanwhile, a day ago, I've just changed my name on Facebook to Sonya Moore, replacing my last name with my mother's maiden name. To avoid a bunch of questions about whether I got married, I posted an explanation of my reasons. The end of my post read, *One thing I love about this change is that when you put Sonya and Moore together, the last two syllables become Amor. Which is for me a beautiful symbol in this journey that has shown me so much love, everywhere.*

Immediately after we finish with the oracle cards, I see this Facebook message from my friend Joanne:

When I saw your name in my feed, I immediately thought, "who is this Sonya Moore?" But I've learned it's the same AMORE woman I've always known.

CHAPTER 32

Learn how to see. Realize that everything is connected.
- LEONARDO DA VINCI

January 2019

I'm in Portugal, chez Cristina and her family. When I talked to Cristina about looking for property here, she was 100 percent enthusiastic and supportive of the idea and she immediately invited me to come and stay with them while we search. They have a big house in Leiria and plenty of room, she said.

They give me a warm welcome, Cristina and her charming kids: Nelson, who's sixteen, and Melvina, who's twelve. Cristina is effusive and joyful and opens a bottle of red wine upon my arrival.

When I connect to their Wi-Fi, I see that the name of their network is *Familledamour*. "Family of love, how beautiful!" I say.

"It's our last name, Damour," Melvina tells me.

Damour. *D'amour.* Of love. I changed my name to love and then I came here, to—literally —the family of love. Unknowingly, because I never knew Cristina's last name. I really am finding love everywhere.

We cover a lot of ground in our property search, because ideally I would love something along the coast, but I'm open to anything anywhere that feels right at the right price. We find one option that my heart says yes to: a two-bedroom right here in Cristina's town, which a bit of renovation could transform into a marvelous Airbnb or boutique bed and breakfast. It has a cozy attic that could become an enchanting yoga studio, and its wrap-around balcony offers stunning views of the valley and the sunset. It feels right.

I meet with a banker who explains the ins and outs of obtaining financing as a non-European in Portugal. As it turns out, Portuguese banks aren't overly eager to lend money to unemployed foreigners.

After some heart-searching, I realize buying the Portugal two-bedroom will tie me down, and I'm not ready to be tied down yet. There are other things I want to do. I want to do more traveling in Myanmar, and see beaches and waterfalls, and do a 300-hour yoga teacher training. And I want to leave a little more time to see what, if anything, will unfold with my French lover.

Maybe I'll come back to Portugal later. For now, I get a twenty-eight-day tourist visa for Myanmar and a ticket back to Yangon.

And speaking of my French lover, I miss him a lot.

He misses me too. He texts charming words. *The apartment is empty without you. The bed is too big since you left. My hands search for you.*

One night, I have a vivid dream that we're making love. I tell him about it the next day. He dreamed the same thing, the same night, but his dream was more detailed. We were at an ashram in India, and then we ended up in Bali. This sets off days of steamy sexting.

I wish for him to miss me intensely enough to ask me to come back to France. Technically, he already invited me, the day I left, but it felt perfunctory. "You're welcome back anytime, if I'm here, but I travel a lot…"

That's not the kind of invitation I want. I'll hold out for a real one. It doesn't seem there's any chance of us seeing each other anywhere outside of France anytime soon, because he's using all of his vacation time to go to India next month for a three-week panchakarma.

But Life or divine forces step in to intervene. As it turns out, Julien and I will meet up again in less than a month, and the way this comes to pass is through a chain of unexpected and perfectly-timed events that interlock with each other with as much precision and complexity as the gears of an exquisitely-crafted Swiss watch.

It starts mid-January when he tries to book his stay at the Ayurvedic center in Kerala where I did my panchakarma. He waited too long—they're full.

I ask if he checked whether one of their other locations might have availability. They have two others, with confusingly similar names whose only point of differentiation is that one ends with "Villa" and the other ends with "Village." One is in Goa and one is in Kerala.

The next day, he tells me he received confirmation of availability at the Village, so he booked it. That's the Goa location.

I've just arrived in Yangon and I'm at Ingyin's apartment when Julien texts me that the Village informed him they can only accommodate him until February 14th, and after that they can relocate him to the Villa for the last five days of his treatment. Those two locations are a fourteen-hour drive apart; that doesn't sound appealing. He's already booked his flights to India, so he says he'll probably just sightsee or something for those last five days.

"February 14th; that's Valentine's Day," Ingyin points out.

That's true. And now memory rings a bell in my head. A couple months ago, a girl in one of my classes had spoken highly of a great 300-hour vinyasa/yin teacher training in Goa. I'm definitely going to do a 300-hour soon somewhere, and I would love more in-depth training in both of those styles. And I've never been to Goa, which is known for having the best beaches in India.

I can't remember the name of the place that girl talked about, but with Google's assistance I find a school in Goa that looks good. Really good. They have a 300-hour vinyasa/yin YTT starting March 5th. That means I could go early, spend five days with Julien, and then explore the beaches of Goa for two weeks before the training starts. I would have to leave Myanmar earlier than planned, but that's okay.

I text Julien. *So, you'll have a few days free in India?*

He calls me immediately. "What are you thinking?"

I explain my brilliant plan. Without hesitation and with undisguised excitement, he says, "Yes! This is great news! This is a great plan."

So I promptly book the training and my flight to Goa, and it's settled: we'll see each other in three weeks, on Valentine's Day.

Julien tells me later that it all unfolded with exquisitely perfect timing, because when the Village wrote to him that they only had space until the 14th, he wrote back and said he absolutely wanted to stay for three weeks and if they didn't have space he wouldn't go. They wrote back and said, *okay, we found space for you.* But it was in the little window before they replied that I told him I could come to Goa, so he told the Village never mind, he was only going to stay until the 14th.

Telling me about it afterwards, he laughed. "They probably thought I was crazy."

In Kalaw, I go back to staying at my house for my last two weeks here. No official approval has been granted, but now that I'm here independently on my tourist visa, there's no chance of my actions creating problems for Hayma. As expected, no problems are created for me either. No immigration officers show up to knock on my door in the middle of the night. My gracious landlady agrees to let me pay rent for half the month and not to withhold any deposit, in view of the circumstances.

I visit Steve's café in its new location. He's avoided homelessness too and the café's new location is bigger and better, with a gorgeous green space for organic gardens out front. I'm no longer officially teaching, and with the responsibilities of the café and the yoga studio off my shoulders, aside from packing and selling furniture, my days are deliciously free for enjoyment.

I host a rooftop picnic for a small group of my closest Kalaw friends. Ruby from the mop store brings artisanal Burmese wine. The sky is blue and the air is fresh and our laughter blends with the sunshine. As per Burmese tradition, they give me goodbye gifts of traditional Burmese clothing, which is heartwarming even though I have absolutely no space for more garments in my luggage. I love them, these three beautiful women with beautiful hearts to match their smiles, who made me feel so at home in this town. We talk about the future, that maybe I'll come back one day—maybe with my Frenchman.

"This is your town," Ruby says, the warmth of her smile reaching her eyes.

But I won't be coming back immediately, because after India I'll be going to Cambodia. That arrangement fell into place shortly after the Goa plan was hatched. Rebecca (the Rebecca of Yogamour who I met serendipitously in Chiang Mai) moved to Siem Reap a few months ago and opened a salon and yoga studio. When she heard I was leaving Myanmar, she invited me to come and teach there for a while.

I already love Siem Reap. I was there five years ago, for what was supposed to be two days at the beginning of a ten-day vacation. My friend Anisha and I had planned a brilliant itinerary that would take us through all the best spots in Cambodia. But we felt so good in Siem Reap, we ended up kicking our fantastic itinerary to the curb and spent an extra week in that charming town. I've wanted to go back ever since.

So I tell Rebecca I'll come in April and teach for a month or so. And just like that, I know where I'll be for the next four months of my life and that fearful uncertainty of Pau is a distant memory.

But there's been a little hiccup with our Goa plan. When Julien gets to the Ayurvedic center, we find out he's not in Goa—he's a fourteen hour drive away, at the Kerala location. At the Villa, not the Village. Whoops.

There's very limited internet at the Villa, so I look for Kerala-Goa flights for Julien and find a perfect option. From the closest airport to him (Kannur), there's a direct flight to Goa for fifteen euros. Bam.

He writes me back that that's a great solution but he found a better one: he's going to meet me in Chennai and fly with me to Goa. He already booked his tickets, and he'll book a hotel for us in Chennai.

Chennai is on the opposite side of India from both Goa and Kerala. My layover in Chennai is from 11:30 p.m. to 4:45 a.m., which will leave us about two hours at the hotel. His solution is completely impractical and also wildly romantic. This man (who's an engineer, by the way, normally a very reasonable and level-headed person) is willing to fly back and forth across India just for a few extra hours with me. I adore him.

And I'm grateful for the Villa/Village mix-up because if I knew he was going to Kerala, I'm not sure I would have come up with the brilliant plan to meet him in Goa.

While packing, I come across my journal from the previous year. I flip through it and find my transcript of the reading my friend Rose did for me just before I left Florida. (It's literally a transcript, because I recorded the reading and later wrote it down word for word.)

One part stands out: "Now let me tell you about the man you're supposed to marry. On the 7th house you have Taurus. Taurus' ruler is Venus. Venus is in Gemini, in the 8th house. So the person that should be coming would be a Gemini. Or a Scorpio."

That's funny because I remember her telling me that it should be a Gemini, and me thinking, *Interesting, Alex is a Gemini...* But I completely forgot the Scorpio part. Julien is a Scorpio.

Three days before I leave Kalaw, Emily calls with the ironic news that she's received her immigration approval. The landlady has agreed to give her a discounted rate so she can afford to live in the house on her own. Can she buy some dishes and stuff from me?

I think she's nervous that I'll be mad, but I'm not. Everything worked out as it was meant to. My time in the house was as brief as that inaugural shooting star, and as bright. I'm glad Emily will get to enjoy the freshly painted walls, and I'm also glad she's buying the dishes.

It's in these final days in Kalaw, as all the details wrap themselves up nicely and I'm bidding farewell to many dear friends, that I understand why I was so happy here.

It was so simple. And that was the key: the simplicity. Because there was such an abundant supply of my favorite things here: love, beauty, nature, kindness, yoga, good food, and because life here was so simple and uncluttered, there were few complications to get in the way of happiness. I had the time and space to feel it.

The current of love and kindness continues all the way up to the very end. I take a dress whose sleeves need to be altered to the girl who has a little shop where I always buy gasoline. She's a seamstress as well as a seller of gasoline. She speaks about as much English as I speak Burmese, so our communication is limited, but we always smile and exchange a few words and end up laughing. She quickly does the alterations for me and then refuses to let me pay her anything.

"You're my friend," she says, shaking her head.

I'm at the bus station with my luggage, waiting for the overnight bus to Yangon, when Mwae appears, breathless. "Oh good, I made it in time!" she exclaims, and hands me a gift. "This is for you."

I don't know how she even knew what time my bus was or which station I would be at. Her gift is the most beautiful of all my goodbye gifts: a modern take on a *longyi,* a Burmese wrap-skirt, that reaches to mid-calf in a gorgeous pattern of pastel blues and pinks and aquas.

"I love it, thank you! I love the colors." I hug her.

She smiles. "I thought they were your colors. I had to go to a few shops to find it."

If I hadn't been kicked out of my house, I wouldn't have met Mwae. I leave Kalaw with my heart full and grateful for everything. And two years later, when Myanmar is shattered by a violent coup that rips democracy and freedom away from its citizens and residents and begins a new chapter of oppression and bloodshed in that beautiful country, the grief I feel is mixed with gratitude for the turn of events that kept me from putting roots down there.

CHAPTER 33

Joy is in fact quite contagious.
– DOUGLAS ABRAMS

February 2019

In Chennai, Julien is waiting for me at arrivals. Fresh from his two-week Ayurvedic detox, he's glowing with well-being and vitality. The two hours we spend in our hotel are more than worth every rupee. I'm exhausted but back in the bubble of enchanted happiness. We doze a little on the flight to Goa, my head on his shoulder and his head on mine.

We arrive at our Agonda Beach hotel around 7:30 a.m. The hotel is beautiful and steeped in nature. Tall hibiscus bushes border the individual cottages and a smiling gray Buddha meditates between palm trees in the garden by the entrance. We drop our luggage at reception and walk to the beach.

The early morning light is soft. Our shadows are long in the powdery golden sand. The waves are longer, rolling in slow and languid, as if to emphasize that here, there is no need to rush. The wide beach stretches toward hazy tree-covered hills to the left and distant bluish-gray mountains to the right. It's beautiful beyond anything I expected. We're here, and we're here together, and that feels like magic. We're effervescent with joy and contentment.

The floor of the hotel restaurant is sand, which according to me is the ideal floor for a restaurant. We choose a table looking out at the beach, with the sea breeze floating in. Breakfast is a flaky masala omelet paratha wrap with garlicky coconut chutney and a fruit bowl garnished with pomegranate, mint leaves, and strips of roasted coconut. I'm convinced the paratha wrap is the best thing I've ever sunk my teeth into. The cushioned chairs are ridiculously comfortable and the location of the table with its beach view and sea breeze is nothing short of divine. I could have happily stayed right here in this chair until sunset. But instead, we get massages and wander down the beach and eat delicious grilled Goan seafood, washed down with refreshing glasses of white Sula. After lunch we walk down the road that runs parallel to the beach, behind the beachfront hotels, our eyes exploring the tempting wares offered by its shops.

Goa is paradise. It has all the spice and energy of India, but with stunning beaches too. (How many paradises are there on this earth? Lately everywhere I go feels like paradise, but Goa is definitely extraordinary.)

Julien rents a Royal Enfield and we visit Portuguese ruins and more beaches. There are countless beaches along the Goan coast and each has its own unique charm and personality. To me, Agonda is perfect, with its wide-open spaciousness and relaxed upscale feel. Julien prefers Patnem Beach: smaller, vibrant and bohemian, full of beachfront cafés with live music.

One of the little shops on the road behind Agonda Beach is run by a beautiful Indian woman with an irresistible smile. Her sales skills are subtle and low pressure, but highly effective on Julien. He can't say no to her. He buys enough mandala throws and t-shirts and jewelry to fill a small suitcase, and she persuades him to get a henna tattoo on his back.

Uninvited, the question enters my mind: *is he a man who can't say no to beautiful, persuasive women?* I wonder if he'll cheat on me one day, if we stay together long enough. I don't want the thought to be there, but it is, with an uncomfortable sense of foreboding. And if he does, what will I do? Will I leave him and end it forever? Or forgive him and give him another chance?

The thing is, with hunches like this, it's hard to know if they're born of intuition or fear. I push the thought to the back of my mind. That's a bridge to be crossed if I come to it. For now, we have a few short days in this paradise, and everything here is coated with a shimmering glow of magic.

I'm happy with this man, and I want the happiness to continue. I've acknowledged to myself that I love him, but I haven't said that out loud because I want him to say it first. We haven't spent much time together, but it feels right. He fits me.

Only, occasionally, small shadows cast themselves over my almost-perfect happiness. I sense sometimes that something's missing, that his walls are still there. I thought they had melted in the aching intensity of missing each other over the past four weeks, but they didn't. Sometimes he withdraws into himself, into a private space where I'm not welcome. He talks sometimes about his future plans, places he wants to travel to, that he's considering switching to 80 percent at his job so he can have twenty more days off a year to travel. But he never mentions me. He never talks about if or when we'll see each other again.

Once, I bring up the subject. One thing on my to-do list is WWOOFing—working at an organic farm, for a month or so. France seems like the ideal place to do this, given the love and passion of the French for their food and wine. I could find a farm in the Basque region and visit Julien occasionally. When I put the idea out there, he goes quiet. I feel the sting of rejection.

That's confusing, because we're so happy together, we miss each other intensely when we're apart, and he does other things that feel like love. One day, he schedules a private yoga class for us at an amazing dome-shaped open-air shala in Patnem Beach. Halfway through the class, I glance over at him and remember the first moment I saw him at that class in Ubud fourteen months ago. I smile. He smiles back. He had the same flashback.

On his last day, I treat us to a couples massage. The massage place is small and their tables are in separate rooms. Julien insists that they bring one table into the same room as the other.

"I want to be next to my girlfriend," he tells the manager.

They rearrange the tables to accommodate his request. I wouldn't have minded if we had been separated by a wall, but his romantic insistence is touching.

That last afternoon, I finally ask him why he never talks about us seeing each other again.

"Because I live in the world of the unspoken," he replies. He adds, "I would like to see you again, and you're welcome in France. But I don't want to get in the way of your projects."

"You wouldn't get in the way," I say. But again his invitation doesn't feel wholehearted.

The time comes for him to leave, and I walk him to the taxi to say goodbye. Our driver is a relaxed Goan named Deepak. Deepak watches us saying our reluctant farewells and says, "If you want to come with him to the airport, I'll drive you back afterwards."

It's a brilliant suggestion; I'm not sure why we didn't think of it ourselves. Along the forty-five-minute drive, we're cuddled together in the backseat, chatting occasionally with the friendly Deepak.

When we say our final goodbye outside the airport, Julien pauses to look into my eyes. I see the emotion in them. "See you soon, I hope," he says.

On the drive back, Deepak tells me that I'm very nice, and Julien is very nice. "Like you were made for each other."

That sentence stays with me. *Like you were made for each other.* That's what it feels like. How interesting, the idea that two people can be made for each other. To fit together like two puzzle pieces, in spite of or because of their uniquely complex character traits and preferences and flaws and idiosyncrasies.

I continue exploring Goa on my own, making the most of the ten days before my training. Julien and I text each other regularly, and then for two days, there's total silence from him.

This has happened to me before, this sudden ending of communication, and it always means it's The End. There's a cold chill in the pit of my stomach.

For a day, all the joy and meaning in life disappears. Goa's magic filter is gone. I swim in the ocean and let my tears blend with the saltwater. Yet all day long the number signs appear: 10:10, 11:11, 4:44, and more. A whole flock of number signs. A flood of winks from the Universe.

That night I decide to keep trusting the Universe and I remember that I am the one responsible for my joy; no one else should have the power to take it away. Not even a charming, irresistible Frenchman who feels like he's made for me. I resolve to wake up feeling joyful the next day.

And I do. I wake up and the ache in my heart is gone and I'm full of so much joy I'm literally dancing around the room. I smile radiantly at all the shop vendors I walk past. Some of them ask me why I'm so happy. I shrug and say, "Why not?"

Julien calls that night to tell me he did a lot of thinking. He says he had a wonderful time with me, I'm a beautiful person, he appreciates me a lot, and we are lovers and friends but he's not ready to be in a relationship. He was married for twenty-five years and it's only been over for three, and he wants to feel free. And besides, he still thinks the fifteen-year age gap is a serious issue. "Imagine when you're fifty and I'm sixty-five," he says. "It will be ridiculous!"

I don't see what would be ridiculous about it or why he's already thinking twelve years down the road. What about four months from now?

He goes on. "You're welcome in France if I'm there, but I don't want you to change your plans for me."

"You have to follow your heart, and I would never try to come between you and freedom," I reply. "You owe me nothing and you are free. But the age difference means nothing and has nothing to do with it."

We have a long, open conversation, and the openness feels good. It makes me sad, of course, the end of this fairytale, but I understand. More than anything, I understand the desire for freedom. And I'm used to endings. I accept his choice with calmness.

After we hang up, we keep texting. The attraction between us hasn't diminished just because we're 7000 kilometers apart or because he decided to end it. I actually don't think it's really the end, not only because the attraction is still alive and sizzling but because our whole romance has felt like a string of magic, divinely orchestrated by the master puppeteer forces of the Universe. I don't think the Universe would go to so much trouble for this to end so soon. But what do I know of the mysterious plans of the Universe? Maybe it is over, and if it is, that's okay. He's free and I'm free too, and maybe there's someone even better waiting for me.

Most importantly, even if I've lost him, I still have me. And I like me. For some strange reason, this ending has made me feel more alive. And strong. And playful. (By the way, this is not my typical reaction to a breakup. The immediate aftermath of any breakup of mine is usually an embarrassing sight involving swollen eyes, mountains of Kleenex, and me convinced I will never again find someone I felt that way about—even if the split was my choice.)

As I'm sitting here, basking in my newly discovered radiance, he texts me a link to a song on Spotify. *"L'eveil des Déesses,"* it's called. The Awakening of the Goddesses. *You are a goddess,* he writes.

That's it. That's exactly what I feel at this moment. Like a playful goddess awakening, stretching in her newfound power.

The next day, I still feel that way. And I'm delighted with myself for this because in the past, I wouldn't have reacted this way. I would have been brokenhearted and devastated. But now I know that trust, acceptance, and self-connection can transform that pain into joy, and that's one of the best life lessons I've learned so far.

The story with Julien didn't end there. In the days that follow, our emotions shift and flow like two dancers twirling in a spirited waltz. Mine change first, because I belatedly fixate on something he said during our last conversation: that he doesn't want to be limited. I interpret this as: *he sees me as a limitation.* That hurts, and the hurt turns my heart cold toward him.

My coldness seems to crack a shell inside him. He writes that he's sad; he regrets this situation. He says this is the first time something like this has happened to him. We shared so many moments of connection, and he misses me.

The hurt and sincerity in his reply thaw the glacial frost over my heart. I consider his words, and everything that happened between us. This is too much for text, and too thoughtful for a phone call. I switch to email, and I write him everything that's in my heart.

I write that I wish him not to be sad. Life is short and he has the freedom he dreamed of … he should enjoy it. He has no reason to be sorry, as far as I'm concerned. I appreciate that he told me what was in his heart, and I also appreciate that he didn't tell me sooner. If he had, I wouldn't have thought to come to Goa to meet him, and we would have missed out on those magical five days.

I thank him for those beautiful days, for the filter of magic that being here with him put on this little Indian paradise. He reminded me what I want in my future. I want almost the same things he does—freedom, travel (with a home base, soon), to enjoy life—but with one big difference: I want love too. I want to share this life with someone I love, who loves me. Love is everywhere and it appears in many forms, but I also want a big fairytale romantic love. I want a love like the one described at Carolyn and Jono's San Francisco wedding a year and a half ago. "Love with freedom … a love that wraps around you like a warm blanket but also lets you fly." That's my dream. To have my true love, a person who sees me as a treasure, who cherishes me, and towards whom I feel the same—and also to have time and space for me, my solitude from time to time, and time to share with my friends. That, and to enjoy life at the same time, without thinking too much about the future—just enough to be responsible. Life is beautiful, but it's even more beautiful shared. And shared with the right person, obviously.

But I understand why he wants something different. I understand the pleasure of being alone, with no obligations to anyone, to be free to do what you want without needing to think about anyone else's preferences.

He writes me back with equal sincerity and openness, revealing some of what was hidden behind the walls he kept up in France and Goa. All the things he couldn't say out loud flow easily in written form.

He writes that meeting me touched him on a level he didn't expect. He loved our time together, but he had no future expectations where I was concerned. He thought I was a beautiful, sweet, cool, connected woman and all the synchronicities caught his attention, but he was always in vacation mode with me. He never thought about the future and he never sought to deepen our relationship because our time together was so short. He always assumed I was just passing through his life.

For him, the only shadow in our time together was when I brought up the future, because as soon as anyone starts to show him the expectation of a relationship, he runs. My idea of WWOOFing in France scared him because he thought it was just an excuse to see him, and that I was going to come and live with him. (Which is funny because moving in with someone uninvited is not really my style.)

He never wanted me to change the course of my life for him, he continues. He felt my expectations on the subject—he's intuitive— but he's not there. He's slowly putting himself back together after his long married life, and he's not ready. He's sorry for not having been able to talk to me about it, our last day together, but he so wanted to just enjoy our last moments together.

He believes strongly in my dream of love. For him? He doesn't know. He's changing. He thought he would end up alone, after the disappointments of his previous relationships, but now he thinks maybe he needs to be able to share moments with another person. But he also needs gulps of oxygen from time to time, to be alone.

He remains convinced that our meeting wasn't by chance. His heart says he would love to see me again one day, but logic and intuition tell him that I still have other things to do and that he was just passing through my path. But time will tell, and in the meantime he'll stay in touch, if that's okay with me.

It is okay with me.

CHAPTER 34

When all blocks and obstacles from the past are cleared
and removed, then there's clarity in a person's life.
They smile and the world around them smiles back.
- MARIA KARASTERGIOU

March 2019

The site of the Goa yoga teacher training is yoga school heaven. It's set up as a little village on the beach, housing five shalas, thirty or so cabins, plenty of comfortable spaces for lounging and outdoor dining, a coffee/tea station, and a coconut station where we can get fresh coconuts anytime we want. Color is everywhere: cushions and pillows of red, turquoise, orange, green, and lavender, prayer flags and mandalas and Buddhas. Everything is well-shaded by palm trees and well-cooled because every square inch of overhead space is covered with ceiling fans. Even where there are no ceilings, the fans are attached to a framework of PVC pipes overhead. (Genius!)

This place is pregnant with creativity and aliveness. Given the experience of my two previous YTTs, I've come here fully prepared to encounter the occasional oversized ego, sleazy director and passive/aggressive teacher—but no. Everyone here is just genuinely nice, skilled, and down-to-earth. Our 300-hour group is small: there are ten of us. All of us have already been teaching yoga for a while, and we're here because we love yoga and we want to learn more.

There are five teachers in our program, a diverse group who have each attained mastery in their respective subjects. They are all very cool humans, and so are my fellow students. The ocean is right beside us, and the food ... ahhh, the food. It's never anything short of incredible. Every meal is a splendid buffet, and the buffet is different every day. I never once manage to eat only one plate.

The combination of yin and vinyasa is perfect. The vinyasa classes are challenging, and fun. It's incredibly decadent to melt into the long hold yin stretches after a day of strenuous vinyasa; to feel mind and body let go. I'm pinching myself because this all seems too good to be true. But it isn't. It's real. So I accept reality and enjoy every second.

Almost every second, that is.

The ongoing communication with Julien is a pebble skipping on the surface of the still pool of my contentment, disturbing the calm serenity of my mind. He's revealed that he wants his freedom more than he wants me, and so I want to move on. But he hasn't let go of me. He's still writing and calling and flirting, and this is keeping me in an uncomfortable limbo. I know how to be all-in, and I know how to walk away, but I don't know how to be in this in-between place.

In his messages I see confusion, and I understand that he needs time for himself. He needs to find his own clarity. I don't want my heart jerked around by a man who doesn't know his own, who doesn't want me as much as I want him. I've gone through that before, and that kind of pain is a chronic, gnawing ache. I don't want to go through it again. It hurts too much.

I'm trying to remain aloof and keep us in friendship zone, but this doesn't feel good either. It feels unnatural, like I'm choking my true self. It's blocking my energy, not only towards him, but in general. For a few days, I am off. Two mornings in a row, as we sit in post-chanting meditation, tears come from somewhere, roll down my face, and refuse to stop. I don't even know why I'm crying, only that I feel so much sadness it has to go somewhere. As if all this sadness has been secretly buried in my cells for decades and now it's all swam to the surface to pour out. Our teacher kindly says nothing, just comes over and hands me a stack of Kleenex.

I try to free myself from this strange sadness by ending things definitively with Julien. When he writes one day that he would love to see me again if I come to France, now that he understands that my

WWOOFing plan wasn't just about him (i.e., wasn't a secret ploy to sneakily move in with him uninvited), I take a long time to think. Finally I write back that I probably won't see him when I go to France. Maybe I'll change my mind later, but right now it doesn't feel like a good idea.

It's my way of setting myself free, of reserving my heart for someone who values it enough.

But his reply surprises me.

My words made him sad. He feels a sense of loss, even though he thinks—at least he hopes—that we'll stay connected. His intuition and even his logic say we will. After reflecting on everything that unfolded the last few months, it's clear to him that I didn't appear in his life by chance. He explains a little more about the ending of his marriage, and his old life. About leaving his wife, breaking up the family, leaving his old group of friends, selling everything, restarting a new life.

His words give me a glimpse of the shock it must have been to his system, to walk away from an entire life like that. I feel compassion. I'm not the only one who's been hurt. We both have our wounds.

He closes his last email with all his affection and love, to a lover and friend who is dear to him.

I've felt love from him before, but this is the first time he's put it in words. Everything makes more sense to me now. Why I felt love from him, and what was blocking it, and why he needs to do his own thing right now.

So I give up trying to fight my own heart and we go back to being long distance lovers, which feels like the most natural thing in the world.

The only other problem here in this Goan yoga paradise is that I am still here with myself. The sunlight of Goa hasn't dissolved all of my secret shadows, hasn't melted all of the happiness-invading insecurities who from time to time rear their unwelcome heads.

The main insecurity making an appearance here in Goa is a quiet but dedicated little voice in my head who has designated himself responsible for keeping me informed about What Other People Are Probably Thinking. He's inhabited that little corner of my mind since I was about three years old. He rarely takes a day off. He means well, but he tends to be pretty pessimistic. When he gets into one of his bouts of negativity, his presence quietly drains my joy and focus.

He's there in his usual spot two weeks into the course, when we students each have to teach a ninety-minute yin class for our evaluation. I love yin yoga, and especially all the new information we've learned about the effect of yin postures on the meridians—the pathways of energy in our bodies. I'm excited to teach the class and I pour my heart into preparing it. I want the students to love it the way I love yin classes.

While I'm teaching, I don't feel that the class is going as well as I wanted it to. I don't feel that I'm succeeding at my goal of transmitting the experience of blissful relaxation. We're at the ocean view shala, and in the beginning I have to strain to project my voice over the sound of the wind and the barking dogs. The background noise gets quieter and my voice gets stronger as I go on, but even so, I don't feel completely relaxed. The annoying whisperer in the corner of my mind is relaying that it is highly unlikely that any students are loving the experience. They're probably bored, or ambivalent at best. I tell myself, *if people are actually loving this class, I'll believe anything is possible.*

Later that night, just at the moment I'm writing that sentence in my journal, my eyes are drawn to the bottom corner of my laptop screen and the time clock shows 12:12.

Wow, Universe. I really felt that my gaze was pulled there as if by a magnet just at that instant. It's the official stamp of confirmation: anything is possible.

Because everyone loved the class. Their feedback was that it was a beautiful class, an amazing class. That everything I said just flowed. That I created a really nice feeling in the shala, a feeling of warmth; with the perfect balance of talking and silence, and it seemed that everything I said came just at the right moment. That they felt comfortable and safe and in good hands.

It was so far from what I thought they were feeling.

I still haven't figured out how to make that pessimistic voice in my mind go away for good, but at least I've learned that it's usually best to ignore its joy-killing interpretations of what everyone else is probably thinking.

❧

There are a few days left in the YTT. I'm on the phone with Julien.

"We need to figure out what's going to happen with us," he announces suddenly, mid-conversation.

This is a change. "You need to figure that out," I say. "You're the one who wants to be single and free."

"I'm changing," he says. "I'm fed up with being single. It's nice to be with someone, to share, cuddle. But you're a free spirit and I'm trapped in France. I don't think I can catch a free spirit."

"It's not about catching. If I want to be with you and you want to be with me, then we'll be together."

"I can't promise you that it will work, that we can live with each other long term."

"I'm not asking for a promise or a long-term guarantee," I reply. "I just want to give it a chance."

This would be an excellent opportunity for him to invite me back to France when I finish my time in Cambodia. But instead, he changes the subject. He tells me that a few days ago he pulled an oracle card thinking of me, and the card he got was *Betrayal*. He sends me a photo of it. It features a scary-looking black cat with demonic orange eyes and a skinny tail sticking straight up. It's the worst oracle card I've ever seen.

"I'm not going to betray you," I tell him. "Pull another one."

Strange, because the oracle cards are usually spot-on.

The day before I leave Goa, Julien gives me promising news. His company has posted a one-year assignment in Doha. From Doha, there are direct flights to Phnom Penh. He'll be able to visit me easily.

He's already applied for the post, and if he gets the job, it means some of his reserved vacation will be unlocked, so he can take vacation in May and come and visit me for two weeks.

There are 3600 miles between Qatar and Cambodia. Doha isn't exactly next door. But it's closer than France, and two weeks with him in May sounds wonderful.

So I say, "Great!! Sounds good!"

And I end my time in Goa full of joy.

CHAPTER 35

Life's gonna hurt but it's meant to be felt.
- INDIA ARIE

April 2019

The day I arrive in Siem Reap happens to be National Smiling Day. The airport is celebrating with lots of smiles, and live music, and a photographer, and they're handing out juices and complimentary *kramas*—traditional Khmer checkered scarves. This festive date feels very appropriate because I can't stop smiling once I arrive.

There's a charm to Siem Reap that's difficult to describe, because it can't be identified by any of our five most common senses. The town itself is not visually remarkable. Although there is a peaceful green river running through the center of town and an abundance of beautiful trees and lotus fields around it, it has neither the mountains nor the ocean that I love so much. Siem Reap's charm lies mostly in the potent energy that it possesses, which it transmits to and though the people who live or visit here. A fresh, aspirational energy that seeps in subtly, energizes, and awakens a sense of aliveness and creativity.

What Siem Reap lacks in natural beauty, it makes up for with the vibrance of its residents and the appeal of its manmade design. The predominant interior design trend here is fresh, natural, and modern, with light airy colors and an open style that merges indoor and outdoor living. Bright white walls are accented with green hanging vines, tropical plants, and French colonial or modern farmhouse touches, or attractive pieces of Khmer modern art. It's also a place that's very easy to settle in as a foreigner, and after my Kalaw experience, this means a lot to me.

After I check into my hotel, I walk to the salon/yoga studio to say hi to Rebecca. She's with her friend Eva, the stylist who came with her from Chiang Mai to open this salon, and their presence is like a bath of light and positive energy. Rebecca invites me to an art exhibition that night at a posh hotel. The only problem with that is that at this point in my travels, my entire shoe collection consists of Havaianas and one pair of sneakers. Rebecca resolves that issue by lending me a dressier pair, and the event is beautiful. We drink a lot of complimentary wine and I meet friendly, interesting people.

Siem Reap is a small town, but after little Kalaw and laid-back Goa, it feels like New York City to me. There are plenty of social events here and more fantastic restaurants than I could count on ten hands, and the restaurants are beautiful and almost as inexpensive as India and Myanmar.

Before I got to Cambodia, a friend of mine who used to live here put me in touch with a realtor who, she said, could help me find a furnished apartment for a month for $350 or so. I meet with the realtor the day after I arrive. She shows me three apartments. I fall completely in love with the third one, but it's not available for the dates I need, so I take the second one. For some reason, I don't love its vibe, but it will do. Aesthetically, it's definitely an improvement on my unfurnished Kalaw house—but because of the love I had for my Kalaw house, we can't compare on a strictly aesthetic level. So I don't compare.

The best features of this apartment are that the wall next to the kitchen/dining area consists of floor to ceiling glass windows that look out over coconut-bearing palm trees, and the apartment has a WASHING MACHINE. I move in on my fourth day in Siem Reap.

Fresh from the YTT, I'm full of new knowledge and creative energy to channel into teaching, and I pour it into classes and workshops.

This studio offers teachers the perk of free attendance to other teachers' classes, and the other teachers are excellent, sincere and inspiring.

With all the social events going on every week and the open friendliness of the people here, Siem Reap is the easiest place in the world to make friends. Whereas almost all of my friends in Myanmar were Burmese, in Cambodia they're mostly all Australian, American, or European, because there are so many expats here. But I make some Khmer friends too, and from them I learn that my name is Cambodian. "Sone-yah, it means promise," they tell me.

This little detail surprises and delights me. It's as if I was always meant to come here, to Cambodia.

One night, I teach a private yin class for Julien via Messenger video. It's a relaxing class focused on the liver meridian. To set the ambience, I instruct him to light candles and I send him a soothing atmospheric playlist to accompany the class. In recent days the words *I love you* are in my heart wanting to express themselves to him, but for some reason it doesn't feel like the right time to speak them, so I don't. Instead I infuse love into the sequence and send it to him through the airwaves while he rests in a rebound savasana. "Through the phone, I'm sending you love. Love crosses through cyberspace and through your telephone and arrives in your house." Eyes closed, he gives me a thumbs up. "Love mixes with the chi in the room, and when you inhale, it flows in with the chi, the prana, into your body. It reaches your lungs, your heart, and there, it flows into your blood, and your heart pumps the blood filled with love and prana through your circulatory system. And love reaches every cell of your body, nourishing and healing every cell." I will him to feel it.

I think he does. Afterwards he tells me, "You succeeded in passing the current."

Later, we lay in our respective beds 6200 miles apart, staring into each other's eyes on our respective iPhone screens. We're so far away but we feel so connected.

That's why what happens five days later hurts even more.

It's the end of April. The anticipation of seeing each other again has climbed to an intense pitch. Julien's still waiting for the Qatar job confirmation and he's become anxious and impatient. He's expecting to get it a few days from now: on Sunday, when the Qatar office reopens after their Friday-Saturday weekend.

On my side of the world, I have an unpleasant issue to deal with. I need to find a new apartment, because the one I'm in doesn't have a backup generator and we've lost power six times my first two weeks here. That's a problem because I've recently started teaching English online, and I can't teach in the dark. After a power outage strikes ten minutes before a class and I have to hightail it to a coworking space, I tell my landlord I need to move out. I expect him to understand, because when I looked at the apartment I told him I need a backup generator. He assured me this building never loses power, because some high-up government official lives in the neighborhood.

Before committing, I reconfirmed the "never" in writing via text message, explaining that reliable power is essential because of my online classes. He assured me "never," in writing. So I take him at his word, and sign a two-month lease, with a one-month deposit. (Two months because my visa gives me sixty days here.)

But when I tell him I need to leave, he says he'll be keeping my deposit since I'm breaking the lease. He's always been very nice to me in person, although he emanates a faint aura of sleaziness, but now the facade of niceness disappears and his true snakelike character reveals itself. I'm not one to back down from a fight when I know I'm in the right, and I'm not inclined to reward his blatant lies by letting him keep my $350, but he doesn't back down from his position, so we take the matter to the real estate company.

The director of the company is an Australian who's lived in Cambodia for sixteen years and, impressively, speaks fluent Khmer. After an hour of discussion between the three of us, during which the landlord grows progressively angrier and nastier, getting to his feet red-faced and jabbing his finger in my face a few times, he reluctantly concedes to the director's suggestion: he'll keep the extra two-weeks' rent for this month and return my deposit.

This behavior is not, by the way, reflective of the Cambodian people in general. The director tells me that in sixteen years, this is the first time he's seen this kind of blatant greed. He wouldn't have stayed here this long if he didn't love the people, he says.

It's a good reminder that a sugary smile can hide a greedy, poisoned heart, but the whole thing leaves me with an unsettled feeling and a bad taste in my mouth. I want to talk to Julien and be comforted. But his texts have been unusually short the past couple days, like he's busy and distracted. Just before the meeting, I messaged him a synopsis of the situation. He replied, *Ok. Good luck. Bisous.*

That's all. I don't hear from him again that day. The next day I message: *Are you ok?*

He replies: *Yes I'm ok. I'm with friends in a big party. I'll call you later. Bisous.*

Apparently he's not sober because he sends an almost-duplicate message a couple hours later: *Yes I'm ok. I will call you later. Bisous.*

I have a cold, funny feeling in the pit of my stomach.

I don't hear from him the next morning. France is five hours behind Cambodia, so he could be sleeping off his hangover. Morning becomes afternoon, and still nothing. The funny feeling in the pit of my stomach is still there and the suspicion that he's slept with someone has firmly planted itself in my mind.

Around 4 p.m., a taxi takes me and my luggage to my new apartment. It's the beautiful one I fell in love with when I was apartment hunting, the one that at the time wasn't available. The other renter fell through and I was able to snap it up. It's an enormous relief to leave the toxic energy of my old landlord behind and to be greeted at the front desk of this beautiful oasis by the warm smiles of two nice Cambodian guys.

I'm standing at the desk while one of the guys looks for the key to my apartment when my cell phone dings. I pull it out to see the message. It's from Julien. It's a long message, longer than my screen. I glance at it and the first paragraph registers.

Hello Sonya. This message gives me immense pain to write. I can't call you to tell you in person, I am ashamed. During my festive night I committed the unforgivable. This gives me no pleasure at all but it is what it is; I met a woman.

A few sentences further down jump out at me:

The distance, the time without seeing each other led to this ... Also I haven't gotten the Qatar confirmation yet, it's probably not going to happen. I don't see any other way we can see each other again... I'm very sorry this is ending like this...

My ears ring. The world spins and expands and pulls away from me and then returns to its normal configuration, and I'm standing there as if the solid ground beneath me hasn't just vanished.

But I can't react because I'm here with these two guys who need to check me in to my new place. I put the phone and the emotion away, smile at the guy who holds up the key, and follow them up the three flights of stairs to my new apartment.

Whenever life knocks you off your feet with a strong punch to the gut, it usually pads your fall with a little cushion of a conciliatory gift, and this apartment is one. The joy sparked by this gorgeous place with its big open kitchen, tall windows, pristine marble floors, leafy potted plants, and spacious bathroom with a granite soaking tub helps to keep the ball of shock and grief under the surface for the fifteen minutes it takes us to finish the check-in.

Then the guys leave. I close the door behind them, say thank you to the Universe for these stunning new accommodations which are costing me a mere $450 a month (which includes a weekly cleaning service and change of linens and towels), and then I sit down to read the full gut-wrenching text message.

At the end, it says the time he spent with me was wonderful. He loved our communication, our meeting wasn't trivial, his life changed somehow after our meeting in Bali. He wishes me the best for the future, he hopes we can stay in touch and he hopes we won't become enemies, but it's my decision.

All of the glittering magic that has surrounded us all this time freezes and hardens into glass and shatters, raining down around me, a million tiny pieces of a broken dream. He's not Prince Charming; he's just an unreliable man.

Grief hits me, layers of it. I cry for the loss of him, the loss of the connection we shared, for the betrayal of trust. I thought our long shared thread of synchronicities and the way I felt about him meant we were destined to be together. But, I had little warnings, didn't I? That preliminary ending-that-wasn't-really-an-ending in Goa. His strong desire for freedom. It's funny that he described what he did as "unforgivable," because in a court of law you couldn't even technically say he cheated. We never had any discussion of exclusivity. I would say it was mutually understood, but he didn't break any promises. And to make it worse, he didn't even give me the chance to decide whether or not to end it; he ended it himself.

In my sadness and disappointment, there is no anger or hatred towards him. Except a little anger about his ridiculous statement *"I can't see any other solution for us to see each other again."* As if there are no flights between Cambodia and France. As if we hadn't already discussed other ideas. It would have been so much better if he had just written honestly, *I don't want to see you again.*

I thought he was the man of my life, but I was wrong. Luckily, I've been wrong so many times in life that by now, I'm quite used to it. Our long-distance situation wasn't easy. Maybe he'll be happier this way. Maybe I'll be happier this way. I tell myself this through the tears.

I write him back.

I'm glad you sent this news in writing, instead of calling. It's not the news I wanted to read, but distance is a challenge and I knew in part of my mind that this ending was always a possibility. It's not the ideal ending, but it's not unforgivable. I forgive you. Like I told you, your heart was always free ... if it didn't bring you to me, I would never try to keep you. I wish you happiness.

The only thing I ask him is to please delete all the photos of me, the ones that were for his eyes only.

Of course, he replies. *Please delete the ones of me too.* 😂

I'm annoyed that he thinks it's appropriate to use the cry-laughing emoji right now. I don't have a lot of X-rated photos of him but there are a few. I don't want them on my phone anymore anyway. I delete them, and as I'm scrolling through the WhatsApp photos I come across the one of the card he pulled a couple months ago while thinking about me and wondering about our future. The Betrayal card, with the scary black cat.

I freeze. The cards were right again. Only the betrayal came from him, not from me.

That evening I go through the stages of grief. They rise up, linger a while, and then dissolve to make space for the next. After the sadness comes nausea. I imagine him with another woman and I want to vomit. Then comes a deeper layer of pain, with more sadness.

I don't try to fight the sadness. I sit there and let myself feel it, and as I'm sitting in the river of heartache, I remember a line I heard recently in a TED talk by Glennon Doyle. "I have all this pain, and I don't want to waste it."

Those words were for me, right now. I am going to take all this pain and transform it into something beautiful. I don't know what yet, or how. Except that I will start by living life as beautifully as I can. And all the love I would have given to my French lover, I'll diffuse it out into the world and spread that love around all over the place.

There is something about pain that awakens; that shocks us out of complacency. Maybe I needed this pain to jolt me into living with purpose.

A little later, I open my laptop for an English session and the time on the screen is 5:55. The wink of confirmation. Apparently this is part of the divine plan. What the plan is I don't know, but I trust that some force greater than me has this under control.

The session is on Zoom so I can see myself, and there's a moment that I smile and in that moment I see the version of myself that I love most. I see that my smile can transmit joy and warmth and sweetness. I understand that I can make people feel good with that smile. And in that moment, I love me for not letting this betrayal make me angry or bitter. I love me for not letting him take away my smile.

I loved him and I lost him, but I also love me, and I didn't lose me.

CHAPTER 36

Wherever you have friends that's your country,
and wherever you receive love, that's your home.
- TIBETAN SAYING

May 2019

It's the beginning of a new chapter, and new beginnings are exciting. Possibilities are limitless, and the good thing about not having a long-distance lover to distract me is that now I can completely absorb myself in the here and now of life in Siem Reap. And there is so much to be absorbed in. My days are full of lots of yoga. I have two great neighbors, Francesca and Luca, a young Italian couple who live next door. They're fun and social and, like me, they love yoga, good food, and everything eco-friendly. They brighten my life. I buy a cute pink bicycle and explore lotus fields and more delicious restaurants. There are, of course, the amazing temples of Angkor Wat just outside Siem Reap, but I don't visit them because I saw most of them five years ago, and there are so many other things to do.

Siem Reap and I have felt aligned since the minute I arrived, so I decide this will be home for a while, as long as I can make a sustainable living here. Until now I've been living on savings. I won't be able to do that forever, so I challenge myself to pretend those savings aren't there and live off what I'm earning. In Cambodia, the cost of living is extremely low—and correspondingly, so are the average hourly wages.

I throw myself into yoga teaching (in person) and English teaching (online). Opportunities unfold quickly. Very soon, in addition to the classes at Rebecca's studio, I'm teaching four weekly classes at a stunning retreat center, weekly staff classes at another hotel, and frequently covering private classes for other teachers when they're too busy – the most beautiful of which are sunrise classes at the lotus fields. (Practicing yoga surrounded by fields of lotuses under a glowing pink and orange sky is an experience I highly recommend for everyone at least once in this lifetime.) At a party one night I meet Sarah, the founder of Plastic Free Cambodia. I join her organization as a volunteer, which turns out to be a fun and rewarding experience. With all of this plus a steadily growing number of English class bookings, my plate is deliciously full.

But these early months in Siem Reap aren't without their moments of challenge.

In the beginning, the town is full of people and classes are full of students. Then, as the weeks go by, the already scorching temperatures reach higher and full low season settles upon the region. Streets are emptier and so are the classes. There are many days when I show up to find just one or two students, or none. After a few weeks of this, my morale is dwindling. I already faced this in Kalaw low season, and here it is again. I start to question whether I'm on the right path. After all, I don't *need* to teach yoga. I never deliberately set out to become a yoga teacher; it just kind of happened. I love teaching yoga, but not when there are no students. This situation doesn't bode well for my financial outlook, either. There are many other things I could do instead, career-wise, and make a lot more money. Maybe it's time to do something else.

One day, after being greeted yet again by an empty shala, I ask the Universe for a sign to let me know if I should continue teaching yoga.

The next morning the retreat center manager messages to ask if I can cover two private classes for him—one-hour yoga and one-hour meditation for the same student.

Absolutely, I reply.

266

The private student is a lovely Aussie from Melbourne named Kristie, and she's a pure pleasure to teach. She's new to yoga but eager to learn, and she learns fast. After the warmup stretches and a few rounds of sun salutations, she says with a huge smile, "Wow! I didn't know it was possible to feel so good!" After a few more standing poses, she says, "This is wonderful. I can't thank you enough."

In the beginning of the meditation class, she tells me she's never meditated before and might be terrible at it. I introduce her to three different meditation styles. After the Samatha meditation, she says, "Wow, that went by so fast! I felt so relaxed." After the mantra meditation she says, again with a big smile: "Wow, that makes it so much easier to concentrate."

After the lovingkindness meditation, she doesn't say anything for a minute. She sits in silence, without a smile this time. I start to think she must not have enjoyed that one. Then she says with quiet sincerity, "That was the most beautiful thing I've ever done."

That evening I write this episode down in my electronic journal. Just as I finish typing *If she wasn't the sign I asked for, then what would be?* I glance at the corner of the laptop screen and it's 5:55. Bam. No matter how often that happens, it wows me every time. Thank you, Universe, for making it unmistakable. Thank you for letting me glimpse the magic. These winks from you and the way the people I need to meet keep showing up at exactly the right times are my ongoing miracle. And okay, I'll keep teaching.

Something else occurs to me the next morning. I don't need to ask yoga to pay for my living. I don't want to feel that it's a job. I want it to stay something that comes from my heart. I believe it has value and if large sums of money happen to flow to me for teaching, I'm completely open to that. But if not, I won't be bitter. I give myself these three months for yoga, English, volunteering, learning, networking, and researching—and probably will give myself high season too—but I plan to eventually find or create another source of lucrative income. So no pressure, yoga. I can just keep teaching you as long as I still want to.

And funnily enough, after that, more students start showing up.

It's all about relaxing and taking the pressure off, I think. That's when everything starts to flow.

Meanwhile, my French ex-lover hasn't disappeared. A week after his sudden text breakup, he writes to inform me that he got the Qatar job. It's a short message, via Facebook messenger. *Nice photos from India (*referring to a belated Facebook Goa post of mine—a post which did not, for the record, include any photos of him.) *Good memories. I got the confirmation of my Doha job. I'm quite happy about it. Bisous.*

The job confirmation wasn't a surprise—I had a feeling he would get it. But the email makes me feel strange.

I tell Rebecca about it. "I don't know what to do with this information. Why is he telling me?"

"Yeah, really. Like, are you telling me as just a friend, or are you looking for redemption and reconciliation here?"

I look at her, startled by the revolutionary idea of just directly asking him. "Oh. I guess I could just ask him."

"Well, yeah."

Maybe that seems extremely obvious to everyone else on the planet. But for me, it's a life-changing revelation. Aside from when I'm angry, when all polite sensitivity tends to temporarily evaporate from my being, I've spent my entire life dealing with delicate situations by avoiding all direct questions that might make me or anyone else uncomfortable and instead getting to the answer by other indirect and sometimes very complicated methods, and if no other options are available, by trying to figure the answer out in my head. I could blame the stars and my Cancerian nature, since we Cancers are reputed to have these turtle-like tendencies of side-stepping head-on confrontation, except Rebecca's a Cancer too.

"Oh no, that skirting around the issue—I've never had time for that," she says.

Armed with this thrilling, empowering, liberating new communication tool, I write back to Julien. *Congratulations. Why are you telling me this, as a friend or for some other reason?*

He seems a little caught off guard by my fantastic directness. *Oh, very good question.* He answers less directly, stammering through his written words. The gist of his reply is that he would like to see me again, but it's really up to me, and if I say no there's nothing he can do.

Something is very blatantly missing here: a big, fat, sincere apology.

I tell him that when he chose to be with someone else, it killed the magic. I always said it was like a dream with him, and now it's like I woke up. I loved the dream; it was beautiful and I'll always be grateful I got to have the happiness of those moments. But knowing now that it wasn't the beginning of the kind of real love I want, I prefer that it ended than to keep living under an illusion.

He replies that it's difficult to express what he feels in writing. His head is full of confusion and a sense of guilt that prevent him from being able to talk about this right now. When he finds the courage, he'll call me, but for right now it's too soon.

I read his email, and then I pick up the yoga manual that I'm in the middle of reviewing in preparation for a class. A quote at the bottom of the page catches my eye:

> *There is a great deal of reality and clarity in confusion. The moment you know you are confused is the beginning of clarity.* —Dr. Vasant Lad

Hilarious. One thing is very clear from all of this: the man is very confused. Another thing that's clear: that is no longer any concern of mine.

A little later he texts me in sincere, polite French: *I humbly ask you to kindly forgive me for everything.* 🙏 😌

I write him back: *I forgive you for everything. As one imperfect human to another. And because there is no freedom without forgiveness. Now if you have someone to forgive, I ask you to kindly forgive them.* 😌 🙏

Now we're free. Our chapter is closed. The day before he leaves for Qatar, I wish him a beautiful new chapter over there.

He's on the plane to Doha when he replies. *As you say, a new chapter is beginning. I need it, in my body, in my soul; so many things have happened these past two years and you were one of them. Thank you for everything, I'm grateful to have met you, to have known you.*

269

I wish you the best for the future.
I love you with all my affection.
Julien
And thus our second chapter ends.

CHAPTER 37

Tonight, for the first time in history,
it's gonna start raining men.
- THE WEATHER GIRLS

May 2019

A little while later, in Siem Reap, things get a little messy.
Siem Reap is a small town where everyone knows everyone, or at least everyone thinks they know everyone. Also, Siem Reap is not known for its large pool of eligible bachelors, to say the least. There are some great guys here, but they're mostly either gay, in a relationship, or not my type. On the other hand, there is a very large pool of beautiful, interesting, intelligent single women in Siem Reap. Considering these statistics, chances are I will be single for years, or decades, or until I take another vacation to a magic tropical island. And that's fine because I have so many other things to focus on.

But I have a friend who's a guy—a friend of my friends, one of the first people I met in Siem Reap. Jesse. He's an outgoing, social guy; a good dresser, in great shape, with skin the color of chocolate. South African born and London raised, he's got a great British accent tinged with African drawl. He's always planning fun things to do with small groups of friends. He's fun, and he would be a great match for somebody, but not for me; he's not my type. Our energy doesn't match. He's too wound-up, too fast-talking, and his occasionally cocky style reminds me of men in Miami, which is the polar opposite of my type.

But he's fun to hang out with, and he knew I had a boyfriend, and when I stopped having one I didn't tell him, to keep things simple. One night he plans a dinner out, and I'm under the impression there will be three of us at this dinner, but it turns out to be just him and me. He's dressed nice (well-dressed men are rare in Siem Reap, therefore this is an attractive detail) and I'm wearing a pretty dress, which he takes to mean something I didn't intend it to mean, and the restaurant ambience is magical, the wine is delicious, and we have a surprisingly great time. After dinner we go back to his place to watch a movie and he kisses me. I kiss him back because of the wine and because kissing is nice and he's a good kisser.

The next day I realize that the kissing was probably a bad idea because he's a fun friend and I don't want to lead him on, but oh well, it was a fun night.

Around this time, my mind has become restless. The business side of my brain has awakened from its long hibernation and is stretching its limbs, impatiently asking to be put to use. I decide to find out if there are any business opportunities for me around here. A friend tells me I should talk to Adrian Schmidt.

I know who Adrian is; I met him at a party about a month ago. We had an interesting conversation that night; he was intense and intelligent. I message him on Facebook Messenger.

Hey Adrian, hope life is treating you well! If you have time this week would you like to grab coffee or lunch? I enjoyed talking with you at Lauren's party and I'm interested in hearing about what business(es) you're involved with.

Adrian writes back that yes, that would be very nice. We meet for lunch the next day. He looks good. The night I met him, he looked a little grungy. Now, his vibe is healthy and upbeat and his hair is freshly cut. He has exceptionally great hair. With this cut, he could be a hair model and I, with my fifteen-year background in the hair industry, appreciate good hair. In fact, he could be more than just a hair model; he's tall and has a very nice bone structure. With my love of beauty and photography, I appreciate good bone structure. He could use a tan and a daily workout regime to build some muscle, but he's definitely a good-looking man … oh right, back to lunch.

It turns out Adrian and his girlfriend broke up a couple months ago. He's just gotten his hair cut and revamped his whole wardrobe and he's feeling like a new person. He's very interested in why I messaged him to have lunch. He refuses to believe it was just about business; he wants to believe I had ulterior motives. I insist my reason was strictly professional, which is true, but the third time he asks, I admit that he is the best-looking and most interesting man I've met in Siem Reap.

Now that we're both single, we have a connection. He's intense, and I like intensity. Our lunch lasts four hours. It's mostly him telling me his backstory. I'm a good listener when I'm interested, and his story is fascinating, so I'm interested. The four hours don't seem like four hours. By the end, I'm tingling with aliveness.

Apparently, so is he. An hour or two after we say our good-byes, he texts me. *When can I see you again? Dinner Wed or sooner?*

I wouldn't have minded seeing him sooner, but I already have plans with Jesse for tomorrow night so I reply: *Dinner Wed sounds good.*

The plans with Jesse are that he's coming over to my place for dinner. I like cooking, and I wanted to do something nice for him since he paid for our dinner date. I also want to tell him in person that the kissing didn't mean anything and that he should expect nothing more than platonic friendship with me.

It's meant to be a simple, casual dinner, but Jesse arrives with not one but two bottles: one red wine, one prosecco. When I open the door, he kisses me on the lips. "I didn't know what you were cooking so I wasn't sure what you'd want to drink," he says.

Uh-oh. My dinner invitation gave him the wrong idea. Maybe I should have thought this through a little more.

We open the red to accompany the Buddha bowls. I wait until we finish eating to tell him that I don't want to lead him on. I want to avoid hurting his feelings with something direct like, "I like you as a friend but you're not my type and I have no interest in any romantic involvement with you," so I take an indirect approach which involves too many words spilling out of my mouth.

"I need to tell you something. I don't want you to have the wrong idea. As you know, I just got out of a relationship, and it was intense and I'm not sure I'm over it yet. I'm not ready to get into another relationship and I'm not interested in anything casual right now. Basically, I'm emotionally unavailable. And you are a really good kisser but I don't want anything more than friendship. And I appreciate your friendship and I don't want to lead you on."

He listens attentively, then clears his throat to respond to the key thing he heard in all of that. "So, I'm a really good kisser?" A gleam of satisfaction twinkles in his eyes and a sly smile spreads across his face.

This is why I really need to get out of the habit of this stupid indirect approach. "Yeah, but the point is, I'm emotionally unavailable and I don't want anything casual…"

"Okay." He reverts to a serious expression and pauses to think for a minute. "Well, I'm not just looking for a hookup." He launches into an explanation of what he likes about me, my personality, my character. He goes on for a long time, including specific details and examples. I listen in surprise. He has been paying attention. I wasn't expecting this from the guy who I had pegged as the cocky-Miami-superficial-player type.

I don't know how to respond to all of that, so I say, "Do you want to watch a documentary?"

He insists on washing all the dishes first, and then we watch a documentary on the catastrophic effects of global warming on the ocean's coral reefs. I have no intentions of letting him kiss me again, but somehow that's what happens. The wise angel on my shoulder hisses that this is not a good idea … but it feels good. This guy really is a good kisser. I ignore the wise angel.

When we say goodbye, Jesse's parting words are, "I'm not giving up. You don't give up on something worth having."

He walks out the door and I'm left standing there open-mouthed. It's been a long time since any man said something like that to me.

One night later Adrian and I are staring into each other's eyes, holding hands across the dinner table.

He picked a nice restaurant and ordered a nice bottle of wine, and again the conversation has pulled me into a spell. The connection is unmistakable. I am excited and completely comfortable at the same time. I've completely forgotten that twenty-four hours ago I was emotionally unavailable.

After dinner he takes me to a wonderful place I didn't know about, a little speakeasy tucked away in one of the small alleys near Pub Street, with plush leather couches and gin cocktails and a dim, sultry atmosphere. It's empty except for the bartenders. We lounge on one of the couches and sip cocktails and keep talking. The moment is perfect for a kiss but he doesn't kiss me so I kiss him, even though in my entire life I've never been the one to instigate the first kiss. It feels natural. He kisses me back. It's a nice kiss; relaxed and sensual. It doesn't feel like a first or second date. Something about being with him feels easy and familiar.

He's cute in his excitement at our connection. "I want to date you—can I date you?"

I laugh. "Of course."

At the end of the night we take two separate tuk-tuks to our respective homes. A little while after I get home, Adrian messages. *I can't find my house keys. :/ I went back to the restaurant but they weren't there.*

Well, I can't leave him stranded out there in the middle of the night. *Oh no! You can come sleep here,* I write. *We can innocently sleep.*

Fifteen minutes later the doorbell rings. I open the door to find Adrian standing there with a big grin on his face, dangling a set of keys in his right hand. "I found them, but you had already invited me, so I came over anyway."

I laugh, and let him in. "You can sleep over, but I'm not going to sleep with you," I inform him.

"I'm happy to go slow," he says.

We sleep spooning, and it feels nice to have the affectionate warmth of another body against me, but ... for some reason, I'm not getting the blissful cloud of endorphins I used to get spooning with my French lover. I'm annoyed that the memory of him has invaded my mind. I push the thought of him away. I refuse to miss him. But I do miss the way everything felt so good with him. The way everything just felt right.

As for Adrian, his six-year relationship ended only two months ago. Maybe neither of us is emotionally ready to get involved with someone else. We talk about this. He disagrees. He says things were really over between him and his ex long ago. As for me—I don't know. I'm just going with the flow.

That weekend, there's an event at a gorgeous hotel in town. It's a beautiful night. I'm there with friends; wine and champagne are flowing and we're having a great time. I'm full of unfiltered happiness.

Jesse is there too. Out of the blue, he asks, "Did you go to that meetup event Wednesday?"

I did, as a matter of fact. So did Adrian; we met up there before going to dinner.

"Yeah, why?"

"Do you know Adrian Schmidt? He's one of my Facebook contacts and I saw he was going and I saw you were going."

Clearly, there are no secrets in this town. I ignore the strangeness of his question. "Yeah, I know him." My attention is pulled away by the laughter of friends nearby.

By the end of the night, an undercurrent of some invisible force of attraction is pulling me towards Jesse. After the event, we end up at his place watching a hilarious movie called *Overboard*. We make out a little between gales of laughter. I didn't expect to be attracted to him like this, but I am. His skin feels so nice and the kisses are so good and it's making me want more. But the thought of Adrian restrains me.

After the movie, Jesse asks, "Is there someone else in the picture?"

Definitely no secrets in this town. "Why do you ask?" I ask.

"It's a simple question."

Not one that I feel obligated to answer at this moment. "I have some things to figure out," is all I say.

He looks straight ahead. "Well, I don't want to get into a competition." Short pause. "Although, I'm not afraid of competition." He tilts his head. "Actually, competition is good. I thrive on competition." As he's talking, his tone becomes progressively brighter, as if he's just realized that in fact, he relishes the thought of some good old-fashioned competition.

I have to admit that's an attractive reaction. This guy keeps surprising me.

He convinces me to sleep over, which is not a hard sell because I'm drowsy and comfortable. He's a good cuddler too. His arm remains wrapped around me while we sleep, and I don't miss Julien while I'm sleeping here, which is nice but confusing.

I keep going on dates with both men. Movie and breakfast and dinner dates with Adrian. Less frequent dates with Jesse, but his are always thoughtful and elaborately planned out. I tell Adrian I'm seeing someone else, so he hears it from me before someone else in Siem Reap informs him. His reaction is calm. He's not thrilled, but he's confident the other guy won't stay in the picture long.

Dating two men is fun, but I don't want to play with anyone's heart, and I don't want complications, and human nature being what it is, people in small towns love to talk, and I don't want to be the subject of their talk. I also don't want to sleep with two men, so my mission is to figure out which one I'm going to sleep with so I can stop holding out, which is getting more difficult as time goes on.

The problem is … it's impossible to make a decision.

With Adrian, I am mentally and emotionally connected. Besides being tall and nice to look at, he's extremely intelligent, articulate, and well-informed on a vast range of subjects. I can talk about anything with him, although we don't agree on everything. He's kind, adoring, affectionate, and he's happy to meditate with me. Being with him is very comfortable. He has a few personality traits I don't love that surface every now and then. But all the good is so good that I find it impossible to stop seeing him.

With Jesse, the attraction is more superficial—a more

chemical/physical thing, even though the more time I spend with him, the more attractive character traits I'm discovering. But still, he's not my type. I don't see a future with him.

And then, there's the memory of Julien, which occasionally returns to annoy me. Am I over him? I really thought he was the one. Maybe I'm over him. I don't know.

Imperfections and all, there's some kind of connection with Adrian that I can't ignore. I can't not date him. Therefore, I'm going to break things off with Jesse for real now. He's been out of town for work and I haven't seen him in a bit, but he's planned a surprise date at his place Saturday night. I have to break the news to him before he goes to whatever effort he's planning to go to. It seems best to do this in person, so I stop by his place in the afternoon.

His apartment is a studio. There's no couch, so all the sitting happens on his bed. He's lounging on it comfortably, propped against pillows and the headboard. He looks good in his white t-shirt and his skin is so nice and smooth, stretched tautly over his muscles. In retrospect, maybe ending things over the phone would have been a better idea.

I sit down next to him.

"I thought I was seeing you tonight …. is this going to be bad news?" he asks.

Reluctantly, I explain my decision. He takes it well. He doesn't show emotion but on some subtle level I feel his disappointment. I hate hurting people and this makes me want to comfort him. I lean against him to give him a one-armed hug. That was a bad idea, because his body feels good. He puts one arm around me. We stay like that.

"Why are you so comfortable?" I mumble. "Your skin is so nice…" and I make myself pull away.

He laughs. "No one can resist the brown sugar."

"What was the surprise going to be?" I ask.

He was going to make Indian food: a vegetarian curry and parathas. He got the spices he needed in Phnom Penh, and a bottle of his favorite white wine.

I moan in despair. I *love* Indian food. The devil on my left shoulder and the angel on my right play tug of war with my mind. The devil wins. "Well, since you already got everything … we could still have dinner, if you want."

He hesitates. I recant. "No, it's a bad idea, we probably shouldn't."

"Well, you're right, I already got everything … okay, let's do it. Come over at seven."

I leave, with the excited anticipation that comes with knowing you're ignoring your wise responsible angel but you're about to have a lot of fun.

The night is a lot of fun. We're both in a good mood. He pours me a glass of wine and I sip it perched on a chair near his tiny kitchen while he finishes the curry and the flaky parathas and the sauteed veggies and we talk. Mostly he talks, about his interesting past in Africa and London and his future plans. I love his voice. The resonant British-African accent is like caramel-scented honey, with layers of subtle complexity and laced with addictive sugar. He's complex too. There are deeper layers to him than I first realized.

We keep talking through the sensationally delicious dinner, and again I end up sleeping over.

In the morning, he prepares an extravagant breakfast: an Indian omelet with rosemary-infused bacon and a sparkling passionfruit mocktail, served with—because he remembered that I once said I like tiramisu for breakfast—a large square of tiramisu on the side, along with coffee and almond milk because he also remembered that I don't drink regular milk.

It's completely over the top and way too much food, but the thoughtfulness and effort is touching. So much for breaking it off with Jesse. I am still fully entangled in the conundrum of these two men—although it has become a sensationally delicious conundrum.

The good thing is that I'm leaving for a week. I'm going on a visa run to Myanmar to visit Kalaw and chase more waterfalls with Ingyin, so for seven days I won't see either of these men and maybe by the time I come back, clarity will have revealed itself.

The week in Myanmar is a beautiful distraction.

In Kalaw I exchange excited hugs with old friends, and visit Steve's new café, which is bigger and looks great, and hug all the café girls. My former home, the fairytale hotel, is as fairytale-like as ever. Ingyin takes me to a majestic multi-tiered waterfall deep in a remote part of the forest a few hours' drive from Kalaw that she found a few months earlier. The waterfall is a dream; seven levels all dramatically different than each other. My favorite part is the section with ten shallow tiers of frothy waterfall cascading over caramel-colored boulders and forming still pools between them. There's no one else here; we have this all to ourselves. We wade and float in the cool water. It's a rare, amazing gem of a place.

By the time I'm on the plane back to Cambodia, I have clarity—I think.

Both men have been texting, but Adrian much more regularly than Jesse. Jesse is indisputably the better cook, but Adrian is the one I feel the stronger pull to. I'm going to see where things go with him.

When I break the news to Jesse, he reacts with grace.

"Okay, I'm out," he says, without hesitation. "I understand. No regrets. I would rather have had all those dates with you than not tried."

With that, he earned my respect—and he rekindled the spark of attraction. So much for clarity. But I've already made my decision, and I'm done going back and forth.

So now Adrian is the only man in my life—for a little while.

Adrian is complex, and how I feel about him is complicated. There is so much in him that is good and wonderful, but as time goes on, I begin to see his shadow side. I discover that his heart is big but so is his ego, and his light is bright but mixed in with it is a dense streak of darkness and negativity that is different than my darkness. I can't relate to it or empathize with it or carry it. I start to notice that the view he has of himself and the belief system he describes to me don't match the day-to-day choices he's making and the way he's living his life. His words are hollow and he doesn't see that.

But towards me, he's affectionate and appreciative and adoring. "Can I just sit here and adore you?" he asks one day, sitting on my couch while I'm making props for an English class on the other side of the room.

I beam. "Absolutely. I thrive on adoration."

I don't want to compare him to Julien, but I can't help comparing how I felt with both men. With Adrian, I don't feel that click of everything being naturally just right. Even though most of the time, being with Adrian feels really good. In many respects, he's the perfect boyfriend. He's a Taurus; we're both homebodies. He's a good cuddler, and the fact that he's always willing to meditate with me is a huge point in his favor.

But gradually I discover more and more qualities I don't like in him, and it becomes clear to both of us that I'm not going to be able to accept him as he is. He could be my dream life partner if he changed about twenty-three fundamental things about himself, and he doesn't want to change all of those things—nor could he even if he wanted to, because many of them are just who he is. I could love part of him, but I'll never be able to love all of him. And he wants someone who will love all of him.

When he recognizes that, he ends it, via a long, articulate, gracious text message, and when I read the message I feel suddenly, joyfully liberated.

Much ado about nothing, you could say, except it wasn't nothing, because the affection and adoration he gave me nourished my soul. He appreciated it too. Maybe we both needed a little dose of love and sweetness at that point in our lives.

Jesse comes back into my life, but I discover another side to him too. Now that the competition is gone, there are no more carefully planned dates, no more romantic words and surprises, no more effort whatsoever. To be fair, this is in part because he knows he wasn't my first choice and in part because his workload has intensified and he's become a tightly-wound ball of stress. But the stress can't take the blame for what I discover: that who he really is is just a big talker. His words and promises are empty. The empty words are a deal breaker for me, but it doesn't matter that much, because it's already become crystal clear that we aren't wired to be together. Again (annoyingly) I can't help but contrast interaction with him to the way it was with Julien. With Julien, everything flowed naturally, smoothly, effortlessly. With Jesse, nothing flows smoothly. We clash all the time. We misinterpret each other's simplest words. We can rarely get through a day without unintentionally rubbing each other the wrong way. Our short texts are so likely to end in misunderstanding and conflict that one day he asks, "From now on, can we only make plans by phone call, not by text, so you don't get mad at me?"

But we keep hanging out in spite of the frequent clashes, because we have a good time when we're not arguing, and he's funny and he can still make me laugh when he's not making me mad, and under all the bravado and big talk, he has a good heart. Deep down, there is something genuine about him. Also, he likes books.

One day I find *Manuscript Found in Accra* on his shelf. I pick it up and leaf through the pages and am spellbound. We all have access to the same words in the English language. I don't understand how Paulo Coelho has the ability to choose from among them and line them up together in such a way that they prick my soul and take my breath away, but that's what he does in this book.

Jesse tells me to borrow it. For that alone, I can overlook a few of his flaws.

I'm going to leave Cambodia for two months the beginning of September, and Jesse's planning to move to Thailand, so I probably won't see him again after I leave. This will effortlessly come to a natural end, which is my favorite way for things to end.

CHAPTER 38

Todo necesita tiempo.
- MY SPANISH HISTORY PROFESSOR,
UNIVERSITY OF SEVILLE, 2002

July 2019

My birthday is the middle of July. This is shortly after Adrian has faded out of the picture, and around this time, I start talking with Julien again. It's been a month and a half since our last email exchange, but it feels like ages.

The correspondence begins like old friends catching up. He tells me about life in Doha; I tell him about life in Siem Reap. In Doha, he's found great yoga teachers and he's doing yoga almost every day and drinking a lot less, because wine is difficult to get and very expensive.

He calls to wish me happy birthday. He switches to video to show me his Doha apartment and we see each other for the first time since our breakup. He's grown a beard, a closely trimmed one. He looks different—and still very attractive.

Seeing him does something to me. I feel immediately the same attraction as before. It's physical, but also more. The most attractive thing about him is his essence. I could search my whole life for the right words to describe this. But to put it simply and unpoetically, it's just energy, or cosmic, or I don't know what.

Under the surface of the conversation there's a current of something more. There's a moment where we're both silent, just looking at each other, and there's a flash. An invisible flash of energy, connection, recognition. His eyes tell me that he feels something, but all I can know for sure is what I feel. In that moment I know that he would have been the one for me. If he hadn't taken himself out of the picture, there would have been no dilemma of Siem Reap men. I would have loved him forever. I don't know how I know this; I just know. But wound together with that flash, there is acceptance of the current circumstances. We're not together, but that fact doesn't make me suffer, and the recognition of that makes me happy. I don't know what the future holds. I don't know if destiny will bring us back together. I know that I won't wait for him, because I don't believe in waiting for someone who doesn't want you. I'm not letting my happiness depend on him. If he wants to continue with his story about the distance and the fifteen-year age difference being a reason to keep us apart, that's fine. I'll keep living my life without him and it will be rich and beautiful and full of joy. I'll keep fully enjoying my time alone and my time with other men, and in time the memory of this connection with him will fade. If he ever wakes up and realizes that what there was between us was the best gift ever and wants to do something about it, well, we'll see what happens.

Soon after the birthday call, he starts writing that he misses me. That I'm in his head all the time.

I'm happy to hear it, but I don't trust that this isn't going to be short-lived. I remain aloof. He keeps texting.

One day he sends a text with a vaguely sexual innuendo, and for some reason that sends me into instant emotional shutdown. I suddenly feel no attraction towards him, just nothing. I only remember how much passion and energy I gave him before and how suddenly and easily he threw it away. And now he thinks he can just pick up again where he left off, just like that, as if nothing happened.

I write him back coldly, and he takes the hint. His messages stay safely platonic from then on.

A few days later, he writes: *I was thinking something crazy.*

What's that?, I ask.

To see you again. Somewhere on planet Earth.

I have to think for a few minutes before I reply. His message triggers conflicting emotions. There is the cold part of me that has no desire to see him again—and there is the part of my heart that jumps happily at the sight of those words.

Well, I rationalize to myself, *I welcome all my friends to come visit me. He's a friend. It doesn't have to be anything more.*

I reply: *It's not the craziest thing I've ever heard in my life.*

We continue our platonic texting, and my emotional shutdown continues, but so does the conflicting secret wish to see him again. We had something very beautiful and he chose to throw it away in the blink of an eye. I'm not sure what we had can be rekindled, but … maybe that will be possible one day.

Where this goes is in the hands of destiny. In the meantime, I have other things to think about. I'm grateful to my heart for this momentary shutdown, actually.

The rainy season has started, but Cambodia's rainy season is pure delight compared to Myanmar's. It doesn't rain every day, and when it does, it pours torrentially for a mere two to three hours. Then the sun comes out again, and the rain has cut the scorching heat, and the sunrises and sunsets are dazzling.

August 6th is the two-year anniversary of my arrival in Asia. That morning I teach sunrise yoga at the lotus fields for a sweet Japanese couple. The sky is overcast and a few minutes into the class, it starts to drizzle. I ask the couple if they want to move indoors, but they say they're okay, so we stay where we are. A few minutes later the drizzle stops, the sun peeks through the clouds, and a magnificent double rainbow appears in the sky. It remains hovering above us for the rest of the class.

If they wouldn't have been willing to wait out the drops, we would have gone back to shelter and missed out on this magic.

It's the only time I ever see a rainbow at the lotus fields. I take this as a spectacular anniversary gift from the Universe and a little reminder: when times get tough, don't let the rain scare you off. Give it some time and wait for the rainbow.

August is supposed to be a slow month in Siem Reap, but the retreat center is busy because they get a lot of European guests this month, and we're down one teacher because the yoga manager is on holiday for a month. Then the teacher who's covering him comes down with dengue, so I'm covering for both of them, and the busyness feels great. Half of Siem Reap falls prey to dengue around this time, in varying degrees of severity, none of which are pleasant. My apartment isn't mosquito-proof thanks to some of its unique architectural features and I get bitten by an average of ten mosquitos a day, but somehow I never get dengue. For this I thank my lucky stars and my valiant immune system, because I have no time to be sick.

When the yoga manager returns, it will be my turn to leave. My travel program will be three weeks of WWOOFing in the south of France and a week in Italy to visit Rome and my former neighbor Francesca, who's moved from Cambodia back to Europe just in time for me to visit her. And then back to the US for the first time in two years.

One August Friday afternoon, I make plans with Jesse for that night. I'll be having dinner at the retreat center after I finish teaching. I'll text him when I leave and he'll come over for Netflix.

I text him when I finish my delicious bowl of gnocchi. When I get home, he hasn't replied. The two little Whatsapp check marks are still gray; he hasn't even seen the message. I start doing my own thing, catching up on emails. A bottle of wine on the counter is calling me. I plan to wait for him to open it, but time goes on and still no reply from him, still no blue check marks.

I've waited long enough. I pour myself a glass and settle back onto the couch with my laptop. I get caught up in typing and lose track of time.

An hour and a half later, I look at the phone. It's 10:30 p.m. Rude of him to stand me up like this, and rudeness is one of my least favorite qualities. But whatever. Add this to the long list of sub-par qualities this guy has. I'll let him know what I think of that later.

I text him, *Waking up early so see you another time,* and go back to my laptop.

The wine is smooth and delicious, and Spotify is playing great music. I'm feeling good—exceptionally good—enveloped in pure, delicious contentment. A song comes on with an irresistible beat. *Bones,* by Galantis and One Republic. *You bring an energy I've never felt before, some kind of chemical that reaches to my core …*

I can't not dance to this song. I put the laptop aside, get to my feet, and start dancing around the living room. *As far as you and me, I've never had a choice, you feel like hooooome …* Wild joy is sizzling in my veins. The music and I are on the exact same wavelength. The song carries the energy of the enraptured state of being in love and that same energy latent inside me comes alive, the energy of being in love with life, and this moment is perfect joy and total aliveness. God bless Jesse for leaving me hanging; I'm having infinitely more fun on my own than I would have had with him.

When the song ends, I play it again and keep dancing. And again, and again. I dance to the song six times in a row, and even when I sit down again with the laptop and let the playlist continue on to other songs, the dancing joy stays with me.

There has been many a time in my life that I let someone's rudeness or other undesirable behavior steal my happiness. This time, I didn't, and it feels AMAZING.

Previously, I knew intellectually that this was possible. I've read and thought about this kind of thing before. But to spontaneously experience what it feels like to stay feeling this good, immune to another person's rudeness: this is another level. This is empowering.

Thank you, Jesse. Thank you for creating the opportunity for me to experience this. Your rudeness turned out to be a gift.

CHAPTER 39

You were thirsty to know more, for greater clarity,
for a greater connection with the mystery of the Divine?
- NARI ANASTARSIA

September 2019

I'm at a bucolic farm in the south of France, surrounded by fig trees, fresh air, and abundant nature. My spirit is festive. As if to symbolize my state of mind, a little physical piece of magic has accompanied me from Cambodia. It's a shimmering strand of pink, blue, and silver foil in my hair.

Four months ago, an American stylist from Las Vegas came to work at Rebecca's salon for a month and she brought packages of festive hair tinsels with her. In May, for Pride Day, she attached them to the hair of many of us lucky girls, giving us headfuls of shimmering colorful highlights. When she put mine in, I said, "I love these! I want them to stay in forever!"

Normally they last a week or two. A couple weeks later, they had all washed out and our hair was back to its normal pre-tinsel state .... except for one glitzy strand that four months later is still on my head. My hair's been washed and blow-dried a hundred times, highlighted twice, dunked in swimming pools, brushed, curled, pulled, twisted, mercilessly windblown on tuk-tuks and motorbikes, and yet against all odds this colorful little tinsel is still there. As if the Universe heard me and said, *oh, you want this to stay? Okay, no problem.* Just so there would be this tiny, insignificant yet magical bit of extra sparkle to remind me every time I look in the mirror that miracles do happen and anything is possible.

One mid-September day, Julien sends me a photo of the oracle card he pulled for himself that morning from his *L'Oracle Cosmique* deck. *Transformation.*

From what he's shared with me of himself, of his inner searching, of his current experience in Doha, it fits perfectly. *A beautiful card,* I tell him.

Now your turn, he writes. *Think about your card and give me a number.* 7.

He sends me my card, a wild, vibrant orange-and-red flower with curling leaf tendrils gleaming under a full moon. *Celebration,* it's called.

Rejoice in your success, dear friend, you deserve it. You are congratulated for all that you've achieved during this trip. Now, celebrate your life, your success and your extraordinary progression. …

You are never alone. You are always guided and supported by the masters and teachers of the highest spheres. All of your material needs and your requests are and will always be satisfied. You are loved and appreciated because you are a beautiful soul. Celebrate life, celebrate you!

With its theme of celebration, this little card couldn't be more perfect if it tried. That is exactly the mode I've been in these two weeks since I left Cambodia. I think back to ten months ago, when I was so frustrated because I couldn't buy a ticket home for Christmas, back when I was in a different place of less groundedness and more uncertainty, and I'm so glad that Life made me wait until I could go back on this joyful high.

And why such a high? What am I celebrating? I haven't accomplished anything incredible, from the outside. I haven't achieved any specific goals. I'm just happy. I found love, beauty, wonder, joy, magic, a home, a sense of belonging, and freedom. It feels like nothing is lacking.

I reread the card and I want to dance. And this is why I can't shake the connection with this man, because of all these beautiful synchronicities and all these little things he does that light my soul with joy.

A few days later, he buys his ticket to Cambodia. I'll be getting back November 6th. He'll come for the last two weeks in November.

My celebratory mood continues through my week in Italy—a perfect country to be in when one is feeling festive. Restaurants in Tuscany even serve wine on tap: white wine that is lightly effervescent, as if even the wine can't keep itself from sparkling.

And yet, mingling with my state of festivity is a current of restlessness.

My mind has been restless ever since Julien bought his ticket to Cambodia. I couldn't put my finger on the exact reason why, until I heard an interesting TED Radio Hour podcast my last week in France. It was about a woman deciding to forgive her ex-boyfriend for raping her in high school. Very thought-provoking.

It made me wonder: had I really, genuinely forgiven Julien for what he had done?

I thought I did. But I'm still carrying resentment. I'm torn between resentment and attraction, and that's what's causing the restlessness. It's not about the other woman. My feelings about that vanished long ago. The resentment is because he hurt me. He threw away what we had. To me it was a treasure, and he threw it away like it was nothing. That's what hurt. That's what I have to forgive him for, if we are to have any kind of future, but I can't. I can't because I'm not sure he's sorry for doing it.

I don't bring it up with him. I don't even know what I would say.

My last night in Florence, Julien sends me a voice note. He tells me he woke up in the morning with a dream vivid in his mind. In the dream he was told he should write down on paper all his regrets, remorse, everything he wished he'd done differently in life. So he got a piece of paper, wrote all those things down, and then burned the paper. It was a significant moment for him, and all day afterwards he kept thinking about forgiveness, and especially self-forgiveness. That night he went to a cacao ceremony, and the theme of the ceremony was The Five Languages of Apology.

The five steps they talked about were:

1. Expressing regret
2. Accepting responsibility
3. Making restitution
4. Genuinely repenting
5. Requesting forgiveness

He found it superb. A really nice experience.

As I listen to his message, I wait expectantly to hear if it will include an expression of regret and a request for forgiveness from me. But it doesn't.

So I ask him about it.

He replies in another voice memo. "I wrote many things on that paper, and yes, you were part of it. Again I ask you to forgive me for what I did to you. When I did that, I didn't really believe in our relationship, with the distance, the age difference, the life you have, and the beautiful woman that you are. I thought you probably also had other men in your life. Now I understand the hurt I caused you, and I'm truly sorry. But we learn from our mistakes, we evolve. You're not obliged to accept my apology, of course. If you want to talk about this more, over the phone or later in person, I'm available. I really want to keep you as a true friend, of course, but also … ever since I've decided to come to Cambodia, it's complicated, how to say … well, it's up to you. Above all, I don't want to impose on you. It's up to you."

It's what I needed to hear. The missing piece. A sincere and specific apology, spoken aloud in a human voice. The resentment I've been carrying around melts like a block of ice on a hot day. I listen to his message twice, and I forgive him.

I don't know what will happen when we see each other, but I know this apology opened a door.

My first two days in the US feel strange. The highways are enormous and the stores are too full of things and everything feels surreal, as if it was in a dream that I've seen all of this before. Then the strangeness wears off and I relax into the familiarity and comfort, although there remains a tinge of the impression that I had often in my adult years, that something about life here is off. Everything is too disposable, too easy to discard and replace. Nothing seems to have any real value because everything is replaceable.

But that's not important right now; the important thing is the people I love here. My month in the US is a whirlwind of reunions with friends and family and joy and celebration, in between garage sales to sell off all my remaining possessions that have been sitting in a storage unit for two years. To my great relief, my little nieces Alyssa and Ainsley haven't forgotten me. They're five and four now, and more fun, adorable, and irresistibly lovable than ever. Within five minutes of my arrival at their house, they've opened my suitcase and are holding an impromptu fashion show in the hallway with all of my clothes, complete with a strutting catwalk for each oversized outfit.

One day I hear four-year-old Ainsley ask her mother, "Can Aunt Sonya live here forever?" I love her forever for that.

But I can't live with her forever, because Cambodia is waiting.

Chapter 40

It's essential to have poor soils. The vines must struggle.
-Christophe Baron, founder, Cayuse Vineyards

November 2019

A few weeks before my return to Cambodia, I messaged the yoga manager confirming my date of availability to resume classes at the retreat center. As of the day of my return flight, he hasn't replied. Has he found another teacher he likes better and replaced me? Rebecca has sold her yoga studio and moved back to the US, and the new owner has found other new teachers too, so I'm not sure what my work situation is going to look like when I get back. Regardless, I've sold everything in the US, so I'm going to make it work in Cambodia one way or the other.

I needn't have worried. When I arrive at Siem Reap airport and recharge my Cambodian SIM, the first message I see is a long one from the yoga manager. He writes that for various personal reasons he's decided to leave the retreat center and asks if I'd be interested in his job.

I've been secretly coveting his job ever since I knew it existed. The Santosha Resort & Wellness Center is a dream—home to an ever-present aura of peace and well-being, soul-nourishing natural beauty, two stunning yoga shalas, a laid-back general manager, and a wonderful staff. Plus, the yoga manager position comes with a salary, something no other yoga teacher in Siem Reap has. Of course I'm interested.

After discussions with the manager, we agree I'll start December 1st. Perfect timing again; right after Julien leaves.

My dream job. That's my welcome-back-to-Cambodia gift.

My first two weeks back go by fast. I buy a fantastic motorbike for $350, a worn-in, ultra-comfortable 2007 Yamaha Nouvo that runs like a dream. I rent an apartment for a month and start looking for a longer-term home closer to the retreat center.

November 16th, Julien arrives.

We meet at his hotel that evening. It's strange to see him again, and at the same time, not strange. I think he's a little unsure of himself. Neither one of us knows what's going to come of this reunion. He doesn't have the beard anymore but in its place is an attractive few days' shadow, like he had in Bali.

We make small talk and walk to my favorite Italian restaurant. I have heavenly melt-in-your-mouth gnocchi. He has a delicious wood-fired pizza with prosciutto and rocket and a generous scoop of burrata in the middle, and we share a bottle of red wine. Later, I won't remember at what point during dinner I knew the spark was still there. I only know that after dinner, in the street outside the restaurant, I turn to look at him and kiss him, and from there we pick up where we left off in Goa, except not exactly in the same place we left off because it's different now. We're different. We've hurt and been hurt and there is no longer a cloud of untainted bliss around us, but under our feet the ground is a little more solid and the cord of connection is still there between us.

Siem Reap is a fun place to have a visitor. We visit artisanal markets, savor the world's best spring rolls, treat ourselves to extremely affordable couples' massages, watch the sun rise over Angkor Wat, and admire the intricate stonewalled carvings of more temples. We have drinks at lush rooftop bars and dine at Khmer and Indian and Japanese and Italian and French restaurants. We do lots of yoga and every day he does a couple hours of work on his shaded balcony. I

find him extra attractive in these moments, when he puts his glasses
on and concentrates intently on his laptop.

My realtor finds a house option and Julien comes with me to see
it. It's a dream: a brand new two bedroom, three bath; furnished,
spacious, and beautiful, full of light with attractive modern
architectural details in the walls and ceilings, large closets, and a big
open kitchen. Construction has just been finished. The big back and
front yards are nothing but sand because, my realtor tells me matter
of factly, the owners ran out of money building the house. But if I pay
a deposit, they'll make a driveway and put plants and grass in.

It's $600 a month, a four-minute drive or ten-minute walk to
Santosha, and I can set the second bedroom up for Airbnb.

The landlords are an older Khmer couple with kind eyes and
gentle smiles. They speak no English and live in a smaller, older house
on the lot behind this one. Their daughter and adorable little grandson
live with them. The grandson is named Magra (pronounced "Mahg-
rah", emphasis on the last syllable), which means January in Khmer.
He's eight but looks no older than five and has the brightest smile in
the world. I pay the deposit and true to their word, the landlords begin
planting grass the next day.

My French lover and I are having a good time, even though the spell
of enchantment has been broken and we're now in real life with no
filters over our eyes. He is kind and classy: a gentleman. He does cute
little things that make me feel taken care of. He insists on taking my
motorbike to a mechanic for a check-up, which seems totally
unnecessary because it runs perfectly, but his insistence is sweet. It
feels good to feel looked after.

But the feeling of adoration I had for him before is gone. My
heart remains a little aloof. Something feels off between us and I'm
not sure what it is.

When he's been in town a week, I take him to my favorite sky
bar, overlooking a sea of treetops and featuring a vivid sunset. We're
here to belatedly celebrate his birthday, which was in October.

"It's also the anniversary of my divorce today," he tells me.

"Oh, it's your freedom anniversary," I say.

He laughs. "Yes."

We're sipping champagne and munching on potato chips and peanuts, waiting for the appetizers to arrive, and everything's perfect, until he casually drops an atomic bomb into the conversation.

Remember when he ended everything between us back in April, because of that "other woman"? Actually, there was no other woman, he informs me. There wasn't even a big party. He made it all up.

He reveals this with an air of perfect nonchalance, as if inventing fake indiscretions to break the hearts of their lovers is something people do every day.

I think I must have misunderstood him. "You made it up?" I repeat.

"Yeah," he says, again with no emotion.

I'm confused. Something must be getting lost in translation. I pull out my phone and scroll way back through all the messages to his long one from April 28th. I read a few lines aloud. "*Hello Sonya. This message gives me immense pain to write … During my festive night I committed the unforgivable. This gives me no pleasure at all but it is what it is; I met a woman.*

"This message? You made it up?"

"Yes," he confirms, taking another handful of peanuts. "There hasn't been anyone else since you."

I'm frozen. He's just unmasked himself as an insane, sadistic sociopath, this man I thought was so good and kind, this man I thought I loved.

"Why?" is the only thing I can ask.

"Everything got so complicated in my head," he says. "With the time of not seeing you and I couldn't see how it was going to work, and I thought it would be easier to end it with that story so you could hate me."

Nothing in my life has prepared me for the shock of this moment. My brain can't process what I'm hearing. I remember vividly what I felt reading that message, everything I felt afterwards. The shock, the nausea, the pain. This man is out of his mind. I don't know anything anymore. The only thing I know is I can't sit here next to this crazy person. I stand up, grab my bag, and walk out of the restaurant without a word to him.

As the elevator carries me to the ground floor, it occurs to me that people walk out on their dates all the time on TV, but this is the first time I've had the opportunity to do such a thing in real life. The dramatic effect gives me a tiny bit of diabolical satisfaction.

I take a taxi back to his hotel, where I've left some of my things and where, conveniently for me at this moment and against all common sense, all the room keys are left hanging on the wall near the stairwell for anyone to grab. I gather all my things, drive back to my apartment, and collapse into the cushioned embrace of the couch in tears of shattered disappointment. I can't reconcile all the goodness I've seen in this man with this bizarre streak of darkness. Nothing makes any sense anymore.

Maybe the Oracle knows. I ask, "Is there some lesson, some message for me in this situation?" and pull a card from my Native Spirit deck.

My card is *Spirit Keeper of the East.* "New beginnings. A fresh cycle is occurring in your life. Wipe the slate clean; it's time to release the old and start again. No matter what has happened in the past, it doesn't need to repeat in the future."

Okay, there are multiple ways to take that...

A few hours later, Julien texts me.

Sonya, I'm not proud of all that. I was sincere. I beg you to forgive me for having hurt you, it wasn't my intention. I wanted to be forgiven, and I obtained the opposite. I was lost, back in that time when I sent you the message. I wanted to set you free and me too knowing that everyone was going to suffer. I'm going to leave, it's the best for you and me.

"I wanted to be forgiven, and I obtained the opposite" pricks my heart. It's only then that I understand there was emotion behind his revelation, even though he didn't show it. That he told me the truth now because he was sorry, and that it took courage for him to tell me what he had done. Then I can see past my own emotion to start to understand his. His lie hadn't been gratuitous and sadistic after all. It was a strange lie, but at least it was motivated by the twisted logic of him trying to arrange for me to suffer less while he set me free. The idea of him leaving and never seeing him again makes me suddenly, devastatingly sad.

Leaving isn't the answer. We should talk in the morning, I text him.

In the morning, over coffee, he apologizes again. His eyes are shiny with tears. "I have this pattern," he says. "When things get too complicated, something happens in my head. I panic and invent a way to get out of it and it makes everything worse. I know that's my pattern and I want to change."

His big lie still doesn't make sense to me, but I can't sit here and say I've never done anything in my life that doesn't make sense. He is flawed and so am I. I look at him sitting across the table from me and I see him as a whole. He is flawed but he is wonderful. He is kind and charming and caring and deep and thoughtful and passionate and he's sitting there with his heart bared, shadows exposed. Sincere remorse is written on his face, and what I feel overwhelmingly from him is the goodness of his essence. I look at him and know that I love him, and my hurt and anger dissolve. My heart forgives him before my mind realizes what's happening.

He suffered too. He hurt me, but the hurt made me stronger. In the end, I think he suffered more than I did. *There is a need for some kind of ending that will make you stronger*, that long-ago soulmate tarot reading in Kalaw had said. Because of this short-term ending I now understand another level of him, and I understand another level of me. I see both his light and his shadow side more clearly, and I feel at peace, and in this peace there is a new kind of strength.

My mind also acknowledges that this unusual flaw of freaking out and inventing a fake cheating story to get us both out of the relationship is preferable to actual cheating. If I was given a choice between the two options, I would have picked the fake cheating.

There's a shift in the energy between us after that. Secrets and lies carry their own kind of energy, and when they're removed, you feel it. He's very loving and adoring that day.

Afterwards, I learn that I misjudged him. I thought he was a suave Frenchman who seduces women easily and often. As it turns out, he's not like that, although he could be if he wanted to. He's a man who was with one woman for a very long time. He's intensely passionate, when he finds a connection, but he's not interested in sex purely for the sake of sex. He finds that idea empty and repulsive. He's never had a one-night stand.

The question that came to my mind nine months earlier in the shop of the beautiful and persuasive Indian woman in Goa, about whether he would cheat on me one day: it wasn't intuition. It wasn't a premonition. It was just a thought, based on prior experience and my impression of who he was. He bought all those things from her not because he can't resist the charms of a beautiful woman; he bought them because he likes to buy gifts for people and he likes to buy nice things for himself when he finds something he likes, and being persuaded to buy things you don't really need by a persuasive saleswoman isn't the same as being seduced to sleep with a woman you shouldn't.

This makes him more attractive to me. It makes me believe it's safer to share myself with him. Some part of my subconscious lowers its defensive shield.

We spend a few relaxing days in Battambang. One morning we hire a tuk-tuk to drive us to Phnom Sampov, where we hike to the pagoda at the top of the mountain to watch the sunrise. We have it to ourselves. The pagoda and the view remind me of Myanmar, and suddenly I feel nostalgic for Ingyin and our Burmese adventures. She would love this place. As I'm thinking about her, I spot an exotic flower I've never seen before. It has a wide, textured yellow center, distinctive red petals with curled edges, and an unusual arrangement of pink and yellow sprigs sticking out of the middle, as if Nature placed them there as a finishing touch of extra decoration. Ingyin loves flowers like I do so I text her a photo of this unusual one.

She replies, *You found me! That's an Ingyin flower!*

I had no idea there was a flower named Ingyin. I google it and the images that appear on my screen exactly match the flower in my photo. It was right there, waiting to be discovered at the perfect moment. A tiny bit of magic disguised as a flower.

When Julien and I say our goodbyes a few days later, I'm not sure what's going to come next. Time will tell. I'm just going to go with the flow, and settle into my new house and my new life here.

The rest of the year flows by smoothly. I'm relishing my new job at Santosha. I love the serenity of its beautiful grounds, and the people who come here for yoga retreats are people I understand. Many of them are versions of me during my corporate life. They are professional, cultured, intelligent, and looking for something. Most are looking for rest, for a break, but often for something else too. I understand them, because I've been in their shoes. It makes me happy that I can be part of offering them something that they've been craving, something I used to crave myself: a mental/spiritual/energetic reset.

Most of my good friends from the summer have moved away, but Siem Reap is the easiest place in the world to make friends, so I make new friends. Lots of them. There are so many wonderful people here: fun, kindhearted souls with open spirits and interesting backgrounds.

When I'm not teaching, eating, or sleeping, I'm shopping to decorate the house and ordering custom furniture from a carpenter who does fast, flawless work at Myanmar prices, which of course brings joy to my heart.

CHAPTER 41

We don't deserve resolution; we deserve
something better ... an open state of mind that
can relax with paradox and ambiguity.
- PEMA CHÖDRÖN

January 2020

It's a new year. I'm always excited about the beginning of a new year because I love blank canvases, but I'm especially excited about 2020 because it's both the start of a new year and a new decade. Also, since 2020 represents clarity and perfect vision *and* it's a repeating number, I secretly believe it's going to be a year of extra magic.

And speaking of magic, just in case you were wondering, that magic little tinsel strand is still in my hair. The color has mostly faded to silver, but it's still there, miraculously hanging on.

January is the busiest month for retreat bookings at Santosha. It's exhausting, but I love it. Sometimes the bookings include private sunrise yoga sessions at little-known ancient temples, tucked away in the jungle far off the beaten path. These bookings require me to get out of bed at 4:30 a.m., but it's worth it. Sunrise temple yoga is as wonderful as sunrise yoga at the lotus fields. Something about the immersion in nature, the quiet morning stillness, the solitude, the space around us, and the synchronized movement of our bodies and breath leaves us high, infused with happiness and vitality.

In February, Julien comes back for another two-week visit. Ever since he got his ticket, I'm less aloof where he's concerned. He hasn't stopped missing me, he hasn't tossed any curveballs at me in the last two months, and that he's coming back means that this is going somewhere.

We spend the first few days in Siem Reap. One morning, he stays home while I go to work. When I get home, I find that he has gotten my cute pink bike cleaned and made drivable again. (I lost the key for the built-in lock so the poor bike had been sitting locked and unusable in my driveway for a month.) And he has set the table and prepared a delicious seafood risotto which he serves accompanied with a refreshing white wine. (There was neither seafood nor white wine in my house when I left that morning.)

I'm amazed. He's very nonchalant about it, like it was as natural as breathing.

A couple days later it's February 14th and we spend Valentine's Day together for the second year in a row. We take a motorbike road trip to explore faraway temples in the remote northeast of the country. We discover the otherworldly wilderness of Koh Ker, the calm beauty of Preah Vihear, and the exquisite pink sandstone of Banteay Srei.

And then, back at my house the next night, I'm in tears and he's asleep on the sofa and the cause of this situation is the 36 Love Questions.

I stumbled across the 36 Love Questions in an article whose title claimed that to fall in love with anyone, all you need to do is ask each other these questions. Which is stellar clickbait, but obviously ridiculous. The planet is teeming with hordes of people I would never fall in love with in a billion years no matter what questions I ask them. But beneath the catchy headline, the actual premise of the article is intriguing: that these questions will reveal whether this other person is a good potential partner for you. Whether you're compatible. That these questions stimulate mutual vulnerability, which fosters closeness.

I want more closeness with this man and I already believe we're compatible, so I think this will be a fun way to catapult us into deeper closeness. When I suggest it, he agrees without hesitation.

The questions are broken up into three sets, and it takes us three days to get through all of them. They start out fun and innocuous, with questions like *Given the choice of anyone in the world, whom would you want as a dinner guest? If you could wake up tomorrow having gained any one quality or ability, what would it be?*

In Set Two, they start to get more personal and more uncomfortable. *What is your most terrible memory? How do you feel about your relationship with your mother?*

We both answer all of them, but the questions are starting to irritate Julien. His answers are becoming less enthusiastic.

We work our way through Set Three that night at my house during and after dinner. *Make three true "we" statements each. For instance, "We are both in this room feeling ..." When did you last cry in front of another person? By yourself?*

His discomfort is now unmistakable. "I don't like these questions," he says, annoyed and squirming.

"Yeah, some of them are strange," I agree. "But we're almost done."

Meanwhile, I'm not having as much fun either, but it's not the questions that are bothering me. It's his answers. They're telling me that he doesn't see me with the eyes of a man in love and he doesn't see a future with me.

One question is: *If you knew that in one year you would die suddenly, would you change anything about the way you are now living?* He answers that he would quit working, travel, visit friends. He says nothing about me.

It's my turn to answer first when we come to the question, *Tell your partner what you like about them. Be very honest this time, saying things that you might not say to someone you've just met.*

An easy one. I give a long, detailed list. He likes my answer. He says thank you and gives me a long French kiss. But when it's his turn, his answer is short, dry, without passion. He begins with, "You're determined; you achieve what you set out to..." He pauses, searching the recesses of his mind for something else to add. "I enjoy the time with you ... you're honest ..."

That's all he could come up with. As if there is absolutely nothing else positive to say about me. He's given me a generous number of compliments in the past, but apparently he's forgotten all of them. I could have answered with much more love and admiration for myself.

"My list was a lot longer," is the only thing I say.

He becomes defensive. "We're different, you shouldn't compare. What I feel for you, I haven't managed to feel with anyone else."

At the end, we fall into an argument. He lays down on the couch and falls asleep, and once again, I'm crying with the disappointment of a broken dream. I don't want to believe what looks very clear: he's not looking for a shared life with me. And in that case, I don't understand why he's here; why he keeps missing me every time we're apart, why he keeps flying across the world to see me, why he surprises me with risotto lunches and repaired bicycles. He looks like a little boy there on the sofa, the way he's laying with his legs crossed and both hands on his heart and a peaceful look on his face.

We have a few remaining days of vacation to enjoy, so I bury my disappointment and focus on immersing my attention in the present moment. We travel by plane and ferry to Koh Rong Sanloem, my magic island, and again it's like coming full circle, to be here together where a year and a half ago that strange Bilbao Guggenheim serendipity happened. The island is as beautiful as ever, serene and uncrowded, and the weather is perfect. To me, it's heaven.

Julien doesn't seem to be appreciating our surroundings as much as I am. The ocean is still and serene but I sense that his mind is not. But we have a great time anyway.

One afternoon while we're on nearby Koh Rong, he gets a phone call with news. He's recently applied for a new posting overseas, in Mozambique. This one is a rotation, meaning that he would work grueling twelve-hour days at a remote site with no days off for four weeks, and then he would get four weeks off. It sounds a bit hellish to me, but he's really excited about the idea of having six months off every year. Which would be a nice perk, I admit.

Several people have applied for the position and he hasn't been overly optimistic about getting it. The phone call is the unofficial news that he got it.

He hangs up the phone, and the light of excitement sparkles in his eyes. His whole mood has transformed. He's not effusive like me, therefore he's not jumping up and down and turning cartwheels down the beach, but I've never seen him this excited, except maybe the long-ago day I suggested meeting in Goa. This will give him the freedom he's been craving.

"And we'll be able to see each other more often," he adds unexpectedly.

Having just come to the conclusion that he didn't see a future with me, I'm surprised to hear that. Being with this man is an ongoing lesson in relaxing with ambiguity.

CHAPTER 42

Take a lover who looks at you like you might be magic.
- FRIDA KAHLO

February 2020

We've planned a private cacao ceremony for the night we get back to Siem Reap. We get back late that afternoon and I'm scheduled to teach restorative yoga at 6:30 p.m. We're both hungry and hoping no one comes so we can go back home, have dinner, and start our ceremony, but one other student shows up. Julien is restless from the beginning and the class does nothing to calm his energy. As we're nearing the end, he slides his eye cover off, points to his wrist, and mouths, *how much longer?*

Twenty minutes, I mouth back.

He makes a face as if he's being tortured and lays back down. Geez Louise.

After class, he's wired. Our energy is completely unaligned. I'm tired, ready to relax, and starving. I start cooking and he puts music on. Usually I love his taste in music, but tonight he chooses electronic music with a heavy, aggressive beat. It's worse than nails on a chalkboard.

"Um, can we have something a little more chill?" I ask.

"You pick the music then," he says.

I select a chill yet upbeat Brazilian jazz playlist and then I go back to looking for the balsamic vinegar, which is nowhere to be found.

"Where did you hide the balsamic vinegar?"

"It's in the fridge, where vinegar is supposed to be."

I laugh. "Vinegar doesn't need to go in the fridge."

Out of nowhere, he explodes, like a volcano that's been dormant for centuries and, with no advance warning, is suddenly blasting molten lava into the air. "It always has to be your way! Every little thing! You're always telling me what to do! I can't take this anymore! You're controlling and bossy!"

I stand there frozen, staring at him. First of all, everyone knows vinegar doesn't need to be refrigerated. It says so right on the bottles. Second of all, because I hate to be bossed around, the idea of bossing anyone else around is abhorrent to me. As far as I'm aware, there hasn't been a single time when I've ever tried to tell him what to do. Unless you count earlier this afternoon when we were shopping for a mattress topper for my bed and I, as usual, had my reusable water bottle with me for both of us, and a lady in the mattress store offered him a plastic bottle of water. He was going to accept, and I said, "We have water already."

"When have I ever tried to tell you what to do?"

He throws out examples like baseballs. The vinegar, the music, the water this afternoon, last week when he wanted to buy water to take on our motorbike road trip and I said, "no, we can just take these," because I had already filled bottles to take with us so we didn't have to needlessly consume more single use plastic that will be used once and then left to rot in Cambodian landfills and spread toxic residues into the earth and our water supply. But I underestimated how thirsty we would be, and we ran out of water in Koh Ker's forest and were forced to open a bottle of wine to quench our thirst.

He adds, "We all have our own things, and I know this plastic thing is your personal crusade, but sometimes your attitude when you're talking to people about it ... it's not nice."

That pricks me and sends tears to my eyes, because it's true. It's something that's been secretly bothering me, and I don't know what to do about it. It kills me to see the constant, unnecessary use of single-use plastic because I understand the consequences of it. I know that only a tiny percent of it is getting recycled. I know that if this trend continues unchecked it will destroy our health and our planet. Two of the things that matter most to me are good health and the spectacular beauty of this gift of a planet that's been generously given to us and that we're not taking care of, and they're both threatened by this irresponsible, unsustainable behavior. I can't stand by and say nothing. Much of the problem is ignorance, and I want to help people see that this is a problem, so they see a reason to change their behavior. But when I say something, my energy doesn't feel good. It feels heavy and negative. It's the same heavy, disapproving energy my mother exudes while pointing out other people's sins. I hate the feeling of it, but I can't just be silent either.

"From my perspective, those things aren't me trying to tell you what to do," I say. "Yes, I do care a lot about the plastic issue and it made no sense for you to accept the plastic bottle of water when I had a full reusable one right there in my hand, but yes, I could have refused more sweetly. And what you're saying about my attitude, I know you're right. That's something I want to change, but I haven't figured out how."

He's told me before that he's a stamp collector: when people do things that annoy him, he says nothing, he shows no hint of annoyance, but he takes that memory and files it away in his collection, until finally the collection is so full that he explodes. This is the first time I'm seeing it happen.

Our conversation goes on for a while. He calms down, but he's cold. I can feel what this means without him saying the words.

"I guess this is the end, isn't it?" I ask.

"I think so," he replies.

"How long have you known?"

"It wasn't a sudden decision. I've been thinking about this all week. It's been wonderful, and I've enjoyed the time with you, but ... it's partly just intuition. I just don't think this is going to work."

I cry; he doesn't. We have a long talk. "Why am I the only one crying?" I ask, sniffling. "I want you to cry too."

"I can't cry right now," he replies. "I might cry tomorrow."

Our mood is somber the rest of the night. He packs his bag, because he's flying back to Qatar tomorrow. At the end of the night he comes in my bedroom. "Do you want me to sleep somewhere else?"

"No, you can sleep here," I tell him. "Break-up sex is the best."

"I don't think that's a good idea," he says.

Oh, it's definitely a good idea. He doesn't hold out. But in the morning, we're not acting like a couple anymore. No more affection, no more holding hands. I'm calm and resigned now. I have to be, because I'm teaching hatha yoga at 8:30 a.m.

He comes to the class. During the final savasana, I place eye covers over everyone's eyes. When I kneel down next to Julien, I notice he's breathing quietly but rapidly, as if he's crying. He is crying.

After class, we walk home for our cacao ceremony, which has been rescheduled for this morning due to yesterday's volcanic eruption. We're both quiet. We prepare the cacao. I light a candle and place it on the floor inside a circle of crystals and the Native Spirit oracle cards, with Mexican blankets for us to sit on. After a few sips of cacao, we each pull a card. Before I pull mine, I silently ask the question, *What is the lesson I'm supposed to learn from the experience with this man?*

The card I get is *Spirit Keeper of the East*. I know I've pulled this card before, but I can't remember when. These words jump out at me first:

New beginnings. A fresh cycle is occurring in your life. Wipe the slate clean; it's time to release the old and start again. Pulling this card means that this is the close of one cycle and the beginning of another. Although it's often difficult to release familiar routines, situations or relationships when they no longer empower you, your native spirit asks that you not cling to the old, but set sail into new waters.

It's the cosmic stamp of finality on the end of this romance. It's really over. It hurts like a knife in my stomach. Tears roll down my face.

"What did it say?" he asks.

I silently hand him the card. He reads it, and then he comes to squat down next to me and wrap his arms around me. "I'm sorry I hurt you." One lone quiet tear rolls down his cheek.

We stay like this for a while, and then I whisper, "I asked what I was supposed to learn from this relationship with you."

He smiles ruefully. "I asked the same thing."

"What was your card?"

He shows me. *Wounded Healer.*

You are a healer, and you provide healing for others, even if you're not conscious of it. Whatever needs healing in your life is being resolved. No matter what happened in your past, the past does not need to equal the future. It's true; the cracks can be where the light enters the soul.

The words ring a bell. I look again at my card. There's one line that's almost identical in both cards. His says *no matter what happened in your past, the past does not need to equal the future.* Mine says *no matter what has happened in the past, it doesn't need to repeat in the future.*

It's not until later I realize my card is the same card I pulled the night of his bombshell confession three months ago.

I reread my entire card, and now I see a different way to interpret it. What if it didn't mean the end of our relationship, it meant the end of some old negative patterns? What if the new beginning was a new beginning between us?

The Oracle speaks, but it's still up to us to interpret her words. I say aloud what I'm thinking. We talk for a while. The energy has shifted, our hearts are more open. We move to the couch where it's more comfortable. I'm resting against him. We're holding hands and his free arm is around my shoulder.

"Are you sure it's the end?" I ask him.

He's not.

I don't know what happened in that ceremony, but something about us, between us, is different. The rest of the day feels like magic. We make love and it's different than before. It's more sensual and somehow, more spiritual. Whatever energetic block was there between us before is gone. We are attuned to each other now, open and connected to ourselves and to each other.

He looks at me again the way a man looks at a woman when he's in love, holding my face and staring into my eyes. In the way that for the past two weeks I had been wishing for him to look at me. My face is puffy and my eyes are swollen from crying, and he's still looking at me like that. As if something clouding his vision has been cleared away and he can truly see me for the first time this visit, and what he's seeing goes deeper than the physical layer.

We go out for our last meal, a late lunch at a quiet little Italian restaurant, and I'm enveloped in quiet bliss. Every sip, every bite is delicious, but that's not why I'm in this cloud of bliss.

And then it's time for him to leave. The tuk-tuk comes to pick him up, and as he drives away he's waving and blowing me kisses and calling, *"A bientôt!"* Which is usually translated as "See you soon!" but literally it's "until soon!" So that could mean talk to you soon, text you soon, see you soon. But who's over-analyzing? In our magic afternoon, we didn't discuss the future. He's going back to Qatar, and soon he'll be in Mozambique, and I'm in Cambodia for the foreseeable future …

We'll just see what happens. Go with the flow, as he said.

When he gets home, he sends me a long email, apologizing for the things he said the night of his explosion. Once again, the words he couldn't express in person flow more easily in written form. I learn he took the 36 Love Questions as an ultimatum: that we must fall in love with each other by the end. He felt under pressure and ill at ease from the beginning, and his discomfort intensified as the questions became more and more direct, invasive. He is private by nature. He doesn't like when people try to figure him out, especially not with spoken words. He prefers when people come to understand each other by their actions—but he acknowledges that sometimes words are necessary.

It surprises me to read that, because he gave no hint of discomfort or reluctance when I asked him if he wanted to ask each other the 36 Love Questions. He said "yeah, sure" and he seemed open and comfortable. He's a hard man to read. And how are we supposed to be in a relationship and not try to figure each other out?

But he seems more willing to be figured out in writing. He answers all my written questions openly. He writes that the night of his explosion, when I asked him, "How long have you known it's over?" the answer he gave me wasn't true. The question put him on the spot and he used the first evasive answer he came up with.

But in the end, his explosion was good for me. The pain he caused me woke me up and left me more fully alive. It was like a healing.

Ever since his explosion, when I'm confronted with the single-use plastic issue, the heavy energy isn't with me anymore. He made me realize there are things more important than that one piece of plastic. The amount of plastic I see wasted needlessly still makes me cringe, but I've learned how to react (most of the time) without negativity or horror. I've learned I usually don't need to say anything. I learned that if I'm offered a plastic water bottle, I can simply lift my reusable bottle and say with a smile, "No thank you." If I take leftovers from a restaurant or buy seafood at the market, I put them in my own reusable container. The eyes of many waiters and merchants light up at this. "That's awesome, thank you," they say.

We've had several temporary endings now, but each one seems to teach us something, to remove a barrier between us, to lift us to a new level. Because of that, part of me doesn't need answers to all the questions in my mind. Part of me is content to flow with the current and see what the future brings. The other part of me would really prefer things to just be plain old unambiguous black and white.

But this is real life, and real life has many shades of gray.

CHAPTER 43

The light is inside you.
– LA LUMIÈRE, LOUNGE DE RÊVEUR

March 2020

Two weeks after Julien leaves, the Covid-19 pandemic shuts Cambodia off from the world.

There is no Covid-19 circulating in Cambodia, as far as anyone knows. There have been less than thirty documented cases in the country, all brought in by people arriving from overseas, and there's been no community transmission. Thank God for that, because Cambodia is a country whose functional existence today, forty years after the horrific decimation of Pol Pot's regime, is a living tribute to the resilience and triumph of the human spirit, but Cambodia's fragile medical system isn't equipped to handle anything close to a pandemic. Like most other countries, Cambodia closes its borders, cutting off the inflow of tourists.

Siem Reap is a tourist town and tourist dollars are its lifeblood. Now, overnight, the streets are empty. Hotels and restaurants close voluntarily, with a handful of exceptions who stay open for the sake of those of us who live here (thank goodness). People stop hugging. Very few people in Siem Reap wear masks, unless they're wearing them because of the dust. That, we were already doing before the pandemic, because there's not a single Covid case here but there is a lot of lung-choking dust.

The perfect timing of Julien's visit isn't lost on me. If we had planned it for a month later, he couldn't have come.

Santosha stays open for the first three weeks of March. Occupancy dwindles to nothing, and then they close too. They continue paying half-salary to all employees, which seems incredibly generous to me because I'm American but seems normal to the owners and manager because they're European.

Globally, Covid is wreaking emotional and financial havoc on large swaths of people, families, and businesses, and my heart hurts for them. In the initial months, for me personally, the situation isn't ideal from a financial perspective, but other than that, I must confess—and I feel guilty making this confession in the context of the widespread loss and turmoil Covid would brutally unleash around the globe, and if I was speaking I would be speaking in a whisper right now, but—for me personally, these initial months of the pandemic are a beautiful time. I make this public confession now only because this is my story, and it's the truth, and I know I wasn't the only one. And because suffering leaves none of us untouched, but it comes to us at different times. I've suffered in the past, and I may well suffer again in the future, but for me, the spring of 2020 wasn't one of the hard times.

My friends and family, so far, remain in good health. After four months of high-season intensity, the break from work is a welcome gift. I'm in the spacious house I love, with my kind, caring landlords (now known to me as Grandma Yae Mwah and Grandpa Ta Baran) and smiling little Magra next door. Right next to my driveway is a little shack that sells fresh coconuts for seventy-five cents, and a handful of great restaurants down the street have remained open. In my yard are two mango trees who provide me with a basketful of fresh, sweet, juicy mangos every morning. Two blocks away is a nursery owned by a sweet woman named Narin where I stop regularly to buy plants for the house and the yard.

Whenever I bring home plants for the yard, Grandma Yae Mwah

and Grandpa Ta Baran reciprocate by going and getting more plants for the yard, and then I go get more, and the cycle continues, and gradually my yard is transforming into a baby tropical garden.

And so, free from the obligations of work, I'm surrounded by beauty, space, time, fresh coconuts, and a plentiful supply of mangos, and it feels like a dream come true. God bless my landlords for building this house.

Secretly, I have a vaguely guilty feeling that this pandemic is something I wished for. To be clear, I never wished for an actual pandemic. But so many times I felt that life was moving too fast, that there was constantly too much happening, that I couldn't keep up with this breakneck speed. In those moments, I wished I could press a giant Pause button so everything would just stop for a while and let me be still and breathe. All of a sudden, that's what's happened … the Great Pause.

With all this beauty and space and time, wild creativity rises to the surface of my being, unbridled creativity that I never knew was lying dormant inside me. I start painting. I paint a giant mandala on the wall in my guest bedroom. I take a month to paint it, painting only when the spirit of inspiration surfaces, and I love the result. (Fortunately, so do my landlords.) I spend untold hours in the kitchen creating magazine-worthy dishes, taking the time to plate and garnish every dish to maximum eye-pleasing effect before devouring them with great pleasure. I make essential-oil scented candles and design labels for them and get the labels printed in town. I host soul-fulfilling Full Moon circles for a small circle of girlfriends on the tiled patio in my backyard. I sign up for an online graphic design course, because that's something I've wanted to do for about twenty years and a talented local designer offers this program at just the right time.

Beauty is the thing that I love, and it's the thing that has often in my life had to be sacrificed in the interest of productivity, efficiency, and other responsibilities. Now, in this period where productivity and other responsibilities have been suddenly grounded to a screeching halt, beauty proliferates in my life. This is no longer a time of "what should I do?" These months are completely about what I *want* to do. And what I want to do is create more beauty in this already extraordinarily beautiful world. Because we were made to create, and there's always room for more beauty.

I also finally start an urban composting program, which is an idea I've been talking about for months, because with all my free time I have no excuse not to. This project comes together beautifully. With the help of an acquaintance and soon-to-be friend named Sam Walker, who offers the use of land at her community center, Siem Reap Food Loop is founded, providing a site where compostable food waste can be dropped off for composting, with a regular weekly pickup service for restaurants and individuals who prefer the convenience of that option. We start with four compost trenches, and with the help of an American carpenter and a resourceful Khmer man, we build three photogenic compost bins and a bamboo and palm frond shelter.

Why composting, you might ask? Composting is my thank you: my thank you to life, to this beautiful earth. It's my small contribution to the preservation of all the magnificent nature around us. It's my answer to the question that was in my heart when I stood in the presence of the indescribable beauty of Spiti Valley, my solution to the burning desire to give something back in return for all the beauty and abundance our planet gives us. It is to literally give back to the earth. Every day, the mango trees in my yard give me a generous supply of fresh, sweet, juicy mangos. The inedible parts of each mango that I don't need: the skin that was the wrapping paper for this gift, the pit that contains the secret code for future generations of mango trees—instead of tossing these into the trash, destining them to finish their existence in an ugly landfill, simply returning them back to the earth. Mixed with dirt and dry leaves who have also completed their cycle of life, in a few short months they will transform back into fertile soil, decomposing into rich nutrients that will nourish the next round of harvest.

It's the cycle of life, of which we are part, into which our existence is woven. Not only is this simple action of composting my thank you, my prayer of gratitude, it's a coming back to harmony, a shift back into balance with the flow of life, to the way things are meant to be.

In Siem Reap, we compost in two ways: in trenches, burying the food scraps and dry plant matter under the soil, and in compost bins. Trench composting is the fastest. In four weeks, all traces of food disappear, blending into the earth, leaving no sign of their former presence except a few eggshells and mango and avocado pits and peels that take longer to break down. In the bins, the process is slower, but it's fascinating to watch the stages of the transformation. It doesn't smell bad. As it transforms, it smells earthy, good, natural.

I dream of a world where everyone composts. Where separating your banana peels, orange rinds, and coffee grinds for composting is as natural as brushing your teeth. Maybe that will come to pass one day. In the meantime, at least I can do it myself.

As time stretches on, suffering reaches Siem Reap. As Cambodia's borders remain closed to tourists, the city streets remain quiet. Many locals and expats who depended on tourism revenue for their income find themselves without jobs and without paychecks. Expats begin moving away in droves. Many teachers find themselves without work, because schools are closed. Some people leave because they want to be with family in this strange, uncertain time. One by one, businesses start closing permanently ... hotels, guest houses, restaurants, boutiques, shutting their doors forever, the creations of years of work and love and life savings gone.

My own personal suffering comes in the form of the forced separation from my French lover. It's okay at first, because we're used to months apart and we don't expect this unprecedented closed-border situation to last long. But as the months stretch on, it becomes harder. It's worse because our separation is not by choice; it's the decisions of world governments that are keeping us apart, and we don't know when this involuntary separation is going to end.

It's a strange feeling. Spoiled by the privilege of my American passport, I'm not used to rules keeping me away from anywhere I want to go or anyone I want to be with. I think of all the immigrant families in my country who have been torn apart by deportations, and now I can more vividly understand the pain and powerlessness they must feel. Why is the right to be with your loved ones not a basic unalienable human right, no matter where you were born or which country issued your passport?

But, thank God for the technology that connects us. We get creative in our long-distance connection. We have virtual cacao ceremonies via Whatsapp video. We write each other erotic chapters. We do online yoga classes together. I give him a private yin class via Zoom, and then he gives me one. He'll probably become a yoga teacher one day; he's a natural.

He's still in Qatar but he'll be going back to France the end of June when his contract ends. We assure each other that France will open her borders in July and I'll be able to come visit. That's my birthday month so it will be perfect; I'll get to spend my birthday with him.

After two months, Santosha reopens but occupancy is very low. Most guests are visitors from Phnom Penh or local Siem Reap residents coming for a staycation. My workload is light.

And during this time, I find enlightenment.

This is not to say that I myself become enlightened. {Huge, knee-slapping laugh at that idea.} What I mean is that I discover enlightenment in human form.

This comes about because one day I turn left instead of going straight and drive down a side street I've never gone down before. There's a small market on this street, consisting of a handful of stalls on each side of the road stocked with produce and a few other assorted items. I stop at one. The girl manning this stall is probably in her late twenties. She greets me with a wide, bright smile and lightly-accented English. We chat a little while I'm choosing vegetables. The light happiness of her energy matches her smile. She teaches me how to say sweet potato in Khmer *(dumlong ch'mooah)*, and she tosses some complimentary spring onions and chili peppers into my bag.

Her name is Nen. I begin stopping at Nen's stand every few days, because her energy adds extra happiness to my day. She's always there, bright and smiling and joking. She's often busy with a fast-moving flow of customers. Sometimes her mother is there with her. Her mother doesn't speak English but she's pretty like her daughter and has a sweet, quiet smile.

One morning, a section of Nen's road is blocked by road construction. Motorbikes are still able to squeeze through while the forklift is angled a certain way so I manage to make my way to Nen's stand. She's there alone today. She greets me with her usual bright smile. "*Su-s'dey!* I haven't seen you in a while!"

I tell her I had been busy and was out of town for a little while. We exchange pleasant conversation while I select my limes and sweet potatoes—she's sold out of watermelon. She adds the complimentary spring onions. It's quieter today because of the construction.

"I get a rest now, it's really good," she says brightly. "Normally I never rest."

"Never? Don't you take one day off? Sundays?"

"No," she says happily. "I work seven days a week."

"Seven days a week! What time do you finish?"

"8 p.m.."

"What time do you start?"

"7 a.m.. I have to wake up at 5:30." She's still smiling, projecting light and happiness.

I stare at her in amazement. This intelligent, trilingual girl (she speaks Thai too) with the charming personality and great sense of humor, always sweet, bright, and smiling, works thirteen hours a day, seven days a week, outdoors in the sweltering Cambodian heat, usually dressed in a long-sleeved turtleneck sweater. (For reasons unknown to me, Cambodian women in Siem Reap love to wear long-sleeved turtleneck sweaters year-round.) In this heat that is so intense it leaves me drained and too exhausted for anything but a two-hour nap many afternoons—and I spend a lot of time in air-conditioned indoor comfort. In the months I've been coming to Nen's stand, not once have I ever seen her look tired or unhappy or heard her complain about anything.

It slowly dawns on me that I am in the presence of a superior being. "You are a superwoman, Nen."

"Thank you," she says, smiling happily.

I thank her, get on my motorbike, and head towards home. The forklift is scooping up small mountains of dirt and I have to stop and wait behind it for a few minutes. While I wait, I think about Nen. I don't know much about her daily life away from the produce stand, but she can't have much of one. She gets up at 5:30 in the morning, she gets home at what—8:30 pm? 9 pm? Her life is work and sleep and repeat. To me it seems grueling, monotonous, horrible. I try to imagine myself in her shoes. I can't even. I wouldn't be able to function. How can her spirit stay so unfailingly bright, day after day?

Tears come to my eyes. They're not tears of pity or sadness for her, but tears of a profound awe and respect. She's a walking, breathing human miracle. She is the sudden, unexpected answer to the question that sometimes floats through my head: *What is enlightenment, really?*

Many definitions have been given for this word, but broken down into the simplest, most literal translation from its Latin roots, it means "in light" or "into light." If enlightenment is to be transformed into light, to consistently embody and transmit light, then Nen is enlightenment personified. She is a girl who, in spite of her challenging circumstances, is always filled with light. It's always there, the light in her eyes, in her voice and her smile, in her whole being. It's tangible and contagious; I feel lighter in her presence. Her light is undimmed by her personal circumstances. She doesn't seem to feel lack or regret or bitterness or to be tortured by an unfulfilled desire for more. She seems content. And yet, the contentment doesn't owe its existence to the absence of dreams of more. Because Nen has dreams.

One almost came true this year. She had passed the final stages of interviews and was about to be hired as a flight attendant for a Thai airline, and then the pandemic happened and her future employment vanished like dust in the wind. She told me about that one day because I asked. But she told me matter of factly, without complaint. She told me about her other dream too: to open a coffee shop someday. She has dreams for the future, but the fact that they haven't become reality yet doesn't seem to impinge on her current state of contentment.

One Buddhist definition of enlightenment is "a permanent state marked by the absence of desire or suffering." She seems to fit this definition too.

In my mind, the memory rises of the overly affectionate swami from Ladakh and other so-called gurus and self-proclaimed enlightened beings who exude no light. They are deluded, empty frauds and this girl is so bright in contrast.

I never told any of this to Nen. I'm pretty sure she would have laughed if I informed her she was an enlightened being. Maybe she's not. I'm not an official judge. All I know is, the Buddha became the Buddha after his long search for freedom from suffering. And Nen seems to have attained this without much intensive effort. She seems both free from suffering and full of constant light.

I don't know how she can do it. I don't know how she can keep this light, this peaceful happiness, day after day after day, but she makes me want to be a better person.

One weekend in June, I visit my friend Olivia in Phnom Penh for the weekend. Olivia is Taiwanese and she's just moved from Siem Reap to Phnom Penh for a job. Her background is in the five-star hotel industry and she's equally elegant and hilarious, with a goofy sense of humor that matches mine. It's rare if ten minutes go by without us cracking ourselves up over something silly.

Saturday afternoon, we take a break from our Aeon Mall shopping extravaganza for lunch at a Chinese restaurant in a corner of the food court. The restaurant has round booths and white leather seats and looks like a place that would appeal to the Chinese mafia. It also appeals to me because I can't resist a round booth, especially one with immaculate white leather seats.

We're starving and we ambitiously order three entrees and hot tea. The waiter brings our tea promptly: a large teapot and two small teacups. A little while later, he makes a special trip back to the table to hand us two paper-wrapped plastic straws. This is mystifying, since the straws wouldn't have a chance at standing up in our tiny teacups.

Tea is served instead of water in Chinese restaurants, so no glasses of water will be forthcoming.

"Uh, thank you, but you can keep those, we don't need them," I tell him. He doesn't speak much English, so he probably has no idea what I'm saying.

"It's okay, these can be useful later, I'll keep them," Olivia says, ever gracious, and tucks them into her purse.

Several hours later our shopping mission is completed and a tuk-tuk deposits us back in front of Olivia's apartment. We walk through the gate and encounter Olivia's landlady, who lives on the ground floor. She greets us warmly and hands us two coconuts and a bag of limes. We thank her for the sweet gift. As the elevator takes us up to the fifth floor, I open my mouth to say, "We have coconuts but no straws" and then I remember that Olivia has two straws in her purse.

"So that's why the waiter gave us two straws!" I exclaim. We burst out laughing. How strange, and perfect.

The limes are the icing on the cake—or we could say, the lime in the coconut, since fresh coconuts are definitely better with a squeeze of lime, and Olivia and I share a sincere love of limes. It's one of our mutual favorite Khmer words—*kro ch'mah*. (Literally translated it means "orange cat." Don't ask me why.) Olivia ran out of *kro ch'mah* that morning and we were planning to buy more but we forgot. We conclude that our magical, whimsical Two Straws, Two Coconuts & A Bag of Limes experience was a message from the Universe: This may not seem to make any sense right now, but this is happening for a reason and everything is going to work out perfectly.

It's a message I'll need to remember a few short weeks later.

CHAPTER 44

Intuition is a powerful thing,
more powerful than intellect, in my opinion.
- STEVE JOBS

July 2020

My birthday is July 16th. In March, I made a wish to the Universe: to spend my birthday with Julien. I felt pretty confident about the chances of this wish being granted. For one, the Universe had been generously granting my wishes left and right lately. And for another, these travel bans couldn't last forever. The world would certainly calm down by July.

As July drew nearer, the situation looked promising. Europe was starting to open up. The EU was compiling a "green-light list" of countries from which they would begin welcoming travelers with negative Covid tests. They would be publishing the list July 1st. Cambodia was a former French protectorate and was currently home to a large French community, and there had been less than 150 Covid cases in the country since the beginning of the pandemic. There was no reason Cambodia shouldn't be on the list. I had no doubt it would all work out perfectly, the way it always had for us.

Also, this birthday would be my 40th. I started getting excited about this milestone a few weeks in advance, when my friend Jon let me in on a little secret. "Life begins at forty," he told me at a dinner party one night. He's forty-nine, and therefore a reliable source. After hearing that, the prospect of joining the Forties Club suddenly seemed much more appealing. Life was pretty great in my thirties, so if it's going to be even better in my forties, bring it on!

But July 1st comes, and Cambodia isn't on the EU's green-light list.

This is a crushing disappointment, and it makes absolutely no sense. Cambodia's next-door neighbor Thailand is on the list, although they have over 1500 cases, and so is South Korea, who has many more. Other countries who made it onto the list include Rwanda, Tunisia, and Uruguay. The list is so sporadic we suspect it was most likely compiled by pulling country names out of a hat, but all we care about is that Cambodia isn't on it. It doesn't help us that Thailand is on the list, because the Thailand-Cambodia border is still closed. I could get into South Korea, but I would have to quarantine there for two weeks before flying onward. We discuss the possibility of meeting in Croatia, which is open, but the rules we find are vague, and Julien has commitments in France, so he wouldn't be able to spare more than a couple weeks in Croatia before he would have to leave for Mozambique. Plus, I'll be able to get back into Cambodia because I have a business visa, but I'll have to quarantine for two weeks and pay a $3,000 deposit upon arrival, which I might have to kiss goodbye if anyone on my flight tests positive for Covid. And plane tickets are triple their usual prices.

Julien is supposed to have a full month off in September. I'm still optimistic that as time goes by, countries will open up and Cambodia will relax its entry restrictions. Therefore, it seems very practical to wait two more months and get four weeks to spend together. If France's border still isn't open by September, we could meet in Croatia or Turkey or anywhere with an open border, because by then I'll be so desperate to see my lover I'll be willing to fly anywhere.

Julien isn't happy about another two months of separation, but he agrees we should wait.

So I don't get to spend my birthday with him. But my 40th birthday is beautiful anyway, surrounded by friends and love and festivity. And Julien makes it extra beautiful, even from 6000 miles away. On the eve of my birthday, he calls to confess that he's been sneakily colluding with the owner of the restaurant where I'll be having my birthday dinner to get me a present, but with so many places closed, and because the lovely owner has met me a total of two brief times and has no idea what my taste is, they couldn't find something he liked.

"I wanted to get you jewelry. Someone told me Garden of Desire is nice. So now the only option is for you to go there and find something that will give you pleasure," he tells me.

His thoughtfulness and effort wrap me in a warm blanket of happiness, and I'm always delighted to shop for presents for myself.

Garden of Desire is an enchanting boutique store. You enter and find yourself in a bright enclave, surrounded by a garden of sparkling, gem-studded creations. It instantly lifts my spirits, the way beauty always does. My eyes immediately land on a ring with a gleaming silver band showcasing a raw smoky crystal, half clear and half black. Yin and yang, the light and dark—my ongoing message. It's love at first sight.

"What is this stone?" I ask the guy behind the counter.

"It's a Herkimer quartz. They also call it a Herkimer diamond."

I've never heard of it. I video call Julien, who agrees the ring is beautiful. I tell the clerk I'll take it.

Later, I look up Herkimer quartz. "The Herkimer Diamond is an attunement stone, useful for attuning to another person, group or environment … and is an exceptional crystal for linking together people who have to be apart," Crystalvaults.com informs me.

They say there's something about crystals—that they choose you. I never really thought there was anything to that, until now.

That night, my last night as a thirty-nine-year-old, I sit myself down, think about what I want my sparkling 40th year to look like, and write down my goal for the rest of 2020. *Flow through the rest of the year in a relaxed state. Leave all pushiness behind. Trust that you decide what you want and the Universe conspires to make it happen.*

If the last sentence sounds vaguely familiar, it's because it's paraphrasing a famous line from *The Alchemist*. As for the first sentence, it will very shortly turn out to be life-changing.

My forties start off beautifully. I keep celebrating for a few extra days, because obviously that's what you should do when you turn forty. (Milk it for all it's worth, that's my motto.) Julien surprises me by starting to send written I love you's. Meanwhile he's busy in France helping his oldest son with the renovation of his new apartment. Sexual frustration notwithstanding, everything seems rosy, in life and between the two of us. In spite of the distance between us, we've grown closer, and the ring on my finger is a constant reminder of our connection.

And then. One week later, life pitches another curveball.

July 24th, two days after the latest I love you, Julien calls with devastating news. The long bony fingers of the pandemic have reached in to wreak havoc on his Mozambique work calendar. Due to required quarantines and other factors, his schedule has been brutally rearranged. Instead of the original four weeks work, four weeks off, it will now be *ten* weeks work, five weeks off.

(How does that even make sense? Do these people not understand basic math? Is this not a violation of French labor laws??)

And the final crushing blow: his departure for Mozambique has been pushed back to October, and his time off has been pushed back to DECEMBER. December is five months away.

This news is incomprehensible to me. How is this even legally possible? "They can't do that! Doesn't your contract state four weeks on, four weeks off? They can't expect you to work nonstop ten weeks straight, fifteen hours a day, without a single day off—that's ridiculous. It's inhumane!"

Apparently no, his contract does not spell out four weeks on, four weeks off, and yes, his giant multinational employer can legally make this inhumane change without batting an eyelid. I offer potential solutions. Can he take time off before he goes to Mozambique? We could meet in Croatia…

No, he can't take vacation before Mozambique.

"Why not? Can't you explain the situation? It's an emergency…"

No, he can't. He's had two hours in the car to think this over and he's already arrived at his own conclusion. "I don't think our relationship can handle this. Five months without seeing each other has been so hard. Five more months is too much. It doesn't make sense. I think we need to end the relationship, and just leave it open. If we manage to see each other again in the future, then we see what happens."

Just like that, he's throwing in the towel. Unbelievable. Once again from him, this sudden about-face and jumping ship. As the wave of disbelief recedes, my heart chills with hurt and anger. "I can't believe we're here again, after all we've been through. Just like that, with a snap of your fingers, you're ready to throw it all away."

"I've thought about this a lot. You haven't had time to think about it," he tells me. (He's thought about it "a lot" … i.e., a whole two hours.)

We agree to talk again later, because I'm too shocked and angry to stay on the phone with him. After we hang up, I shed a few tears of hot, disappointed anger. Then I'm suddenly filled with an intense desire to clean my cluttered bedroom. I may no longer have a long-distance lover, but I will have a spotless bedroom God damn it. I've been procrastinating for weeks on this task, but now I channel all my fierce anger-fueled energy into ferociously cleaning and organizing the entire room, leaving no corner untouched. I even tackle the closet. Marie Kondo would have been proud.

By the time my sleeping quarters are returned to a state of pristine order, I'm calm enough to look at the situation from a broader perspective. Both of our patterns are playing out again. His pattern: he's overthinking and the intensity of thwarted desire has built up to a level of pressure that feels unbearable, and the only escape route he can see is to run away. In other words, his prefrontal cortex has temporarily shorted out and he's making irrational decisions. And my pattern: I immediately lose my temper and react as if it's the end, instead of giving him a little time and space. In all fairness, I also had doubts about our relationship a few weeks ago, but when I talked to him about them, he responded with calmness and understanding, and my doubts evaporated. So, let me just chill out for now. Just because he felt this way today doesn't mean he'll feel the same tomorrow. Also, today was one of the days where I constantly saw repeating numbers: 1:11 and 4:44 and 5:55, maybe a 12:12 too. Extra winks from the Universe. Whatever happens, I will trust that this is all part of the divine plan.

I pull an oracle card later, curious if it wants to offer any insights. To my surprise, I get one of the most beautiful and joyful cards in the deck, the *Nature Spirits* card. *Joy. Delight. Peaks of carefree abandon. Living wildly, magically and free. Beneath the surface, mystical interventions are occurring in your life. Relax. All is well.*

Well, okay then.

The next morning, I wake up with a light heart, full of joy and the belief that anything is possible. In the history of the world, across millennia, countless people and civilizations have faced staggering difficulties and challenges. The little hardship Julien and I are facing now is comparatively nothing. My mind, always the collision of left brain and right brain, can see both sides of the argument. From the logical perspective, yes, you could acknowledge that the total number of days we've spent together so far is a little less than seven weeks. 1 ½ days Bali + 12 days France + 5 days Goa + 2 weeks Cambodia + another 2 weeks Cambodia. And you could make the argument that it would be crazy to keep yourself in a committed long-distance relationship for ten long months with someone that you never had time to build a solid foundation with.

Yes, I can see and appreciate the rational value of that argument, and then I can instantly brush it off the imaginary table with one dismissive swoop of my hand. I know what my heart feels. And the other day Julien said something I loved. *Il y a quelque magie dans notre relation.* "There is some kind of magic between us." I believe in that magic.

Two days pass before we talk again, because he's been busy with friends visiting. It's an amicable conversation, relaxed and open on both sides. I'm at home on my couch. He's on a sunny beach in Biarritz. He hasn't changed his mind.

The intensity of his frustrated emotions has become oppressive; he wants to free himself from that weight. He doesn't want to feel restricted and limited anymore, and he doesn't want me to either.

I know what he means. It's a strange feeling to be away from your lover for so many months. It's as if to be able to endure it, you have to shut down some part of yourself—some part of your natural passion and desire. Because I treasure and adore him, and because I waited so long to find someone I feel this way about, I would have endured it longer. But I understand the logic of his choice. Maybe he isn't wrong to end it—but my heart thinks he's wrong. I suspect that he'll regret his decision later, and something in me knows that if he ends it this time, I might not be able to go back. We've been through this too many times now, and I love him, but I want to love someone I can count on.

"You know that if you end it this time, you risk losing me for good?" I ask him.

"I know that I am risking losing you," he replies.

I want him to say that to me while looking me in the eye. The sun is too bright on the beach for him to use video chat, and his friends are waiting, so we agree to talk again later by video. When we say goodbye, I notice the time. It's 10:10 p.m.

So, this is part of the plan? But what is the plan exactly?

After hanging up, I sit on the couch in silence. I can't ignore the feeling that it's over. That his mind is made up, and all that needed to be said has been said. There's no need to look him in the eye. There's no need to talk again.

He felt that too. The next morning I wake up to find a text from him waiting. *Sonya, I've thought a lot about all this: I wish to end our relationship because I don't believe in it anymore. I ask you to forgive me for hurting you. I wish you the best in your life. Take care of yourself.*

There is something about written words—their power to hurt is stronger than spoken words. If only spoken, words can become hazy in your memory and fade away. Written words are permanent. You can go back and read them over and over again. You can't deny or unsee them. And in this case, they carry the finality of the last nail in the coffin.

When I read that text, that's when I accept that it's really over.

I'd like to tell you that I took it all in stride, bolstered by unshakable faith in the Universe and all the repeating numbers and the zen energy accumulated from so much yoga and meditation over the previous years—but no. I react to this breakup the way I traditionally react to all serious breakups: by mentally dissolving into a puddle of grief and sobbing my heart out.

It's interesting how much emotional pain hurts; how it's as painful as physical pain. And this breakup has an extra level of hurt, because after everything we've been through so far, my heart really believed he was the one brought specially to me by destiny—that all the magic and all the serendipities of our story meant something. Just like that, it's all gone—vanished like smoke in the wind. For a moment I question everything I ever believed in. Maybe there is no magic. Maybe everything was nothing more than a string of meaningless coincidences. Nothing special.

The feeling of hopelessness temporarily sucks away all my joy and energy for life. I don't even have the energy to keep standing upright. I collapse on the floor, tears spilling on the cold tile.

After a cathartic few minutes of dramatic sobbing on the floor, the emotional tidal wave starts to recede and common sense begins to resurface. True, this is a painful turn of events, but, to bring things back into perspective, the world is not ending. And luckily, I have a few things going for me. First of all, I've been wrong many times in my life. Being wrong about Julien being the cosmically ordained love of my life is not the first thing I've been wrong about, and that makes it easier to accept. Also, I've been through plenty of breakups, and I've survived them all. After all the practice, I might even be starting to get really good at dealing with them. What is there to do but adjust to this new reality and move on?

I sit up and start to pull myself together. Yes, I loved him, but he wasn't the only thing I love in life. I also love me, and I still have me. I love my friends, and I still have them. And I love life, and I'm still alive.

At that moment, I remember the resolution I wrote on a notecard two weeks ago: *Flow through the rest of the year in a relaxed state.* I burst out laughing. Sitting on the floor with swollen eyes and tearstained cheeks, I'm not exactly the poster child for this mantra.

But when I wrote that, I knew I was going to slip up. I wrote it with permission for myself to make mistakes, and then pull myself together and restart. I'm not going to permanently fall off the wagon just two weeks into my new decade.

I exhale a deep sigh and breathe in to reset into relaxed, go-with-the-flow state.

Tears purify. Pain can leave you with a new beginning and a fresh canvas waiting to be painted. Energy starts to seep back in. I get to my feet and prepare to get on with life.

CHAPTER 45

If you seek the light, be prepared to face the darkness.
- UNKNOWN

Now that (once again) Julien is no longer my primary focus, I am fully invested here, in the present moment. Now that I no longer have him to love, what else do I love in life? What makes me happy?

Dancing. Dancing makes me happy. So for one thing, I will keep dancing. And second, dinner parties. I love dinner parties. I used to host so many back in Florida. Why aren't I hosting dinner parties here? So I keep dancing and I start hosting dinner parties, and in return I get invited to other dinner parties, and friendships deepen through the shared deliciousness, and life becomes richer.

In the days that follow, my happiness stays with me. At first, I'm hesitant to claim it as real, true happiness. I wonder if it's just a temporary manic state, masking the pain below, an ephemeral veneer that could vanish at any moment with the suddenness of a popped bubble, plunging me into the ocean of sadness waiting below. But the days turn into weeks, and my buoyant happiness lasts. I expected to suffer, but instead I feel light and energized and full of defiant joy. All of the energy I'd been channeling towards my absent lover through the pathways of my thoughts and attention is suddenly liberated to flow through me, to be used for something else. There's so much energy buzzing through my cells, I have to keep dancing. So I do. I blast my Spotify dance playlist and dance wildly and blissfully around the house to my heart's content.

My ex-lover doesn't stay completely out of my thoughts, of course. I wonder sometimes why he was in my life. Why all those serendipities? What was the point?

I have no answers and that's okay. I still wish for true love with the man of my dreams. I am open to meeting that man at any time. I am also open to living fully, beautifully, and joyfully with or without a man. And I wish for Julien to be happy. He is still a good man, and at least this time, with this ending, he was honest with me.

One day while he's in my head, I ask, *Why was he in my life? Why did this end?* and take out the deck of wise and all-knowing oracle cards. I pull the *Storyteller* card.

> *Make the most of every experience. You can choose the meaning that you give events. Find interpretations that empower you rather than diminish you.*

An answer and not an answer at the same time. Fine. I will go on making the most of life.

I go on making the most of life until the next full moon, and then I temporarily backslide. Julien has started texting me again, and memories are surfacing of all the fairy tale parts of our story, all the good things about him and the beautiful things he said. *I love you … I'm giving myself all the chances with you…* and then a few days later I said *if you love me don't let go*, and he let go.

He had sent me a beautifully written message three days after his breakup text.

> *Dearest Sonya, the fog is clearing and now I know why you were in my life, on my path. You brought me many beautiful things, much positivity. I wonder and will always wonder if it would have worked out in France or the USA, or elsewhere, if we could have seen each other more often. I'll never have the answer. Know that I'll continue to appreciate you as a person with whom I have a deep connection, with whom I shared very*

*beautiful emotions I've never experienced before. You are a beautiful
person, and you deserve the best. I'm grateful to life for having met you.
For having loved you with all my heart. Thank you for everything.
Of course, I feel the deep pain of this separation but for me, it was no
longer reasonable for you or me. Our energy was dissipating.
Take care of you. I love you with all my affection. A bientôt, somewhere
on planet Earth physically or mystically.*

That would have been a lovely ending, really, except for that incongruous *à bientôt*. But he didn't leave it at that. A week later, he sends a screenshot of a plane ticket and an ironic message. *What a mess. Everything's been flipped around. I'm leaving tomorrow for Mozambique. I'm sad.*

That means that he'll have five weeks of vacation two-and-a-half months from now. I'm not shocked. This is very much reminiscent of the Qatar situation a year ago.

I don't reply. He keeps texting, full of sadness and regret. He regrets his hasty decision, he's sad and in pain. But it's too late. I feel cold towards him, and annoyed by this sudden flip. He should have let his goodbye message be the last one. He made his choice, now he has to live with it.

I ignore him. He keeps texting. I don't want to think about him anymore. I want to get him out of my head. I want to kiss somebody else. And I know who I want to kiss.

There's a Spanish guy in town named Elias. He owns a wine and coffee bar on the other side of town, and they have irresistible oat milk cinnamon lattes, good wine, a great vibe, and live music sometimes. Elias also does mechanic work on the side, and he's really good at it. That's how I met him, because after a string of bad luck with my motorbike and mechanics, a friend put me in touch with him and he had my bike running perfectly in under twenty minutes.

Elias's warm brown eyes are the color of coffee dappled with golden specks of honey. He has a thing for me. I know because he told me so, and he tried to kiss me a couple months ago, and even before either of those things I could feel it. I can't deny that I felt a spark of attraction to him too—he's attractive and likeable and has smooth olive skin and a charming Spanish accent—but I met him when I was with Julien, and I wouldn't have done anything to mess that up. I told Elias I had a boyfriend and that I loved my boyfriend and that was that.

But now, I'm free.

So I have dinner at Elias's bar and stay until everyone else leaves and then he locks the door and pushes me against a wall and makes out with me. He's a good kisser and there's no shortage of chemistry, but he's too aggressive too fast. I just want kisses. I have to keep pushing his hands away.

"It's late now and I have to wake up early, but do you want me to come over tomorrow night?" he asks. "I'll have more time then. I'll bring a bottle of wine."

I hesitate. I don't know if I want that. He kisses me again.

"Okay … come. Just don't come with any expectations."

"Okay. I'll come around eight or nine."

But around eight he messages me that he can't leave the bar yet, there are too many customers still there. He'll call me when he can get away.

While I'm waiting, I decide to browse through his Facebook profile. I click on it. The first thing I see is that his relationship status says *in a relationship*. Well, surprise, surprise.

Facebook shows the woman he's in a relationship with; she's a Cambodian woman. I click on her profile, which likewise says she's in a relationship with him. It's clear from her posts that she's the mother of his son. I knew he had a four-year-old son, but I didn't know he was still with the mom. It's highly unlikely that they broke up and neither one got around to updating their status. I feel a little sick to my stomach.

Maybe there's an explanation, although I doubt it. I'll ask him about it when he gets here. But the hours pass and no word from him. Around 11 p.m. I message him that it's late, better another time…

He replies: *I'm really sorry, still 5 people here—yes next time hmmm! Buenas noches*

He messages the next day to apologize again and tell me he ended up closing at 2 a.m. He doesn't try to reschedule, and I'm certainly not going to instigate that, and I'm not going to ask about his relationship via text. Maybe his conscience got the better of him. It leaves me with a strange feeling, but whatever. He isn't the first shady guy I've met in this town. At least I got one fun night of kissing.

Meanwhile, Julien's texts continue. *I ask you to kindly please forgive me for all the hurt I've caused you. You don't deserve it. I'm an imbecile. Everything reminds me of you: yoga, meditation, music, photos, our conversations of the last months, so many memories. It's exhausting. I can't sleep. I'm searching for solutions.*

My heart softens a little. I have the benefit of decades of breakup experience; I know this is typical breakup aftermath. He spent twenty-seven years with the same woman; breakups are less familiar terrain for him. I write him back.

> *Julien, give time time. Your emotions change very quickly. A few weeks ago, you told me, "I'm taking all my chances with you." Two weeks ago you told me, "I wish to end our relationship because I no longer believe in it." Three days ago, you were going to cut the cord. Also remember, you always had doubts about our relationship. You decided to end it after Goa. And before Doha. And in Cambodia in February. And again, this last time. Now you have the freedom you wanted. There's no point in suffering. The pain and the sadness aren't going to last forever. They might even disappear very soon.*

Really, there's no arguing with these cold hard facts. But skillfully, he doesn't bother to argue. Instead he does something completely unexpected. His reply is a long message that reads like the first chapter of a novel.

Sunday November 25, 2017, it begins. *I'm on a plane headed to Bali. Why this destination? Intuition tells me it's the right place, to find a thread of sense in my life, to forget these terrible past few years.*

That was two weeks before we met, that fateful day in Yoga Barn. His chapter continues, well-written, surprising, captivating, reaching backward into the past to explain things that I never knew, revealing things that had always remained hidden behind his walls, events and circumstances of his past that hurt him, scarred him, shaped him. He weaves my name into it, then with a "but I'll come back to Sonya later…" segues back into the past, leaving a wisp of suspense hanging. He writes of his adventurous flight to Bali, which was rerouted to Chengdu, China due to the eruption of Mount Agung while they were in the air, of how he got himself a last-minute seat on a flight from Chengdu to Surabaya, arrived in Surabaya, hired a taxi to drive him the two-day journey to Gilimanuk where he could take a ferry to Bali. The taxi cost an arm and a leg; he didn't care. After everything he'd been through in the last few years, he needed this vacation. He was getting to Bali, whatever it took.

The taxi driver was a great guy, a sincere, authentic soul who spoke lovingly of his wife and children. Julien asked if he'd ever cheated on his wife. "Good God no, one is enough," the driver replied. Julien burst out laughing. He liked the answer.

In Bali, he spent three days in Jimbaran. There was almost no one around; the island felt empty, thanks to Mount Agung. It was relaxing, but this wasn't where he wanted to spend his vacation. Someone told him about Ubud. He hired another taxi to take him there. He rented a scooter, explored the town, met people. Someone told him to check out Yoga Barn. He'd never done yoga. He wasn't flexible and the idea of yoga had never appealed to him before, but for some reason he decided to try it.

He made his way to Yoga Barn and signed up for a beginner's class. The teacher was a sunny blonde with curly hair who emanated goodwill. Her confidence was gentle, her explanations were clear; there was no judgment in the room. The sounds of birds and insects hummed around them. Time stopped. Halfway through the class he decided this was where he would spend the last two weeks of his vacation. Too bad for the rest of his plans and the rest of the islands. This was where he wanted to be. He signed up for the unlimited class package.

In spite of myself, I'm hooked. Our fateful meeting is burned into my memory forever. To read his perspective, to discover the background story that led to our meeting, in these clear words that lift the veil of privacy over his mind and let me in, this is something I never expected and can't resist. In spite of myself, I wait with bated breath for the next installment.

It arrives the next day.

At Yoga Barn, he tried three different classes a day. He loved everything. The quality of the teachers; the diversity of the classes; the small numbers of students in each class which he knew was rare here and for which he could thank Mount Agung; the discovery of everything new. He tried Thai massage, pranayama, Shamanic breathing, meditation, Tibetan sound bowls. Some of the classes were powerful. He felt at home here. He felt at peace. His mind was clear and quiet. This was the break from life he'd dreamed of taking for so long.

He met interesting people, including some women. Lucy, a British writer, with whom he shared some deep, open discussions. A Polish woman, with whom he took an adventurous ride to see Mount Agung closer up. They stopped to do some trekking; visited a magnificent waterfall. They met more interesting people along the way and fell easily into conversations that were real, authentic, absent of superficiality. These were all moments that both quieted and awakened his mind. He was reinvigorated.

Now it was his second and final week in Ubud. One morning, in a vinyasa flow class, he noticed a pretty blonde near the front. Her flexibility and the birthmark on her right arm caught his attention. (My attention perks up in anticipation here because he's referring to me.) He returned to his asanas, he didn't think anything more about her; anyway, she was too young for him and he was leaving in a couple days. Also, he wasn't looking for anything; he'd had beautiful connections with people here and he was content.

The next morning, he placed his mat a little closer to the front to be able to see the blonde better. (Me: *Oh really? Well, that clearly contradicts that previous statement "I didn't think anything more about her."*)

His story continues:

Unfortunately, she arrives just before the start of class and she's behind me. Darn. But afterwards, she comes up and asks me how I liked the class. She's pretty, young, with a little red scar on her nose close to her eye.

I wrinkle my nose, remembering the temporary bright red scar that thankfully has completely healed now. But I kind of like that we met when I had this blemish and he saw past it.

He continues:

We talk a little. I find her very attractive in her yoga outfit, but I don't think farther, she's at least ten years younger than me. Age has always been an important detail for me. We talk about the Ecstatic Dance Friday. I hope I'll see her there.

A few days later, at the Ecstatic Dance, I look for her everywhere. I spend a while looking for her, actually. I was thinking about her all day.

(Yet another contradiction of that 'I didn't think anything more about her' ...)

A blonde like that should be easy to spot here, but I don't find her. I circle around the room a few times. I come across a blonde who resembles her, it's not her; I apologize. I resign myself to reality; she must not have come. Maybe she wasn't able to get a ticket or something else came up. Anyway, we barely talked at all. Too bad. I come across Lucy, the British writer. She's completely ecstatic. We talk a little. She's high. She looks at me. Our hands meet. I leave her; we won't see each other again. I go back to my room a little disappointed by the evening.

Good riddance Lucy, you hussy! As I read, so many different emotions are surfacing inside me that they should all take a number like customers at the deli. First, the elevating sense of new discovery. We've talked about that night at the ecstatic dance, but never in great detail. I never knew he was thinking about me all day and made several laps around the room searching for me. I always assumed we each made one circle around the room and it was at the same time so we missed each other, and that's the only thing that makes sense because if he circled around several times, it should have been impossible for him not to find me. This wasn't an enormous space we were in—it was a yoga shala that could hold about sixty yoga mats max.

On another level, there's also the rekindled spark of there-is-some-mysterious-divine-cosmic-magic-at-work-here-and-we're-meant-for-each-other, and that is a dangerous and unpredictable spark that the simultaneous but contradictory left-brain emotion of you-don't-care-anymore-what-this-man-has-to-say-it's-all-over wants to furiously stamp out with its army-booted heel.

It's all very confusing, but whatever. I don't want to analyze my emotions, I just want to read his version of the next couple Balinese days. Fortunately, he sends the next installment without delay.

His memory matches mine about seeing each other in kundalini yoga a couple mornings later. While we're talking after class, he feels the current pass (I like this expression of his) and he invites me to coffee. *I find her charming, beautiful energy, I adore her already even though nothing's happened.*

I'm really looking forward to reading what comes next, but he disappoints me. *After breakfast, I take her to another place—pfff, let me take a break, it's too vivid, all these delicious memories.*

In the messages that follow, he is swallowed up by the present and goes back to reminiscing in regret over his recent decision.

I'm still attached to you. I don't know why I ended it. I wanted to give freedom to both of us since I was trapped and I didn't believe anymore in this long-distance relationship. Sooner or later, one of us was going to cheat. I was afraid of that. I lost you. I regret it. You are what I've never known in any other woman. I've felt good with you since the beginning in Bali. I love to be with you, I love your attitude. Time passes quickly with you. But every time, this recurring question about not being able to see you again soon. And this clumsy pattern of mine of stopping our story because we couldn't see each other again and I didn't want you to waste your time with me.

The summary: in 2 ½ years, we've spent less than 2 months together. How sad, this distance. I would so have loved to spend time with you. I honor life for having met you; I hate it for not letting me see you more often.

341

This is annoying. I don't want the present to interrupt, I just want to read his account of The Divinely Ordained Balinese Encounter of Sonya and Julien: As Experienced by Julien.

He continues: *Can I ask you just one question: what did you think of our first meeting in Bali? And the following year before you came to France?*

First of all, that's two questions. Second of all, it's annoying that there are questions here at all. I just want to sit back comfortably as a relaxed observer of the past and read. He's trying to drag me into a dialogue and I don't like it.

I tell him that for a long time I would have loved to hear those words, but now I don't trust him anymore. I don't want a love who's willing to drop me so easily. I want a love I can count on.

He writes more, and I try to ignore him but he says things I can't not respond to, so the dialogue continues. It's devouring my energy like a vacuum and I'm starting to feel angry at the world in general and I can't explain why.

A couple days later Julien asks if I want us to see each other again one day.

I reply honestly. *I don't know. Right now I have no desire to see you again. I think that writing about your past will help you sort out things from your subconscious, as you said. If you want me to read that, keep sending it. But please stop asking me questions.*

He replies: *Okay, I won't bother you anymore. Thank you for your honesty.*

He follows that with a lovely message, apologizing again and asking for my forgiveness.

I write back the truth. *One day I'll be ready to forgive you but I can't yet. I'm a little angry and I need time to understand the roots of this anger.*

He understands that I need time; he hopes that one day I'll be able to forgive him. He adds, *there's no excuse for me. I am lamentable.*

It's a little harder to stay annoyed with someone when they describe themselves as "lamentable." The sentence makes me laugh, but my bad mood returns later. It's Friday night and I'm angry at the world. I know I'm angry because of Julien but I don't understand why.

It's not until the next morning that I understand where this anger came from.

From fear.

With his messages, Julien got under my skin. I had let him go, I had cut the cord with him, I was feeling free, strong, and happy, and then he started opening up and sharing all of these deeply personal things, with many words that I wanted to hear for so long mixed in with some annoying ones. His messages have triggered a tiny seed of hope that maybe it's not really over between us. Maybe his love for me is real and this latest "ending" is just part of the journey. But I'm afraid this hope is a mirage; I'm afraid his love isn't real, isn't strong enough to stand up to the challenges of life. I'm afraid to trust his words and emotions; I'm afraid his emotions are a yo-yo and his words are manipulation. I'm afraid that if I let him back into my heart he's going to repeat this pattern again. Afraid he'll give up too easily again. And I'm angry because getting pulled back into the spell of attraction to him feels like weakness. I'm afraid that to give him another chance would be weakness, and that being strong would be to ignore him and let him fade out of my life, and I want to be strong.

Then I read something in *The Seat of the Soul* by Gary Zukav that makes me consider the situation from another perspective. It's about how we always act from love or fear. How acting from fear creates painful consequences.

> *Eventually we see everything as an opportunity to create with love instead of fear. Fear creates the illusion that something should not have happened, that painful experiences are negative, and love dispels this illusion.*

What if my fear of being weak is blocking me from the future and the love I really want? Is keeping him shut out strength or stupidity? What if we had to go through this, if something inside him had to feel enough pain and loss to be cracked fully open, and meanwhile, it gave me the chance to step past my fear and my ego? Would giving him another chance to get my heart and trust back be naive and stupid, or an act of love and courage?

I don't know for sure, but the sea of anger inside my head is gone. I feel peaceful.

Halfway across the world in Mozambique, his emotions have shifted too. He sends me a long message, apologizing for breaking his promise not to write me anymore.

He's sad, he says, but something has shifted. He has come to understand certain things about himself, and for him that has enormous value. He feels a kind of joy, and he knows it may not last, but he appreciates it for the moment. He appreciates that I was part of his life, and he just wanted to share that with me.

The calmness in his message matches the calmness I feel inside.

I write him back what I came to understand that morning. All of it, the roots of the anger and the fear and the love and what I read in *The Seat of the Soul.*

He writes back quickly. He loved what I wrote; it surprised him, touched him. A little later he sends me a photo of a page from a book.

It's strange, looking through the photos from Bali, I came upon this one. Maybe I sent it to you? I don't remember it, but rereading the lines, I find them very beautiful.

I don't remember seeing the words before, but I have read them a couple years ago because they're from a little book he gave me in Bali: *L'Ame du Monde (The Soul of the World)* by Frederic Lenoir.

Don't reject the shadow side of you; the fog, the darkness that you carry within you. ... The flaw in each being is the cleft through which life links one to another through love. We are linked to each other not only by the synergy of our strengths and our gifts but also by the complementarity of our deficiencies and our weaknesses. Life wants us to need each other so we can support each other in love. The Creator made it this way: each being is blessed with a gift that will allow him/her to be a support, a light, a consolation for others, but also with a flaw, a crack, a weakness, that requires the help of another.

I'm speechless. I look at the ring on the middle finger of my right hand; my half-dark, half-clear Herkimer quartz, my constant reminder that darkness and light are part of the whole. The dark side of my ring is beautiful. The words on that page just made the dark side of humanity beautiful.

One of Julien's shadows is to panic and run away when his mental pressure gets too high. Do I have the light to balance that particular shadow, to forgive him and start again? I don't know yet. I'm not ready.

Just then, my phone dings. It's a Whatsapp message from my friend Anisha: a meme featuring a lion and a warrior princess. It says, "If you seek the light, be prepared to face the darkness."

It seems the metaphysical forces of the Universe really want to hammer this message home.

Two days later, Julien writes that he's looking at flights to Cambodia in October. The travel situation is still complicated. Cambodia isn't issuing tourist visas. He could possibly get a business visa, but he would have to go in person to a Cambodian embassy and there isn't one in Mozambique. He may only have two weeks off, and if anyone on his flight tests positive for Covid, he'll have to quarantine for two weeks in Phnom Penh.

Then, if you only have two weeks, it doesn't make sense for you to come, I write.

I don't care, I'll come anyway, he replies.

That's nice to hear, but, it's all very complicated. The woman at the visa consultancy recommends that we wait till the middle of September; she expects that they're going to be relaxing the restrictions in October. So for now we wait, in limbo.

CHAPTER 46

The mind can never deny the heart.
— AUSTRALIAN PROVERB

August 2020

As if I needed more complications in my life, one morning my motorbike won't start.

I message Elias. Can he come fix it? Yes, he can. He comes that afternoon. It's a quick fix; just the spark plug. Afterwards, we talk. He tries to kiss me on the lips. I pull away.

"That night you were supposed to come over, I saw your Facebook profile says you're in a relationship," I say. It's so much easier to say these things face-to-face.

He looks at me in surprise. "Yes, I am. I told you that, the other time I was here."

Now I'm the surprised one. "You told me?"

"Yeah."

Somehow I missed that in the stream of rapid-fire Spanish. "So you have an open relationship?"

"Kind of. She's Khmer; her culture is very different, very conservative. As long as I don't come home with lipstick all over my face or something, it's fine."

What I hear in this is that it's a one-sided open relationship and his Khmer partner chooses not to ask questions whose answers she

346

won't like. He explains the situation in more detail, and while I feel uncomfortable for her, I can also empathize with his point of view. He doesn't use the word unfulfilled, but that's what I sense he is, and when he finds what he's missing elsewhere, he goes after it. He has no guilt about it; to him, it's natural, and you can't fight nature.

It isn't the kind of relationship I want for myself, but maybe it's the best for them. I can only guess at how his girlfriend would feel about this based on how I would feel in her shoes, but we don't wear the same shoes. Maybe she prefers ignorant bliss to the alternative of him leaving her. It isn't for me to know, but I appreciate that he's being honest with me and that he's comfortable with who he is.

He's telling me all this as we stand a few inches apart, leaning against my kitchen bar. The chemical attraction is still there and the relaxation of the air being cleared enhances the attraction. He puts one hand on my lower back and pulls me toward him.

Kisses are delicious, and he's such a good kisser. I kiss him back for a few seconds, and then I pull away. "When I saw you last, I kissed you because my boyfriend and I broke up. We're still broken up, but we're talking. We're probably going to get back together. And if we do, I won't be kissing you anymore."

He smiles. "You're not together now." He pulls me back to him.

We keep kissing, but that's all. He gestures toward the bedroom, but I won't move from the safety of the kitchen bar. Kisses are safe. Anything more is crossing into a land I might not be able to come back from.

"I want to make you come," he whispers.

Oh, God. After such a long hiatus, it's a tempting offer. But this is a crossroads, and I don't know which way I want to go. We stick to kisses. He can't stay long anyway, he has somewhere else to be.

After he leaves, I'm confused. I don't know what's the right choice here. On the one hand, I am free. I am talking with Julien, but we are not back together. I'm not 100 percent sure I want to get back into a complicated long-distance relationship with him. No matter how beautiful his apologies are, no matter how many gorgeous apology bouquets he sends (he's sent two), after all his flip-flopping it seems logical to remain uncommitted until we can see each other in person again. Life used to always orchestrate situations for us to be together. It doesn't seem to be doing that now. Maybe it's trying to tell me something. And I've been feeling so good the past few weeks, so fully alive. I want to stay fully alive. I would love a freaking orgasm, and this attractive Spanish man wants to give me one. And my motorbike broke down so I would have to see him—is that a sign?

But—Julien. We're not together, but I know his intentions. What's going to happen to our connection if I'm with someone else? Do I want to have those memories in my head forever, a secret from him? Maybe it's okay. Again, we are NOT together. I'm free. But, Elias has a girlfriend, and semi-open though his relationship may be, for me, I don't like that. I accidentally found myself the other woman once before; it's not a position I intentionally want to put myself in again.

But just one time … but it might not be just one time. Orgasms are like chocolate; once you have one, you want more. Would being with him be like opening Pandora's box? What's going to come of it? Pleasure and the afterglow probably … that would be really nice. But, after that? I can think of four possible scenarios. A, the sex isn't good and neither of us wants to do it again. (This seems unlikely.) B, it's really good, too good, and I want more, and I want to stop but it's too hard to stop and I get caught in another triangle. C, he likes it too much and falls in love with me, and I don't want that. D, we both fall for each other and he ends up leaving his girlfriend and then I'm a homewrecker.

None of these scenarios are appealing. My attraction to him is physical and chemical, but it doesn't involve the vision of a long-term shared future. My body doesn't care, however; it's tantalized by the idea of some physical loving.

Aaaargh. I don't know what to do. I want someone else to tell me what to do.

I turn to two different sources: my friend Anisha, and the oracle cards. I leave Anisha a voice memo, explaining the conundrum and inviting her to give me a lecture on morality and talk me back into my senses. Then I pull a card, hoping for one with a really specific answer like *Yes, indulge in that chocolate,* or *Sure, you can have your cake and eat it too!* or *Don't be caught up in old-fashioned morality and misplaced loyalty or held back by an over-active conscience, just go enjoy all of the pleasure life has to offer.*

But what I get is the *Storyteller* card. Again. That card is coming up a lot lately. *You can choose the meaning that you give events. Find interpretations that empower you rather than diminish you.*

When I wake up the next morning, Anisha's reply is waiting. She doesn't give me a moral lecture and she doesn't tell me what to do. Instead, her response is perfect.

"Sonya, about your dilemma, I don't think this is about justifying anything, it's about getting super clear about what you want. Yes, you are broken up with Julien and if you want to hook up with this other guy, you can do that with a clear conscience. But I want to remind you about what you said about the box of chocolates, and that you described him as Pandora's box, {she laughs} so I think that subconsciously you already know this is a dangerous situation, and it might be best to avoid a dangerous situation. I think it's really hard for women to sleep with anyone and stay emotionally disconnected. There's always some attachment that comes from it. I know you gave those examples of being on vacation, but it's not the same, because neither of you are leaving.

"I think you could go either way here. I don't have any moral lecture for you. I think it's unfortunate that he has a girlfriend, but I think it comes down to what you guys are okay with. The only part of the story I have a question on is, it's great that he's totally clear and was up front with you, but his girlfriend who's the mother of his child, does she have the same okay in her head? Or is she thinking she's in a committed relationship and if she found out, would it break her heart? From a karmic perspective, I think that's the only place where this could backfire and bring you bad karma. That's my take. I think you're free to do whatever you like; you have free will and the universe is giving you this chance to think about it and if you want to have some fun short-term and you're happy about it then you should enjoy that guilt-free just like you would indulge in a piece of chocolate, or if you feel like the universe is giving you this opportunity to decide, *no, I don't want chocolate, I want something else*, then that opportunity is also revealing itself."

So much wisdom she has, this friend of mine. That's what it all boils down to: what do I really want?

I sit down and meditate in silence for twenty minutes, and by the time I open my eyes, the knowledge of what I really want is crystal clear in my mind.

Short-term pleasure and orgasmic ecstasy with this attractive Spanish man would be nice, but that isn't what I really want. What I really want is what I've wanted for years: my fairy-tale true love, and as complicated and inconvenient as it may be, the man I've fallen in love with is this Frenchman who lives halfway across the world in a country whose border is closed to me, who constantly tells me I'm too young for him, who's injured my heart multiple times but who has evolved afterwards every time and is now asking for another chance. Maybe it's going to be many more months before we can see each other again. Maybe he's going to break my heart again later. I don't care. If it doesn't work, it's not going to be because I didn't give it every possible chance. I know that maybe I could have both, the short-term pleasure and the fairy tale, but even if I wouldn't be technically cheating, I would feel like I was cheating on true love. It would feel like a betrayal of trust. It's not worth it.

"The mind can never deny the heart," an Australian engineer told me one day last year. Despite all the logic my mind can come up with about why it doesn't make sense to stay loyal to this man, my heart doesn't care. It wants what it wants.

Clarity is the best thing. When I stand up, I feel clear-headed, and lighter.

A couple hours later, Julien calls. "I have a question for you," he says.

"Okay."

"How did you feel about our time apart, all the time we spent apart, since Bali?"

There's no use being cagey. I have no games to play, nothing to hide. "For me, meeting you was something magical. It was the first time in my life I ever had the feeling of being struck by Cupid's arrow. With you in Bali, I was just in this cloud of happiness and everything was beautiful and felt so good. When you left, if you would have asked me to come see you in France … well, at that time I was totally free, I had nothing holding me back, I would have happily jumped on a plane to France."

He's astonished. "What? Noooo … I saw it completely differently. I thought I was just a passing adventure in your life, and you had chosen this life as a nomad, and I didn't want to hold you back."

It's true that there are many things we didn't say to each other in Bali. It was too soon to talk about anything like that. Then we rehash the serendipitous timing of the following November, when I got my one-way ticket to France.

"And I was so happy in France, and I would have loved nothing more than for you to invite me to stay longer, but you didn't, so I went to Portugal."

"What?" he huffs. "That would have been wonderful if you stayed longer! I missed you a lot after you left. That month between France and Goa—it was very difficult!"

I remember that he missed me, but he never invited me back. "Well, I wasn't going to invite myself to your place. And I was hurt actually, because there was so much contrast in Portugal, with Cristina and her whole family trying to get me to stay there, and you saying nothing about wanting me to come back. I felt so wanted by them and not wanted by you."

He's astonished again. "I thought I would be holding you back. You have your life, you just came to enjoy France, to enjoy Julien, and then leave."

"Well yeah, but I would have been happy to enjoy Julien for longer. That would have been my dream."

"I can't believe this," he says. "I've always seen myself as a limitation in your life, and I've always been asking you, how long are you going to stay in Cambodia…"

He definitely came up with that idea on his own. I've never said anything to give him the impression he was any kind of limitation.

"Well, Cambodia is really nice, and I'll probably stay here as long as I don't have a reason to go anywhere else. But I don't really know what I'm doing here. I'm living my life and I have to live somewhere, and this is a good place, but really I've just been waiting for you, Julien, to realize that you're so much happier when you get to cuddle me and kiss me and make love to me every day instead of spending all this time apart missing each other. I've just been waiting for you to say, 'okay Sonya, let's have a common base.' I understand if you have to travel for work, that's fine, but can we make it so we have a common base so we can see each other, I don't know, at least half of the year, instead of just a couple weeks here and a couple weeks there?"

He's completely blown away by this. "I … I … I never thought this was possible. That's what I've always wanted, but I never wanted to get in the way of your life. *Quel gâchis, quel gâchis.* What a mess, what a waste. So much lost time."

"I don't know…" I say thoughtfully. "I think maybe we needed the time apart…. I don't think you were ready before. You needed time. You've changed. And me too, I've changed. I loved the experiences I had living on my own in Asia. I think maybe it all worked out perfectly."

He wants to continue the conversation, but he has to go back to work. He texts me afterwards. *You're right. I think it all happened the way it had to.*

He calls again that night when he gets off work. "I still can't believe you would have come to France," he says. "But anyway. Enough about the past. Let's talk about the future. You are welcome in France. You can live in either of my places, Pau or Biarritz, you can choose. Your costs will be zero, you will have no expenses, you will have lodging, you will be fed."

I wasn't expecting the generous offer of financial support, but the invitation to share a common base with him in France is my dream come true. It's so sudden that I can't even feel emotion about it, but— I'm in. Of course. Except my independent side needs to speak its part, even though my practical side appreciates the financial offer, since I'll have to figure out what to do for income over there. "Thank you for that very nice offer, but I'll pay for my own food at least."

He continues on to other practical details. "How long is your work contract for? When can you leave Cambodia?"

I don't have a formal written contract, but my verbal agreement with Santosha is through the beginning of December. My house lease will also expire the beginning of December. Therefore, what seems like a good idea is that Julien should come visit in October, assuming Cambodia reinstates the tourist visa by then. Because we shouldn't get ahead of ourselves. It would be smart to have a little trial run and see if we get along for three or four weeks before I move across the world to move in with him. And if his visit goes well, I can move to France in December. He agrees.

"If I can't get into Cambodia then we can meet in some other country," he adds. Then he switches topics. "Talking about the future, there are many projects I would like to share with you."

His choice of words is remarkable, because that's something we've never talked about, but it's almost word for word a wish I've written in my journal. It was a point that always secretly hurt me, that he never envisioned things we could do together in the future. Did my higher self whisper into the ear of his higher self?

He lists off some of the projects he has in mind. He wants to go back to the Kerala Ayurvedic center for a full panchakarma. He wants to go back to Thich Nhat Hahn's Plum Village. He wants to go back to Bali. He wants to explore more of France—there is much of France that he has left to discover. And so on.

"At Plum Village, they have a side for women and a side for men, but also rooms where couples can stay together," he tells me.

"That sounds nice, but if we're there to be all zen and meditative, maybe we should stay separately."

"Then we're not going," he says immediately.

Laughter spills out of me. He's the cutest.

This is all music to my ears, but it's also a dramatic difference from the Julien of the past. "This seems like a very sudden change," I tell him. "When did this all happen?"

"Mmm … since I was in quarantine in Mozambique. Since then, I've been thinking a lot about all this."

"How can I know that you're not going to change back, that you're not going to just flip again and want to run away?" I ask cautiously. "How can you be sure?"

He answers without hesitation. "I'm sure. I'm ultra-sure."

What other assurance could he give me? How can any of us be 100 percent sure about anything in the future? At least he's sincerely ultra-sure at this moment. There is no life without risk.

The next time we talk, he tells me he's been wanting to redo the bathroom and kitchen in Biarritz. This is more music to my ears, not only because I love to remodel anything I can get my hands on, but also because although the Biarritz apartment is really cute, the bathroom and kitchen could use some updating. He starts describing the tile he wants for the shower. It sounds exactly like the Turkish stone tiles I put in one of my bathrooms in Florida. I send him a picture of it.

"Yep, that's it! That's what I want."

This is incredible, because I loved that Turkish stone so much. It turned every shower into a spa experience.

"I've been wanting to do this for a while but I haven't started because someone needs to be there overseeing everything and I'm always traveling."

"Well, I would be delighted to oversee it," I say brightly.

"That's what I was thinking."

Once again, I have the feeling I had with him in Bali, that the great and powerful Universe Genie has scrolled through my mind, identified my deepest wishes and wildest dreams and with elaborate attention to the minutest of details is rolling everything out in real life, down to my favorite shower tiles. This is wild.

I can't help but notice that this new batch of magic began unfolding the very same day I made my decision about Elias. Maybe it was just coincidence, but I don't think so. I think it was the Universe Genie checking one final time to see if I was really sure about what I wanted before handing it over.

It's not until much later that I remember the words of the soulmate tarot card reading from December 2018. *When you no longer settle, when you decide 'this is what I want,' it's gonna come.*

It's the end of August. Julien pulls an oracle card and gets the *Clair de Lune* card. *You will soon go on a very special voyage.* That's perfect, because it's now confirmed that he'll have two and a half weeks off in October. Cambodia is still not issuing tourist visas, so we've decided to meet in Turkey, where both European and American citizens are allowed in without so much as a negative Covid test or a quarantine required.

A couple days later, we're on the phone. He's reading something on some website and he says: "Oh! This says travelers from Turkey are allowed into France."

"Really?!" I say. "Well … then I guess it doesn't make sense for me to come back to Cambodia and try again two months later to get into France … I guess I should just go for it now."

That's exactly what he was thinking. So we come up with Plan A and Plan B. Plan A is: we'll meet in Istanbul, spend a week in Turkey (because Turkey is an amazing country), then fly to France together. Ideally, they'll let me in and everything will be easy as pie. At least he'll be with me to protect me from any cold-hearted, overzealous immigration agents. And if they turn us away at the French border, then we pivot to Plan B (which is entirely Julien's idea): take a boat from Turkey to a Greek island, then fly to France from Greece, or else he'll buy a car and drive us into France.

You have to understand that this man is, generally speaking, a very practical, grounded, responsible person who doesn't say something unless he means it. He's an engineer, for crying out loud. Although I hope we won't have to resort to Plan B, I find it wildly romantic that he's willing to buy a car and smuggle me into his country if that's what it takes.

There are a lot of risks and unknowns here. All the country border rules are so fuzzy and keep changing so fast that I'm a little nervous that Turkey might change its mind and decide Americans aren't welcome before I get there, and I'm not at all sure France is going to let me in. I'm following Facebook groups of other expats trying to leave Cambodia and reading horror stories of travelers turned away at various gates because an agent decided their PCR test was the wrong format, or because boarding eligibility rules changed while they were en route to the airport, or because their flight was canceled at the last minute.

But this is what we both want. I remember a time in India when Nesha and I were so intent on getting on a sold-out train to Shimla that it seemed that our sheer force of will overcame all obstacles to make it happen. Something tells me it's going to be like that now. Julien and I are going to be reunited and I'm going to get to France.

This means I have less than a month to dispose of the houseful of possessions I've accumulated, and resign from my job, and help them find a replacement, and try to find someone to take over Siem Reap Food Loop, and let my landlords know I'm leaving, and pack, and … and, and, and. Plus I have a lot of temples to visit because four days ago I bought the three month temple pass thinking I would be here until December and I've just discovered how incredible it is to see the temples of Angkor with no one around. Now I've got just three and a half weeks to get my money's worth out of it, but that's all fine. This is my heart's biggest wish coming true. I need to be pinched.

The next day we buy our tickets to Istanbul and Toulouse.

The following month is a whirlwind, but a beautiful whirlwind that feels blessed by divine grace, as though the forces of the Universe have ordained that everything will go perfectly and smoothly and my four angels are diligently arranging all details for my greatest ease and pleasure. Out of the multitude of things that could have gone wrong during this time, nothing goes wrong. Everything goes more right than I could have hoped.

With the assistance of Jake, my realtor/translator, I let my landlords know I'm leaving two months early. We sit at my dining room table and I explain the situation. "I'm sorry to be leaving early—but it's for the best reason! I'll try to help them find a new tenant, but if I can't, they can just keep my two-month deposit and we'll call it even, if that's okay with them."

Jake translates my words and Grandpa Ta Baran's reply, which is made with no hesitation. "That's too expensive. It will be great if you can help them find a new tenant, then they'll give you the whole deposit back, but if not they'll give you one month back. The other month they already paid as commission to my company."

Their generosity and purity of heart warms mine.

Five minutes after they leave, my hairstylist friend Tanya arrives to cut my hair. She walks in and I announce my news. She covers her mouth with her hands in surprise. "Oh, wow! I'm so happy for you … wait, what's happening with your house?"

"As of October 1st, it's available!"

Excited interest dawns on her face. "Well, I am very interested," she says, looking around. "This is the most beautiful house I've seen around here, and my mother's coming here next month. I think this would be perfect for her. She's been bouncing around a lot and is feeling ungrounded and she would love this. I think it's just what she needs."

She takes a video and sends it to her mother, who does in fact end up renting the house. The deal will be solidified and the contract signed two weeks later, but by the time Tanya leaves my house that day, she's pretty sure she's convinced her mother and we're both jumping up and down in excitement. My sweet landlords don't lose a single month's rent and I get my full deposit back. Tanya's mother buys most of my furniture and assorted other home goods, which simplifies my moving out process enormously. I post everything remaining on the local Siem Reap Facebook page and it sells in the blink of an eye. I sell my motorbike to the first guy who comes to look at it, for the same price I bought it for. Everything I can't bear to part with, which includes a lot of Khmer ceramic dishware, I pack into two suitcases for the plane and three boxes to ship to France.

My employers are kind and understanding about my departure. I ask my friend Tingting, who's been teaching at Santosha the past few months, if she's interested in replacing me. She is. She meets with the owner and manager; they love her; that's settled. When I tell Sam I'm leaving, she volunteers to take over Siem Reap Food Loop. Hurrah! The little baby community composting program will continue.

I've felt supported by Life many times in my life, and I've also experienced the feeling of everything going wrong, doors repeatedly shutting in my face, like Life telling me gently but firmly, "Nope, honey, you're not going that way." But I've never felt so completely, unequivocally supported by Life as in those weeks following my decision to start a life with Julien in France.

CHAPTER 47

When love beckons you, follow it.
- KAHLIL GIBRAN

September 2020

Tingting and I are walking down a path made of dirt and rocks and tree roots and we're surrounded by tall trees, green vines, and giant boulders. We've wandered into the dinosaur age. We haven't really, but that's what it feels like. Something about the jungle, the massive boulders, and the stillness here, devoid of the sounds and energy of other humans, give the impression a longnecked brontosaurus could come lumbering through the trees at any moment. Tingting bought a temple pass the same day I bought mine, and we've become temple visiting partners. Yesterday we visited Banteay Srei and camped nearby, and now we're hiking to Kbal Spean, the River of a Thousand Lingas. It was Tingting's idea to come here. I visited Kbal Spean briefly last year, and the short cylindrical lingas carved into the riverbed didn't make much of an impression on me. But Tingting wanted to see this famous place and since we were so close, I didn't mind coming back.

We've taken a different route than I did last time. This path and the dinosaur forest are unfamiliar to me. It would be worth coming here just for this hike. After about an hour, we reach a fork in the path. From the left we hear the low hum of a waterfall, so we go that way.

The path opens up into a wide circle of open space featuring a short waterfall that spills over a rock ledge to form a shallow pool between the rocks below. It isn't a visually spectacular waterfall, but there's something enchanting about it. Having it all to ourselves makes us free and playful. We set our backpacks down and wade into the pool. Tingting lounges happily on a wide comfortable boulder. I strip down to my bathing suit and walk into the waterfall, letting the cool water pour over me. It's deliciously refreshing in the hot Cambodian air.

We linger here for a while, then continue our trek upriver to find the lingas. We come first to a section of a couple hundred, carved on a raised portion of the rock riverbed, clearly visible under the shallow water. They're what I remember from before, like upraised circles, not that impressive. We continue farther and we come to something I didn't see last time. In the middle of a wide section of the river, a large symbol is carved into the stone riverbed. Here too the crystal-clear water is only a few inches deep and the carving is clearly visible. It's the outline of a geometric shape: three sides of a square and fourth side that morphs into a long, skinny triangle. The two long sides don't quite meet at the bottom, leaving the triangle open at the top and bottom, like a funnel. Five large lingas are arranged symmetrically inside the shape. Seven more lingas are carved outside it. Beyond them, hundreds of lingas cover the entire riverbed.

I don't know what the geometric symbol is, but I can't take my eyes off it. My peripheral vision registers that this section of the river is beautiful, with its shallow glimmering water and banks of tranquil green foliage shaded by leafy trees.

We've been here for a few minutes admiring everything when I notice that there's an unusual energy coursing through me. It's not like the energy burst of coffee or sugar. It's an energy of power, of aliveness. It's strange because it's unfamiliar, but—fantastic. I feel … taller. Stronger. Possibly invincible. As if every cell in my body has just been fully charged. As if until now my batteries have been running around 60 percent and now, suddenly, they're at 110.

I don't know what this feeling is or where it came from, if it's from the symbol or if this is a sacred place, or both, but I love it. It's too strong to be my imagination.

Tingting is sitting ten feet to my left, staring at the river. "Tingting … do you feel anything different here?"

"It feels very peaceful," she replies.

Okay, so she's not feeling what I'm feeling. I keep this heady power rush to myself. It stays with me on the hour-long hike back to our bikes.

I investigate later. I casually drop Kbal Spean into separate conversations with two friends. Their reactions are identical. "The energy of that place!" I research and learn that the captivating symbol in the river represents the yoni and the lingam, symbol of fertility and the union of Shiva and Shakti, masculine and feminine energy. It was carved into the riverbed to make the water fertile. But fertility is only one aspect of the union of masculine and feminine energy. The yoni and the lingam together are also the symbol of union and creative energy, of creation and regeneration. The yoni symbolizes Shakti, the goddess, feminine energy, primordial energy, uniting with the lingam, Shiva, Divine Consciousness. Shakti allows consciousness to materialize, to become manifest in the physical world. When united, the power of these two energies is magnified dramatically.

So that's the energy I felt that day. Maybe standing under the waterfall and letting that supercharged water pour over me had something to do with it. Because I didn't know what the yoni-lingam symbol represented until afterwards and because I had no special expectations for Kbal Spean, the cynical half of my mind has no comment to offer here. Energy is real.

My American friend Sarah went back to California for what was to be a short visit just before the pandemic broke out and got stuck there for eight months. She comes back to Siem Reap just as I'm packing up to leave. Because who doesn't love a good excuse to celebrate, we plan a Welcome Back Sarah/Bye Sonya bar-hopping extravaganza for the end of the month. It's a gorgeous evening and I get to say a joyful farewell to most of my favorite Siem Reap people in one long festive night.

September 30th, I meet Grandma Yae Mwah, Grandpa Ta Baran, and Jake for the exchange of keys, electricity payment, and deposit refund. My electric bill hasn't arrived yet, but on average it's around $120 for the month. They want to charge me just $50. I protest. "That's not enough!"

Jake says, "They just want you to leave feeling good and happy." Then he adds with a big smile, "The house was beautiful when you moved in, but you made it more beautiful."

They were so beautiful, Yae Mwah and Ta Baran and Jake. I'll never forget them.

October 1, 2020
Phnom Penh, 6:15 a.m.
I'm curled up in a comfy cushioned chair at a riverside café, watching the sun rise on the other side of the Mekong River, waiting for the clock to reach a reasonable hour before I go over to Olivia's. It still feels like I'm in a dream. It feels like I've been in a magic waking dream the entire past month. Even the overnight Giant Ibis bus ride here was marvelous. I was the only passenger, so it was like my own personal supersized limo. I had booked two tickets to make sure I got a double sleeping bunk all to myself, but I got the entire bus for that $28.

Olivia and I spend the day eating Indian food, lounging at the pool, and getting our nails done, and that night we say our goodbyes and now I'm at the airport checking in. My flights were booked separately, but Asiana and Turkish Airlines are part of the same alliance and they conveniently check my bag all the way to Istanbul. My bags are overweight but they don't charge me. No one gives me a hard time about anything.

In Seoul, I have a sixteen-hour layover. The airport is a ghost town. Except for a handful of isolated holdouts, all of its shops and cafés are closed and it's almost empty of humans. It feels surreal. But there's one open restaurant selling hot kimchee and noodles, and I find a huge carpeted empty space on the second floor with a couple tables and chairs next to a closed café. I convert this into my private oversized office / yoga studio for the day. Fortunately, the airport Wi-Fi is still functioning.

And then finally, after an uneventful eleven-and-a-half-hour plane ride to Istanbul, the immigration officer stamps my passport and says, "Welcome to Turkey" and then I'm pushing my luggage cart through the exit doors into the cool 5 a.m. air and searching the faces of the small crowd for Julien, who arrived last night at 7:30 p.m. And he's there, wearing a black sweater and a light blue surgical mask and holding a bouquet of a dozen red roses. And this all still feels like a dream but it's real, he's really there, and he hands me the roses and wraps both arms around me. I set the roses in the basket of the luggage cart so I can wrap both of my arms around him, and this is the best hug ever, this solidness of his torso against mine and the warmth of his arms tight across my back and my cheek against his neck, this hug we've been craving for seven months. Then we start laughing because we can't kiss each other through the masks and we pull our masks down so our lips can find each other, and the seven months was worth the wait, and I'm everlastingly grateful to the country of Turkey for its open borders during this time. Later, when I'm writing about our first dinner date back in Bali at the restaurant Kismet, I look up the word kismet. I knew that its definition is destiny; fate. I didn't know that kismet is a Turkish word, which made its way into the English language in the 1800s.

So it seems like a poetic touch that Life brought us here to reunite in Turkey. Like bringing us full circle.

CHAPTER 48

Maktoub.
It is written.
- ARABIC SAYING

esides its fantastic open borders, Turkey is a phenomenal country
any time and our short stay here is marvelous. When we're not in
the hotel room making up for the seven months of separation, we
wander the streets and drink Turkish coffee and eat kebabs and *köfte*
and *meze* and *künefe* and way too much Turkish delight. We walk
barefoot on the carpeted floors of the Hagia Sophia and through the
underground pillars of the Basilica and we take a short flight to
Denizli to visit the stunning thermal travertine pools of Pamukkale.

Now, this is the strange part. A couple days into our stay, I check
to make sure France hasn't changed the regulations for travelers
arriving from Turkey. To my dismay, Turkey is no longer included on
the list of countries from which travelers may freely enter France.
There is Thailand, Tunisia … no Turkey. We have a problem,
Houston. I show Julien, and then I mildly freak out.

"I think I'm going to have to fly to Croatia, and quarantine for
three days, and then try to fly to France…"

He shakes his head. "No. That's too complicated. We're going to
try. We're traveling together. They're not going to ask you for
anything."

I'm not convinced about that. But I look closer at the list of requirements for travelers going from Turkey to France on the IATA website. Entry is forbidden to non-French citizens, but there is a list of exceptions, none of which I remotely qualify for except possibly one: travelers from Turkey are allowed into France for medical treatment.

Well. I haven't had so much as a standard health checkup in over three years, so I'm probably due for some medical treatment. Come to think of it, I've recently been getting dizzy sometimes and my ears ring occasionally. That could be vertigo. I should have this checked out. And Julien's doctor in Pau just so happens to have a special TRV chair to treat vertigo.

Meanwhile, the lead story on all Turkish news stations is the increasingly hostile relationship between Turkish President Erdogan and French President Macron following Macron's recent unveiling of a proposed law to combat radical Islam in France. Erdogan, outraged by this proposed legislation, is urging all Turkish citizens to boycott French products and appearing frequently on Turkish news channels saying angry and probably not very nice things about Macron. Julien worries that the Turkey-France border may be closed any day now and moves our flights ahead two days earlier.

I search the internet for an announcement of when Turkey was taken off the EU's green-light list, but I can't find anything. Were Turkey-France borders ever really open? Both Julien and I saw that in writing a month ago. We couldn't have both imagined it. Did Fate just make those words appear to both of us, like a written mirage, just to get us here? I don't know, but it's really odd, because that was the detail that initiated our whole Cambodia-Turkey-France plan.

Anyway. We've made it this far; now to see if they'll let me across the French border.

In Istanbul airport, the two Turkish Airlines agents at the entrance to the check-in line ask for our passports. I hand mine to one of them. He opens it, looks at his colleague, and asks a question in Turkish along the lines of "Are Americans allowed into France right now?"

"Do you need to see my paperwork?" I ask proactively.

"Yes please."

I hand him the two documents printed from IATA's website along with my negative PCR test. He leafs through them and hands them back. "Okay, thank you. Have a good day."

The agent at the check-in counter asks only for our PCR tests. And then we're on the plane. So far so good. I start to relax a little.

And then, when we're already in the air, a flight attendant passes out a form that all non-EU residents have to complete. It's the same form I printed from IATA's website, except there are two options missing and one of them is the medical treatment option. My blood turns cold. I show Julien. "What am I supposed to do?" I whisper. They're definitely going to turn me away at the border now.

His forehead wrinkles, but he doesn't panic. "They must have the wrong form. Yours is up to date; you downloaded it two days ago. Just use your form instead."

So smart. I shove the other little paper into the seat back pocket, safely out of sight. I remind myself that the Universe is in charge here—but this is nerve-racking nonetheless, and the Universe is known for throwing curve balls occasionally. My heart is beating faster than normal.

We land in Toulouse. There are two extra checkpoints before immigration, one asking for PCR tests, and one asking to see passports. The passport agent looks at our passports and asks, "You're traveling together?" We smile and nod and he waves us on.

We reach the immigration window and hand our passports to the woman behind the counter. She looks at mine, and then at me. "You have a visa?"

"I came for medical treatment," I tell her and hand her my printed forms. She studies them. She asks which clinic or hospital am I going to.

"*Poly...technique de Navarre,*" I say slowly. That first word is a tongue twister.

Julien laughs. (His spur of the moment strategy to stimulate a sense of solidarity between us women, he says later.) "*Polytechnique!*" he repeats mockingly. "*Polyclinique de Navarre.*"

I sigh in embarrassment. "Sorry; it's not my first language," I tell the agent, even though my American accent has already made that obvious.

She feels sympathy for me, I think. "And you live in the US?"

"I'm American, but I've been living in Asia for the past three years, in Cambodia. And trust me, you don't want to go to the hospital in Cambodia."

"I can imagine. I had to go to the hospital once in Peru and that was enough for me." She stamps both passports and hands them back to us. "Have a good day."

And thus, I am officially welcomed into France. It feels surreal. I don't fully believe it until we're outside the airport. Until we pass the exit doors, I'm afraid someone might decide they've made a mistake and escort me onto a plane back to Turkey. But that doesn't happen. We made it.

We drive to Pau that night. I want to turn cartwheels with happiness, but my psyche isn't yet fully registering that this is real. Throughout my last month in Cambodia and then during our five days in Turkey, I felt no emotion about the end of my time in Asia. I was so focused on getting to France, on wrapping my arms around Julien, and on the underlying fear that someone at the borders would stop me—that I wouldn't be able to get to him. I know that deep emotions must be inside me somewhere, but I can't feel them. On some subconscious level I must have them locked away. I couldn't afford to feel them before. There were still too many hurdles to get over, too much up in the air, too much to lose.

I know me, and I figure it's only a matter of time until the emotions unleash themselves.

That happens the following night when we pull oracle cards, cozily ensconced in Julien's living room. It was his idea to pull three each: past, present, and future. We pull them from his *L'Oracle Cosmique* deck, by Nari Anastarsia.

My Past card is *New Chapter*.

A change and an inner transformation have taken place inside you. Today your soul is impatient to reach the next phase—a leap of faith into the unknown. A new chapter awaits you with new opportunities and adventures. For some time, your heart has pushed you to move forward, but your prudent mind has held you back. Don't allow the fear of the unknown to hold you where you are or you won't have any chance of progressing. More than anything, your soul is eager for growth and evolution. In staying where you are, you won't lift yourself toward higher spheres of spiritual consciousness and full awareness. Follow your heart, your intuition and guidance. Believe in yourself! Don't take into account the opinions and expectations of others. It's your life and you know what is really best for you. You don't realize it, but the next chapter will bring you wonderful lessons for the growth your soul needs. Be always sincere and confident; the spirit will guide you in your life. Be assured, easy routes will appear on the horizon.

How do these cards always know?? It was a perfect description of my inner landscape leading up to that life-changing decision in Johannesburg three and a half years ago, and the years in Asia that followed. Those words crack open whatever invisible wall had kept my emotions at bay and I start to cry. Julien brings me Kleenex.

A few days later we drive to Biarritz.

I couldn't have imagined a more beautiful ending for that Asia journey, than this one—in the south of France, with the man I adore, the man I felt this pull of attraction to from the first moment I laid eyes on him, this man who is kind and intense but relaxed, serious but playful, educated and classy but low key and adventurous, loyal and true to his words, thoughtful, affectionate, generous, caring, cosmopolitan, well-traveled, funny, romantic, hard-working, deep, who knows how to live life fully ... who has never, even for a moment, tried to pretend to be anything other than who he is. With him, in the charming, light-filled apartment in magical Biarritz, a few hundred meters from stunning beaches with hazy mountains in the distance, with sunsets and surfers and bakeries full of fresh croissants on every corner, a thirty-minute drive from the Spanish border. Once again I have the feeling that the Universe Genie peered into my heart, read my deepest wishes, and with his magic wand, wrote them into the script of Real Life.

And the future? The future is a mystery, but the future card I pulled that night in Pau was *Without Limits*.

Epilogue

We are here to love. The rest is silence.
  - Paulo Coelho

Part 1: October 2020

Three weeks after we arrive in France, President Macron locks the country down a second time. Internal Schengen borders remain open; external borders, "without exception," close. Only French citizens retain the right to reenter the country from overseas. The first day of the lockdown, I sit on the couch with tears of gratitude filling my eyes, absorbing the full impact of our lucky timing.

In December, when Julien returns from seven weeks in Mozambique, we get hitched, and by hitched I mean PACSed—a form of civil union commonly chosen in France as an alternative to marriage, a perfect short-term solution for us and the beginning of the next chapter of our adventure.

Part 2: June 2023

Nearly three years later, now that this book is finally almost ready for publication, I can add one more update.

After a year and a half in France (that is, France for me, Mozambique/France for Julien), we moved to Papua New Guinea for Julien's job, where the adventure continues.

We now know each other a lot better than we did when we decided to officially become life partners. Lest anyone have the wrong idea, let me assure you that we are not one of those perfect couples who never ever have an argument. We get mad at each other occasionally. Sometimes I drive him crazy and sometimes he makes me want to throw things. But those occasions are becoming much more rare as time goes on.

A month ago, we went back to Bali. We spent a day retracing our original steps. We found that a lot has changed: the Ubudian has closed, Kismet has relocated and downsized (but still serves good wine), and the streets of Ubud are congested with heavy traffic. But many things are still the same. Yoga Barn is still there, with some of our favorite teachers. Bali still possesses its quiet glimmer of magic.

In Lovina, in north Bali, the owner of the retreat center where we stayed recommended that we do a palm reading with a woman named Padmi. "She has a gift," she told us.

So we got readings from Padmi, a beautiful Balinese woman with an aura of sweet, pure serenity and charmingly imperfect English. She did the readings individually for six of us. I've never had a palm reading before, so I don't know what they're usually like, but this one involved Padmi taking one of our hands in both of hers, looking into our eyes, and proceeding to tell us very specific and highly accurate things about ourselves, describing the fundamental qualities of our characters, our jobs, events from our pasts, our fears, our loves and desires. She blew us all away, even the most skeptical among us.

We recorded our sessions with her, and Julien let me listen to his later. Halfway through his reading, she said to him, "I think you have been married before, yeah? Two times, you now married, yeah?"

"One time," Julien said.

"Now, not yet?"

Julien explained the PACS in simplified terms. "In France, it's not a religious wedding, but it is legal. I went to see a legal person and said, 'we are partners.'"

Padmi said, "That is, partners or married, is same, because you happy with her. Even you not married in legal, your soul already married. You already together, you feel already good, click together, growing together. You happy together, with her. Because you sensitive man and your spirit, your angel inside, choose the right one for you. She is the right one for you.

371

"In the past, I know you have many experiences not happy, like specially about love. You a lot of giving love, giving giving, but you not get what you want. That in the past. Now, not anymore. Now happy forever. The rest of your life, you happy."

I was listening with tears in my eyes.

In my session, while discussing the state of my heart, Padmi told me, "You're happy with your love now. And also you love traveling. You love to move to other countries. That is your life, you love that, you enjoy that."

I can't argue with any of that. I couldn't argue with her either when she informed me "sometimes I see, about your character, not really patient … you difficult waiting sometimes." Or when she said, "Your spirituality grow very well. But only sometime you need control your ego and emotions. That you must control."

At the end of my session, she added, "Oh, I see about the love there. Only that I see for you: keep this man, because he really good for you. He give you freedom."

When she said it, I thought: *that's so true, he is good for me and he does give me freedom and of course I'm going to keep him.*

Later, listening to the recording, it struck me that love with freedom was very specifically my biggest wish during the journey of the previous few years: the wish that crystallized in my heart at Carolyn and Jono's wedding right at the very beginning. Padmi couldn't have known that. It was as if some divine force or the Universe itself, speaking through her, wanted to remind me that my heart's deepest wish had been granted. As if to bring this whole adventure full circle, with a final sparkling flourish of magic.

And what is magic, anyway? Is there a connection between it and love? I've seen so much of both of those things over the past few years, and so often they seem to be intertwined, to exist together.

My theory is that magic is the way love operates—the way it sometimes shows us little glimpses of itself. The way love draws us closer, sometimes down a long, winding path.

I think magic is love winking at us.

EXTRAS

If you'd like to see some pictures from the journey, you can find them at **sonyamoore.com**.

Chapter 29 mentioned a post-run yoga sequence which very effectively eliminated post-half marathon muscle soreness. (I still maintain that this qualifies as a minor miracle.) If you want to try it out for yourself, you can find an abridged version at **youtube.com/@breathemovebliss**. It's the **Yoga for Runners | Post-Run Recovery | 35 Minute** video. There's also a link to it on **sonyamoore.com**.

If this book touched or impacted you in some way, I'd love to hear from you. Feel free to message me at **sonya@sonyamoore.com**.

If you enjoyed this book, would you mind taking a few minutes to leave a review on the site where you purchased it, and/or on **goodreads.com**? It would mean so much to me.

Thank you, and may love & magic surround you always.

Sonya

Acknowledgements

First, to my love: so much gratitude for so many things. For being who you are. For brightening my life with love, laughter, adventure, and delicious home-cooked food, for skillfully resolving my many IT issues, for being a person I can count on AND dance with in the kitchen, for your immense patience during the long writing process, and for being awesome enough to be okay with this book being put out into the world.

Heartfelt gratitude to Anisha, for being an incredible friend, occasional unofficial therapist, and the world's best cheerleader. Without our ongoing correspondence during the journey years, many sections of this book could never have been written, and your encouragement and moral support during the writing process brought so much joy to my heart.

To Lauren, our past emails also turned out to be essential for the writing of some of these chapters, and I'm so grateful to you for the ongoing connection, encouragement, and good vibes.

Bucketloads of sincere thanks to Maria, Fatima, Michelle, and Laura for the encouragement, critiques, feedback, and inspiration.

A big thank you to Jocelyn, my editor, for the valuable insights, feedback, humanity, intensive knowledge of all grammar rules, and for being okay with my occasional free-spirited deviations from said rules.

To all of those who gave me permission to use your real names, thank you; that meant so much to me. While all the names that have been changed were changed voluntarily by me, in the interest of protecting the privacy of those individuals, there were some that I wanted to keep true to life.

And to all the souls who crossed my path during the journey described in these pages, thank you so much for the role you played in making these experiences possible. There are too many of you to list by name, but I am deeply grateful to all of you: to those who became true friends, to those who shared wisdom, to those who cooked and served me delicious meals, to those who created and maintained the accommodations that kept me warm and safe and sheltered, to those who provided the transportation that let me move freely from place to place, to those who guided me on adventures, to the many beautiful souls who were bright lights along the way and who brought me joy and connection with your presence, conversation, and laughter.

I'm also indebted to the writers of the books that inspired and influenced me along the way, especially Douglas Abrams for *The Book of Joy*, Paulo Coelho for *The Alchemist* and *Manuscript Found in Accra*, Carmine Gallo for *The Storyteller's Secret*, Gabrielle Bernstein for *The Universe Has Your Back*, Paramahansa Yogananda for *Autobiography of a Yogi*, Helen Keller for *The Story of My Life*, Elizabeth Gilbert for *Eat Pray Love*, Walter Isaacson for *Steve Jobs*, Sunil V. Joshi for *Ayurveda & Panchakarma*, Frederic Lenoir for *L'Âme Du Monde,* Joe Dispenza for *You Are the Placebo*, Candace Pert for *Molecules of Emotion*, Gary Zukav for *The Seat of the Soul*, Glennon Doyle for *Love Warrior*, Leslie Kaminoff and Amy Matthews for *Yoga Anatomy*, and B.K.S. Iyengar for *Light on the Yoga Sutras of Patanjali*.

And to the writers of the oracle cards that inspired, mystified, and delighted me throughout the years— Nari Anastarsia, Toni Carmine Salerno, and Denise Linn—thank you for creating those printed portals of beauty and wisdom which became an indelible part of my personal story.

BIBLIOGRAPHY

Anastarsia, Nari. *L'Oracle Cosmique Guide d'accompagnement.* Rockpool Publishing, 2018.

Aron, A., et al. (1997). *The Experimental Generation of Interpersonal Closeness: A Procedure and Some Preliminary Findings.* Personality and Social Psychology Bulletin, 23(4), 374–375.

Bernstein, Gabrielle, and Hay House. *The Universe Has Your Back: Transform Fear into Faith.* 1st ed., Kindle ed., Hay House, 2016.

Isaacson, Walter. *Steve Jobs.* 1st ed., Kindle ed., Simon and Schuster, 2011.

Joshi, Dr. Sunil V. *Ayurveda and Panchakarma: The Science of Healing and Rejuvenation.* 1st ed., Kindle ed., United States of America, Lotus Press, 1997.

Lama, Dalai, et al. *The Book of Joy: Lasting Happiness in a Changing World.* Illustrated, Avery, 2016.

Linn, Denise. *Native Spirit Oracle Cards Guidebook.* Hay House, 2015.

Lenoir, Frederic. *L'Âme Du Monde (French Edition).* Pocket, 2014.

Mata, Sri Daya. *Intuition: Soul-Guidance for Life's Decisions.* Self-Realization Fellowship, 2019.

McMahon, Christina Sian. "How to Attract Love into Your Life," *Insight Timer.* https://insighttimer.com/meditation-courses/course_how-to-attract-love-into-your-life.

Salerno, Toni Carmine. *Gaia Oracle: Guidance, Affirmations, Transformation.* Blue Angel Publishing, 2018.

Solluna, Shashi. *Tantra: Discover the Path from Sex to Spirit.* Hay House UK, 2016.

Yogananda, Paramahansa. *Autobiography of a Yogi.* 13th ed., Kindle ed., Self-Realization Fellowship, 2019.

Zukav, Gary. *The Seat of the Soul: 25th Anniversary Edition with a Study Guide.* Anniversary, Kindle ed., Simon and Schuster, 2014.

QUOTES

Chapter 8: Mata, 3

Chapter 9: Lama et al, 150

Chapter 14 : Bernstein, 9

Chapter 16 : Solluna, xiii

Chapter 18: Bernstein, 175

Chapter 19: Joshi, 18

Chapter 20: Yogananda, 173

Chapter 24: Salerno, 68; Salerno, 38; McMahon, ep. 4.

Chapter 29: Salerno, 77

Chapter 30: Gilbert, 148-149

Chapter 39: Anastarsia, 33

Chapter 41: Aron, 374-375

Chapter 44: Isaacson, 48

Chapter 45: Zukav, 317; Lenoir, 123

Chapter 48: Anastarsia, 69